This Book:

- Helps you recognize and understand some of your basic personality traits.

- Recognizes that an accurate and comprehensive self-awareness will give you the self-control that allows you to choose who you will be in life.

- Recognizes that only you can have the ongoing self-observations, insights, and self-reflections necessary for an accurate and comprehensive self-awareness. Therapy can help, but only you can do this.

- Helps eliminate the endless dead-end work on surface symptoms that you, and possibly your therapist, have never recognized as arising from more basic personality traits.

- Helps you better understand your relationships and family life.

- Helps you recognize a dysfunctional or abusive relationship or avoid these relationships in the future.

If you don't know the trees you can get lost in the forest, if you don't know the stories you can get lost in life.

—A Siberian Saying

WHY YOU DO THAT

*How to Gain the Self–Observations, Reflections,
and Personal Insight You Need for a
More Accurate and Comprehensive Self–Awareness*

JOHN B. EVANS PHD, LCSW
with illustrations by Hilary M. Larson

bookVillages

Why You Do That: How to Gain the Self-Observations Reflections, and Personal Insight You Need for a More Accurate and Comprehensive Self-Awareness

© 2020 John B. Evans PhD, LCSW

All rights reserved. No part of this publication may be reproduced in any form without written permission from Book Villages, P.O. Box 64526, Colorado Springs, CO 80962. www.bookvillages.com

BOOK VILLAGES and the BOOK VILLAGES logo are registered trademarks of Book Villages. Absence of ® in connection with marks of Book Villages or other parties does not indicate an absence of registration of those marks.

The names, details, and circumstances have been changed to protect the privacy of those mentioned in this publication. This publication is not intended as a substitute for the advice of health care professionals. The reader should regularly consult a physician in matters relating to his/her health and particularly with respect to an symptoms that may require diagnosis or medical attention.

ISBN 978-1-94429-870-8

LCCN:

Cover and Interior Production Design by Niddy Griddy Design, Inc.

Poet: William Ladnier
ladnierw@gmail.com

Artist: Hilary M. Larson
https://simbi.com/hilary-larson/art

Printed in the United States of America
1 2 3 4 5 6 7 8 9 10 Printing/Year 24 23 22 21 20

Dedicated to all who receive this book as an anonymous gift

TABLE OF CONTENTS

HOW TO USE THIS BOOK *xi*

INTRODUCTION *xv*

PART I

PERSONALITIES —GENERALLY SPEAKING 1

Lack of awareness 7

Isolation 11

Personalities in Relationships & Families 14

Nature vs. Nurture 30

Personality Change 34

PART II

THE SEARCH FOR SELF-KNOWLEDGE 41

The Quest for Self: Getting Started 42

Specific Aspects of Your Basic Nature 45

PART III

DESCRIPTIONS OF SPECIFIC PERSONALITIES   71

The Abusive Personality / Abusive Relationships   72

The Obsessive-Compulsive Personalities   96

The Shy Personality   127

Mild Depression   148

Anxiety   160

The Borderline Personality   170

The Schizotypal Personality   179

The Narcissistic Personality   188

The Histrionic Personality   198

The Dependent Personality   204

The Passive-Aggressive Personality   211

The Antisocial Personality   217

The Sociopath / Psychopath   227

The Paranoid Personality   235

The Schizoid Personality   241

Cyclothymia (Mild Bipolar)   245

PART IV

PARENTS DO COUNT   257

The Family Systems of Murray Bowen   258

Murray Bowen's Triangles   268

PART V

CONTINUING THE JOURNEY INTO THE SELF   277

Counseling / Therapy   278

With Perseverance, Expect Success   285

PART VI

DEFENSE MECHANISMS   291

ACKNOWLEDGMENTS   298

BIBLIOGRAPHY   299

ABOUT THE AUTHOR   319

How to Use this Book

TO DEVELOP A more comprehensive understanding of your basic thoughts, feelings, and behaviors, that is, your personality, read the introduction and Part I so that you have some perspective and general information about the nature of personalities and personality development. Then read Part II and mark any trait in which you recognize yourself or another person of interest, in any way at all. Next read about the relevant personalities that you think may describe you in Part III. Reading about family systems in Part IV may offer you new insights and perspectives about how your personality formed and continues to be influenced by the family in which you were raised or about the effects you may be having on your own children. Part V discusses the counseling process and then offers ideas and suggestions about how to use the information you have learned about yourself. Finally, since we all use defense mechanisms to some extent, reading the descriptions of the defense mechanisms in Part VI may help you recognize the defenses you may favor from time to time.

...he turned left at the trail-marker on a whim of wind,
knowing from that faded, carved
and yellow-painted wood sign only that this way winded.
Feet slipped steep in the dirt-rock-dust of the new slope
and the first traces of coming wind were welcome feelings.
In the bending of branches and leaf-rustlings
he seemed to hear the first half of a song that
came soft and simple, like the subtle
saying of a name, meaning 'come here'...

With varying shades
in many tones
Comes the dream
and what seems
is shown.
And seeds are sown
when well it's known
That beneath one sun
are gardens grown

and he stopped.
Beneath the long shade, and small
beside the trunk of an old tree, he
stopped and looked back.
In his previous path, amongst the puddles,
around the rocks; in the soft mixes of earth and water,
there, in the footprints he realized a story had been
written. And turning back to the winding path,
wished only that he had paid more
attention to its writing...

From *With Visions, Not Plans In Their Pockets*
By William Ladnier

Introduction

Personality traits are enduring patterns of perceiving, relating to, and thinking about, the environment and oneself that are exhibited in a wide range of social and personal contexts.

DSM-5

AFTER TEN YEARS of full-time graduate school in the behavioral sciences, and many more years working as a psychotherapist and family therapist, I finally woke up one day and realized that I was as poorly trained as the therapists my parents sent me to in high school. These expensive therapists, in hindsight, were helpless when it came to understanding my personality and behavior, or spotting the dysfunctional environment in which I was living. Decades went by before I walked into a bookstore and just happened to pick up a book with the information I needed to begin my journey towards understanding myself as well as the family that raised me. Amazingly, my ten years of full-time graduate school and three graduate degrees in the behavioral sciences were essentially useless in this process. With this accidental increase in my self-knowledge and self-understanding, and further research, I became a more adept observer of myself as I interacted with other people and the environment. These self-observations afforded me increasingly accurate insights into my personality and the characteristics of the family that raised me. My own life finally began to make some sense, and the dysfunction in my extended family of origin began to crystallize into a comprehensible whole of genetic and environmental influences. I now believe there are many people experiencing a similar struggle while receiving little information and help from therapists whose training was as inadequate as my own academic experience. Most self-help books are little better, with some authors displaying fake degrees on the cover.

Today, my most important goal as a therapist is to help my clients understand their basic personality, the family in which they were raised, and their current family or living environment so they can begin to observe their own life experiences from a more knowledgeable perspective. Reflecting on their self-observations, my clients have their own increasingly accurate insights into their ways of thinking and being. Of course, developing a better understanding of their past and present family functioning is a natural part of the process. The inevitable increase in self-awareness gives my clients the ability to "choose" new ways of responding to other people and the environment. They can also choose new ways of responding to their own thoughts, feelings, and behaviors, even as their thoughts, feelings, and behaviors are changing via their new insights and self-awareness. In a real sense, my clients become their own therapist—the only therapist who can get inside their head twenty-four hours a day.

This book is designed to help you finally discover aspects of your basic personality that you may not have previously been aware of and to help you better understand yourself, your relationships, and your past and present family life. This book may also help you avoid dysfunctional relationships in the future by helping you to more readily spot dysfunctional personalities in other people.

John B. Evans, PhD, LCSW

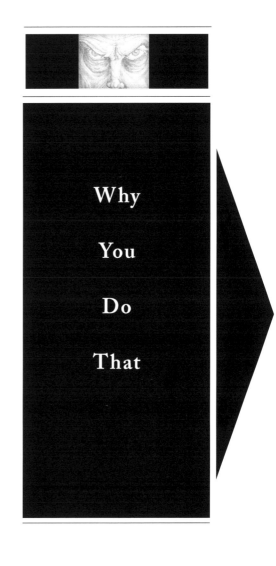

Why You Do That

PART 1

Personalities–Generally Speaking

We are all apprentices in a craft where no one ever becomes a master.
—Ernest Hemingway

PERSONALITY REFERS TO our enduring patterns of thinking, emotions, emotional control, motivations, and outward behavior with reference to self, others, and the environment in which we live. Generally speaking, *personality* refers to how we view and react to life, and personality plays a central role in an individual's self-concept and the values they embrace. Although no two personalities are the same, there are many common patterns and categories of inner experience and behavior that, if recognized, can contribute greatly to our self-knowledge, self-awareness, and self-control. Some people are inflexible in their responses to life, while others seem to drift with the prevailing winds. Some people are shy, while others are more outgoing. Some people seem to think too much, while others appear overly emotional. And on and on. How often do we think we understand someone's behavior, or what they are thinking or feeling, when, in fact, we understand very little—or nothing at all? Unknown to most people is that this same lack of awareness about others may also apply to ourselves. As a rule, society expects us to "fit in" rather than maintain our individuality, but struggle as we may, most people will sometimes say or do the wrong thing, be misunderstood, offend someone, or just create some awkward moment when they wish they were somewhere else. For those less able or less willing to play the game, the child may be bullied at school, or become the bully, and the eccentric employee may be ridiculed openly by an equally dysfunctional boss or more quietly by coworkers at the water cooler. Of course, these judgmental coworkers may have equal difficulty making some aspect of life work for themselves. Some personalities just quietly blend in while feeling considerable anxiety and tension from the struggle to do so. Elsewhere on the personality chart are successful people who seem to be admired by everyone except, of course, the people they scam and cheat all the way to the top of the corporate ladder. These personalities can seemingly do no wrong, except when it suits them, and if there is a problem, it's someone else's fault. Unfortunately, most people, and frequently their therapists as well, never recognize the underlying personality that contributes to the dysfunctional coping styles they have adopted. While many people may attempt to change some aspect of their personality, others make little effort to modify their personality because they have so little self-awareness in the first place. This is not surprising, since personality problems sometimes cause less distress for the sufferer than for those who must deal with the sufferer.[34] Few of us are able to observe our own personality in an objective manner since our self-observations are influenced by the very personality we are trying to assess.[76] A further complication is that most of the information we have about ourselves is learned via the reactions and observations of others,[34] and we do not always accurately perceive the reactions of others. Of course, the reactions of others may have their own dysfunctional content.

Unfortunately, learning from our mistakes may seem like a very slow process, taking years or decades during which we continue to use poor judgment and display personal flaws we do not understand. The results for some may include lost relationships, estranged children, or problems at work, while others may hold themselves back through indecisiveness, procrastination, or withdrawal and isolation. Maybe you have been in therapy in an attempt to figure yourself out, but although you find you feel better after seeing your therapist, long-term changes in your life still seem elusive. Struggle as we may, some dysfunctional thoughts, feelings, and behaviors appear hardwired into our bodies. They just seem to come out of us, especially when we act spontaneously, an essential ingredient in healthy relationships. Paying strict attention to our thinking while we slowly compose a response might improve the response choice itself, but this kind of slow, deliberate response at all times is not feasible and would itself be viewed as odd or eccentric behavior.

In my work as a psychotherapist and family therapist, I have found that many of the thoughts, feelings, and behaviors that create problems for people come out of known personality *styles* that most of us experience to some degree, although usually outside of our awareness. Research indicates that even the more severe personality *disorders* are more common than past estimates have suggested,[39] with estimates falling somewhere between 10 percent to 20 percent of the general population.[5] Determining the number of people with a diagnosable level of a personality disorder is difficult and involves some guesswork, since these individuals tend to be reluctant to seek treatment, participate in research, etc.[11]

Less well known and even more difficult to detect is the prevalence of milder forms of these same personalities. While most people do not have the more serious and diagnosable levels of a personality or mood *disorder*, most of us do have a recognizable personality *style* where we may exhibit mild levels of some of the same traits associated with more serious disorders. The more serious and diagnosable personality *disorders* are now recognized as just more extreme versions of normal behaviors.[7,36,48] Psychology professor Svenn Torgersen of the University of Oslo points to the "…continuous relationship between those with no or small personality problems, those with moderate problems, and those with severe problems. No natural cutoff point exists."[39] Even the mildest personality traits can have maladaptive effects on our thoughts, feelings, and behaviors throughout our lives. People considered to be relatively normal may still exhibit some odd or eccentric behaviors, and their eccentricities may sometimes get in their way, causing problems in their career, relationships, parenting, etc. For example, one of the features most commonly associated with the more serious personality disorders is some level of inflexibility in the responses to different or changing circumstances.[34] I have found those with milder personality styles to also repeatedly exhibit the same dysfunctional behavioral patterns, making the same mistakes over and over again.

Compounding the issue is the fact that many people experience more than one personality style,[6] creating personality patterns of thoughts, feelings, and behaviors that are derived from varied sources yet commingle into the unique personality that defines each of us. Arising from multiple sources, our more normal behaviors seem to blend into the eccentricities that contribute considerably to the individuality by which others know us.

LACK OF AWARENESS

How often we make circumstances our prison and other people our jailers.

—Sheldon Kopp

WHILE SOME PEOPLE may have some awareness of their personality traits, for others there may be little or no self-awareness at all. Personality patterns tend to appear gradually during childhood and adolescence, and this gradual process may contribute to a lack of awareness within the nuclear family. With this slow developmental onset, parents have time to become accustomed to the child or adolescent's changing behavior and may fail to notice the nature of the developing personality. Even with more serious levels of personality dysfunction, parents frequently fail to notice the gradual changes occurring in their children because the normal turmoil and angst of childhood and adolescence mask these changes. Of course, parents' lack of awareness about their own personality and/or the dynamics of their marital relationship will negatively effect their awareness of the overall family functioning.

For many people, it is only years later that they begin to sense the chronic nature and intransigence of their problems, and some people may never recognize the role their basic personality plays in creating their problems. For these individuals, the problems they do recognize always seem to be caused by their spouse, children, boss, coworkers, bad luck, etc. So how is it so many people miss the elephant sitting squarely on top of them?

One of the main reasons people do not recognize the irrational aspects of their personalities over long periods of time is that our brains are wired to look outside of ourselves to make sense of the world. While this external search for understanding may help us solve various problems in our life, or put footprints on the moon, most of us will experience some level of ignorance, an irrational bias, or outright denial about our own thoughts, emotions, and behavior. Research scientists have elaborate research techniques specifically designed to prevent our biases from distorting the results and interpretation of scientific studies, but we do not have a scientific method for daily life experiences. Consider these examples of the tendency to look outside of ourselves for explanations that actually reside within:

Example 1: *An individual suffering from mild depression goes into an art gallery and thinks the art is just awful. She is not aware that she is wearing "depression glasses" and that many things she looks at, experiences, or thinks about appear negative in some way because she is projecting her depressed mood onto the person, object, or event—the art, in this example.*

In a similar way, depression glasses may cause a depressed father to severely punish his child because his depressed mood interprets the child's minor misbehavior as a severe infraction, or he may criticize his wife over trivial issues. He fails to recognize that he is in a bad mood, i.e., depressed, and that his poor state of mind preceded the perceived infractions of other family members. Unfortunately, most people suffering mild depression are not aware of the depression and its effect on them.

Example 2: *Individuals with some level of an obsessive-compulsive personality come to my office after seeing multiple therapists about their seemingly intractable anger and temper tantrums. In most cases, the other therapists missed the obsessive-compulsive aspect of their clients'* *personality and never explained to their clients that their quick anger and temper tantrums, need for control, need to be right, and willingness to publicly humiliate others may be symptoms of an obsessive-compulsive personality.*

In some cases, these individuals are aware they have some degree of an obsessive-compulsive personality, with traits such as a need for perfection, orderliness, cleanliness, etc. They just don't know that the need to be right, a quick temper, etc. can also be symptoms of the same personality. For years these clients have told their therapists and their anger-control groups that their anger was caused by other people, events, circumstances, and on and on. Simply realizing their anger stems from some level of an obsessive-compulsive personality, or some other personality, can give motivated individuals considerable conscious control over their irrational emotions and behavior.

Example 3: *This same external focus to make sense of the world is evident in the individual who suffers even mild paranoia and interprets his or her spouse's extra time at work as obvious signs of an affair.*

We tend to look outside of ourselves for explanations rather than seeking to understand that which is within because we usually do not even know about that which is within. Another difficulty is that our dysfunctional responses may initially seem appropriate and effective to some extent, even if only at reducing stress. The problem is compounded by years of blaming other people or circumstances for various problems. Needless to say, we cannot seek to understand that which we are not even aware of in the first place. Unfortunately, most people never make the connection between their personality traits and their thoughts, emotions, and behaviors.

ISOLATION

SYMPTOMS OF A dysfunctional personality may be reflected in the level of relationships with, or detachment from, other people.[34] Problems dealing with other people may be the most common symptom of personality-related issues. An inaccurate self-image, shyness, difficulty understanding others, being overly emotional or emotionally constricted, impulsive, rigid and inflexible, moody, angry, or just exhibiting a consistent pattern of social missteps and blunders may create difficulties when dealing with other people on a daily basis. For some people, their verbal or behavioral eccentricities may alienate them from effective participation in the community, and they may experience some degree of isolation. There are people who prefer their isolation and care little what other people think about them, but for others, life may be a combination of chronic loneliness and stress.

It is common for those with more serious personality issues to live alone, as they are more likely to experience divorce or just never marry. Yet those with less severe symptoms may also suffer some impairment.[34] Isolation not only helps maintain one's unusual nature, but can be a major contributor to ever-increasing oddness and eccentricity. A vicious circle begins when other people distance themselves from the unusual and unexpected behaviors of the eccentric. While isolation may be the product of an individual's eccentric or dysfunctional personality, isolation also creates the conditions that exacerbate the individual's dysfunctional symptoms. Isolation offers fewer opportunities for individuals to practice modifying their behavior, and serious isolation almost invariably leads to an increase in low self-esteem and depression, accompanied by ever-increasing odd or eccentric behavior that may result in even more isolation. The individual who goes over the edge in some way is often described by neighbors as a loner who "just kept to himself."

When people with dysfunctional personalities finally seek professional help, they frequently come in complaining about loneliness and depression. Those feeling the loneliness of isolation may not be aware of other symptoms or underlying personality traits, and overcoming the effects of isolation may be one of the most difficult challenges some people ever face. Efforts to make changes in self and life are much more difficult and challenging for those who are cut off from their fellow struggling souls. Therapy, individual at first and group counseling later, can be very effective at helping isolated individuals learn to understand themselves and develop the coping and interpersonal skills they need to better relate to other travelers on their own life journey. A very important step in this process, of course, is for lonely and isolated individuals to recognize that they are, in fact, not alone in their lonely world. There are many isolated people who long to reach out but do not believe anyone is interested.

PERSONALITIES IN RELATIONSHIPS & FAMILIES

A COMPREHENSIVE READING of the personality descriptions in this book may help you understand not only yourself, but also someone you are involved with in a relationship or have been involved with in the past. Since our personalities obviously play a major role in the level of stability in our relationships and family life, reading the personality descriptions in this book may help you understand your past or current family situation or help you avoid becoming involved in a dysfunctional or abusive relationship in the future. The ability to more readily spot the red flags exhibited by others is a serious skill.

Many dysfunctional personalities tend to be rigid in their responses to new or changing circumstances, while other personalities react with logical reasoning when some emotional expression would handle the situation better—or vice versa. Others may be known for their offbeat way of thinking, unusual sense of humor, negative or pessimistic view of the world, or displays of anger. Still others may exhibit overly loose or overly strict values and ethics, a tendency to blurt things out without forethought, or they might be manipulative or abusive in some way. Some people may have a somewhat blank outward demeanor that gives no clue to what they are thinking or feeling, while others may overreact to the slightest stimulus. But these are not the traits we typically encounter when we first meet someone.

Everyone puts on a fictional front or facade, sometimes referred to as a *persona*, that they present to the public. While some facades are thicker than others, it is not very often—if ever—that we meet a completely authentic and unvarnished person. It is only with time that we begin to get to know the real person beneath the false front that is offered for public consumption. Initially a dysfunctional personality may come across as exciting, brilliant, adventurous, sexy, caring, confident, and on and on. People may be attracted to one of these characteristics or by the individual's physical features, musical or artistic talent, success in business, or high position with power and authority. Maybe potential partners are not sure why they feel attracted to someone and view their love interest as somewhat mysterious. It is our attraction to shallow surface features that makes it so important that we remain aware of the personality traits in others as well as ourselves, especially the traits associated with abusive personalities. With an ability to spot the red flags given off by all but the most artful manipulators, and by not allowing love's denial to cloud one's reasoning, it is usually not that difficult to put together a picture of where a relationship might be headed.

Needless to say, most of us are a little nervous and feel a little awkward when we first meet someone, and experience tells us the more we worry about screwing up, the more likely we are to do so. But whether it's worrying about making an embarrassing social mistake or actually making one, these are usually normal human responses rather than dysfunctional responses, and the relaxation and familiarity that come with time usually resolve the issue. The crucial point here is that it is this same relaxation and familiarity over time that allow an individual's basic nature, whether dysfunctional or not, to surface.

With time, the brain chemicals that induce the infatuation, or *honeymoon stage*, of a relationship will subside, and only then does the initial persona, the full-time act put on to impress and win favor, begin to give way to the true self. This initial honeymoon stage typically lasts from six months to a year or more, although some personalities are prone to less infatuation or shorter honeymoons. When someone becomes less vigilant and more spontaneous in their thoughts, feelings, and behaviors, their true nature will begin to make itself known to those who are not too blind to see. Where the initial facade is more entrenched, the lack of authenticity itself usually becomes apparent over time and becomes its own red flag. Where alcohol or drugs are involved, the false fronts people put on tend to be thicker, more irrational, and more deeply entrenched. This includes people who are in extreme denial about their personality, have poor self-control, or have a need to self-medicate.

Personality plays a role in who people choose as mates,[106] and people who are in a dysfunctional relationship, or have a history of dysfunctional relationships, need to take a look at their own personality to see why red flags given off by their mates in the past were missed or ignored. Are you a caretaker or overly trusting and gullible? Did you think the relationship itself would eventually change the dysfunctional partner? Did you think your partner would change when children arrived on the scene? Those having experienced dysfunctional relationships must also consider whether they contributed to the problems via their own personality and lack of self-awareness. It is infinitely easier to spot the red flags in yourself and others if you possess a higher level of self-awareness along with some understanding of personality traits and characteristics. It is common for people in dysfunctional relationships to look back and recognize that they were aware of some of the red flags displayed in the early stages of their relationship—but ignored them. With hindsight, they may recognize that they went into some level of denial and were unable to be assertive and demand to be treated differently or just leave the relationship altogether. For some people, painful or abusive relationships may be less scary than being alone. For example, it is critical for those with some level of a dependent personality or an avoidant personality to remain aware of their fear of being alone or venturing out without a caretaker. A fear of being alone can result in a very irrational choice for a mate, since the sufferer may choose almost anyone who comes along. Knowledge and self-awareness of their personality allow dependent and avoidant personalities to consciously overrule their irrational tendency to settle for the lowest common denominator.

The goal for most people, presumably, is to find someone who has a high level of self-awareness, good self-control, and a value system that allows for true empathy and caring for another. These characteristics are sometimes referred to as *stability*, and all potential mates should be subjected to the same educated scrutiny over time. While meeting someone who is undergoing some form of therapy could be considered a red flag, it may also be the sign of someone who is not in denial, can admit personal flaws, and, most important, work on them. On the other hand, abusive personalities frequently get into therapy so they can manipulatively tell their partner and others they are in therapy and "working on myself."

While a given dysfunctional trait or symptom in a potential partner may not be a deal breaker—no one is perfect—it is important to keep a balanced and reality-based running tab in the back of your mind as you get to know someone. People with severely dysfunctional personalities tend to give off red flags in multiple areas of life. You want to be very careful if you meet someone who has been divorced three times, has poor credit, lost his home to foreclosure, has an unstable job history, or talks

about how awful his ex-girlfriend or ex-wife treated him or how the ex-wife turned their children against him. You also want to be very careful with someone who has poor relations with his parents and siblings (See Part IV). On the other hand, some people become absurdly picky and high-maintenance. For these people, the grass is always greener at the next social event, and they can spend decades looking for Mr. or Ms. Perfect. These individuals seem to want only what they don't have.

If you want to have children or already have children from a previous relationship, you must consider how the potential partner's personality will impact the children. It is frequently the children who suffer the most in dysfunctional families. It is recognized that the level and kind of parental attachment a child develops in early life may affect the individual's adjustment as an adult. As young adults, people may form similar styles of attachment to future romantic partners. There is also evidence that a parent will tend to form the same kind of attachment pattern with their child that they experienced with their own parent when they were a child.[125] Will the future parent's personality result in irrational and excessive punishment that replaces both rational explanations for decisions and logical consequences for discipline?[45]

Of course, the way children are raised plays a major role in passing the parents' dysfunction on to their own children. As stated by Geri Fox of the Department of Psychiatry at the University of Illinois-Chicago, "Children rehearse and internalize their parents' style of emotional responding from an early age. We find ourselves reacting as our own parents did."[128] Fox points out the importance of parents understanding their child's personality and temperament as well as their own so they can adjust their parenting style according to the child's needs. Ideally, there is a good fit between child and parent. An anxious child would

benefit from growing up in a home with less anxious parents, and there could be serious and ongoing conflict in a home where an overly cautious parent routinely stifles and inhibits a naturally outgoing child. Of course, children's needs change as they grow into later childhood and adolescence. As a child changes, the parents must also change.

Research indicates that inadequate parenting that does not rise to the level of official abuse or neglect may still lead to maladaptive personality traits and disorders in children.[41] Will the potential mate enjoy spending time with the children or be so obsessed with work or his own personal projects that both the partner and the children will be viewed as interruptions to be sidelined and ignored? Parents' lack of affection, communication, or quality time spent with the child, as well as a controlling parenting style, are associated with personality problems in both adolescents and the adults they later become. A child who grows up with parents who take the time to explain the reasons for treating other people a certain way and model empathic behavior toward others is much more likely to grow up displaying more empathy for the feelings and needs of others. This is important, since developing the ability to care for others becomes the basis for a person's general moral code.[125] One study obtained descriptions of the amount of warmth children received from their parents and found a significant correlation between these descriptions and the level of physical and emotional health of these same individuals 35 years later.[123]

Spanking? The research is in.[109,110] Physical punishment is harmful to children, even though research suggests that up to 90 percent of parents in the United States resort to this quick fix for child misbehavior. With this level of social support, even a minimally unstable personality, especially those emphasizing power, control, and a lack of empathy, are given license to do serious damage to a child's emotions and self-esteem. The American Academy of Pediatrics (AAP) does not endorse spanking for any reason, and 32 countries have passed laws designed to eliminate the physical punishment of children, although the United States and Canada have not joined the club. Spanking creates fear in a child and lowers a child's self-esteem. Spanking also models aggressive behavior as an appropriate response to problems, and spanking aggressive children sends a mixed message to the child.[125] Physical punishment has been associated with later problems, including depression, anxiety, and the abuse of drugs and alcohol. Children may learn to lie to avoid punishment. Physical punishment also damages the parent-child relationship and causes the child to feel anger toward the parent, and these negative emotions may continue into adolescence and adulthood. I cannot count the number of clients I have seen visibly tense up when they talk about one or both of their parents. Unfortunately, many people may not know of any other method of discipline, especially if they were spanked as a child. Parenting classes that teach appropriate parenting skills are rarely a part of school curriculums.

Parents experiencing marital strife or personal difficulties may unconsciously choose one particular child on whom they focus their anger and hostility. This child, referred to as the *scapegoat*,[112,127] receives the brunt of the parents' criticism, punishment, blame, rejection, and isolation, as the parents essentially use this child as a diversion from their marital problems or other personal problems.[111] The scapegoated child may grow up with the lowest of self-esteem, as the child repeatedly internalizes the parents' negative messages. Further damage may occur when children raised by critical, hostile, or neglectful parents grow up to treat themselves in the same negative way they were treated by their parents.[37] Not surprisingly, research has found that maladaptive personalities and behaviors in children may have further negative effects on the parenting style of the parents,[41] resulting in a two-way downward spiral of poor parental responses to worsening behavior on the part of the child—back and forth—for years.

So how many children have a "normal" childhood with little dysfunction in their family of origin? I have always believed that you could drive down any street in America, or the world, and pick out any number of houses at random, and if you could go inside these homes and really get to know the families living there, including the so-called "family secrets," you would almost always find some problems. You might find a depressed father, obsessive-compulsive mother, a shy adolescent who is withdrawn or into drugs, a pregnant teenager, an eating disorder, depression, anxiety, problems at school, chronic unemployment, and on and on. Or you might find lesser problems, but still problems, that the family must deal with on a daily basis. It is very common for family members to have little or no awareness of the problems in their midst or, at least, the severity of their problems. Some families are healthier than others, but I have found the normal family to be a convenient concept—more the exception than the rule. Many children grow up without the parental support, attention, empathy, affection, communication, and quality time known to help children develop confidence, resiliency, social skills, coping skills, and a sense of optimism about the future (see Part IV).

I am sometimes asked how some people can have so little apparent self-awareness about the ill treatment or abuse they dish out to those they profess to love. You may be aware of people who

are rude or abusive to their "loved ones" or, from the other end, allow themselves or their children to be mistreated or abused. Most abusive relationships involve verbal and emotional abuse rather than physical abuse, and most abusers are probably aware at some level that their behavior is unacceptable. In some cases, though, such as the paranoid, antisocial, narcissistic, or obsessive-compulsive personalities, individuals' ill-mannered or abusive behavior and their lack of empathy for others may be built into the structure of their personality. Their behavior makes sense from their way of thinking, so they feel entitled to be that way and see no reason to change. In some severe cases, the perpetrator may be a sociopath, which is someone who does not experience the feelings and emotions necessary for a fully functioning conscience. Without a conscience, the sociopath is not capable of feeling guilt or remorse and cannot develop accurate concepts of empathy, caring, or love. Sociopaths are not just the serial killers we read about. Approximately one in 25 people is a sociopath,[75] and they walk among us every day. But these are the extreme cases. In most cases involving the mistreatment of others, the explanations are more mundane.

An abusive personality may have been raised in a chaotic household where he watched an abusive parent reap the entitlements and privileges that come from intimidation, control, and always getting his way. From the other end, being abused may seem normal to the victim who grew up watching her mother suffer abuse for years or who was raised in a conservative religious environment where she was taught that a woman's role is to be submissive. Of course, her own daughter may, in turn, learn submissive ways from her. Some circles need to be broken. Still, in many cases involving an angry, manipulative, and controlling personality with little empathy for others, it is just an angry, manipulative, and controlling personality with little empathy for others.

It is typically the partner who brings an abuser in for counseling, possibly after an ultimatum with a threat of divorce. I usually recommend couples counseling at first, because individual therapy with an abusive personality tends to be ineffective. In most cases, abusers attempt to manipulate the therapist by rationalizing or downplaying the severity of events, while trying to focus the blame for most problems on the abused woman. As part of couples therapy, it is essential for the therapist to also have a private individual session with the abused partner or spouse so that a more accurate account of the couple's dysfunctional relationship is offered. Many abused women find themselves unable to speak frankly while the abuser is sitting right there, since past attempts to do so at home have usually ended badly.

The couples sessions will allow the therapist to gain a sense of how the two partners respond to each other by watching how they interact during the session. This is most important where an abusive personality is involved, since the abuser's manipulations and control are usually deeply ingrained in the way he interacts with his partner. The exceptions here are abusers who have already been busted in previous therapy and have now learned how to better manipulate their partner, the therapist, and even the criminal justice system.

It is critical to understand that just telling yourself that you can leave a relationship if it becomes dysfunctional or abusive does not reflect the difficulty and complexity of actually doing so. I have had many clients who would always feel an extreme sense of guilt at just the thought of leaving even an extremely abusive relationship. Needless to say, if one partner has a propensity for

PART 1: PERSONALITIES—GENERALLY SPEAKING 27

guilt and self-blame, this gives the other partner enormous control over how the guilt-ridden partner responds to the relationship. The longer an abusive relationship continues, and the more abusive and dysfunctional the relationship becomes, the more difficult it can be to end,[12] and this is the case if there are no children involved. Add children to the mix, and it can be almost impossible for a victim of abuse to eliminate the abuser from her life.

It is not always just one dysfunctional personality that creates difficulties in a relationship. Dysfunctional personalities seem to attract each other, and dysfunctional responses to dysfunctional behaviors will always complicate things. Difficult relationships are frequently avoided early on, since people frequently stop dating those who appear unstable, eccentric, less self-aware, or emotionally unhealthy. The more self-aware individual eventually recognizes the unusual thinking, insecurity, critical nature, eccentricity, need for control, etc. displayed by the more neurotic personality and moves on to greener pastures. The point is that we tend to recognize dysfunctional or eccentric behavior in people who are more dysfunctional or eccentric than we are or, at least, who are dysfunctional in a different way.

Eventually, the neurotic individual will meet someone who is just as neurotic as he or she is, and they may form a relationship where both partners are somewhat blind to both their own, and each other's, dysfunctional traits and symptoms. This may result in a long-term relationship in which two neurotic personalities play off of each other, creating a highly dysfunctional relationship that is greater than the sum of its neurotic parts. This environment does not bode well for the relationship or family life, especially the children. Of course, some relatively normal people do marry eccentric or somewhat unstable others because they fall in love with the positive traits they see, and these sometimes turn out to be very good relationships. In an accepting and nonjudgmental environment, the dysfunctional individual may grow into a relatively normal-functioning partner and parent—or not.

A process of mutual growth sometimes occurs in relationships where both personalities are dysfunctional. It is a truism among family therapists that if one member of a dysfunctional family does the work to increase their self-awareness and modify their own dysfunctional behavior, a ripple effect may cause other family members to change their behavior as well, even if they are not consciously aware of the changes occurring in their midst. Of course, attempts to change a relationship in this way offer no guarantees and are almost never effective in relationships involving abuse or personality patterns where one partner consciously and calculatingly manipulates the other partner. Serious abusers usually do not change, although they do get really nice for even extended periods of time to keep their spouse or partner from leaving the relationship (see chapter: The Abusive Personality / Abusive Relationships).

NATURE VS. NURTURE

THE NATURE VS. nurture debate refers to the effects of our genetic endowment—the *nature* part—as influenced by the environment in which we were raised and live—the *nurture* part. Since the fifth century BC, there has been an awareness of the uniqueness and predictability of individual behavior patterns, and even in ancient times, it was recognized that our behavior patterns had biological correlates. The ancient philosophers, of course, did not know about genes and neurotransmitters, so they referred to irregularities in blood, black bile, yellow bile, phlegm, etc.[35]

While many personality issues may stem from the family environment we were installed in at birth through no fault of our own, it is also clear that many aspects of personality may be products of the genes we inherit.[35] Today mental-health professionals recognize the ongoing interaction between the genes we inherit and the environments in which we grow up and live. It works both ways. Just as the experiences we have in life may become hardwired into our brains, genetic connections may, in turn, play a role in our life experiences.[14] For example, neurobiological research has demonstrated that stress and childhood mistreatment can modify the brain circuits that respond to stress. This may lead to deficient brain activity with an increased risk for psychological and psychiatric problems later on.[14,41]

Glen Gobbard of the Menninger Department of Psychiatry at the Baylor College of Medicine points out that even our self-image and our emotional connectedness to other people involve repetitive patterns of thought and behavior that become a physical part of our brain chemistry during development.[42] All of us have genetic predispositions that may lead to problems, depending on the environment and stressors to which we are exposed.[44] Keep in mind that a genetic connection does not necessarily imply recognizable problems in the family history. Behavioral styles or disorders with a genetic connection may skip generations or appear to show up for the first time in a family's known history.

While we know it is the combined effects of both genetics and environment that shape our personality, predicting the outcome of these influences on personality is a risky endeavor. The interplay of environment and genetics does not lend itself to absolute rules. If an individual's genetic makeup predisposes him to develop a dysfunctional personality style or disorder, but he is raised in a stable and supportive home environment, his genes may have less of an impact on his behavior both in childhood and later on as an adult. An example of this is the individual who has a genetic predisposition toward anxiety and worry, a common symptom by itself, but frequently accompanying a larger personality pattern. This tendency toward anxiety and worry may not develop into a problem if there is a stable childhood, but if this genetic predisposition is exposed to a neurotic parent who is punitive, critical, or helicopters over the child, the result may be an insecure child with low self-esteem, little self-confidence, and some level of depression as well. This child's difficulties may then be exacerbated by teasing by other students at school, and the child's symptoms may endure as the child grows into adulthood—or maybe not.

Some people, raised in what appear to be the healthiest home environments, may descend down a path of increasingly counter-productive behaviors at various levels of severity, while others who are raised in severely dysfunctional homes may end

up psychologically healthy in most respects. Genes do count. As stated by James D. Herbert, "Just as estimates of heritability derived from family studies are limited by shared environmental effects, so too are studies of parenting effects limited by shared genetics."[30] The environments that parents create for their children are, in part, due to the parents' own genetic makeup. On top of that, since biological children carry some of the same genetic makeup as their parents, the environment created by the parents may have a greater impact on their biological children than it would have on adopted children with a different genetic code.[19]

Regardless of how these interactions play themselves out in a given individual, the results may persist into adolescence and adult life in the form of personality-based traits, as well as fluctuating moods and dispositions. Yet, with some degree of an accurate self-awareness and self-knowledge, choice can play a decisive role in the personality outcome. Perseverance and a desire to be the CEO of your own life can definitely make a difference in how you handle the cards you are dealt.

PERSONALITY CHANGE

QUESTION: Can we change those aspects of our personality that seem so endlessly intractable? The answer to this question is an unqualified *YES*—but an essential first step is to develop an accurate self-knowledge about the personality-based characteristics that influence our thoughts, feelings, and behaviors. Understanding our personality helps us to separate our symptomatic thoughts, feelings, and behaviors from those that are more rational and less problematic. Personality traits that are not understood, or not even recognized, will influence an individual's behavior for life, although the severity of problems may vary over time, depending on a person's disposition, life circumstances, and level of stress.

Many people experience diminishing symptoms over the years.[34,40] Although childhood personalities are clearly linked to the adult personalities they become,[104] there is considerable evidence that personalities can change at any age through the experiences people have via work, social relationships, marriage, etc., although some people are more amenable to change than others. Over time, personality change may occur when we observe other people or hear what others think about us. Our personalities may also change when we observe ourselves in various circumstances, including social situations.[107] Personalities may change in a positive way when there are positive experiences such as a supportive family during adolescence, a first serious relationship as a young adult, getting married or remarried in late middle age, or experiencing other satisfying relationships generally.[104] A child's personality may change according to the parenting style the child is exposed to.

Over time, some people with impulsive or aggressive symptoms seem to grow out of their dysfunctional character. On the other hand, introverted behaviors tend to increase with age,[34,40] and a negative change in personality may occur if an individual is on the receiving end of an abusive relationship.[12] Still, for those whose symptoms lessen with age, there may remain some cognitive, emotional, or behavioral inclinations that will alter and shape their behavior for life unless they develop some conscious control over themselves.

Understanding your childhood and other past influences can definitely contribute to an understanding of your past and present thoughts, feelings, and behaviors. Yet understanding your past history may still leave you perplexed about your personality until you first recognize and understand your underlying basic nature. Increased self-awareness will help you get your personality off automatic pilot. The greatest stability for individuals who make no effort to modify their behavior and just allow their personality to run its course may occur around the age of 50 or so,[47] and not everyone is happy with themselves at that age. The choice, of course, is yours alone. While you may not be responsible for creating your personality, it is your responsibility to work on your personality in the present, simply because no one else can do it for you. The idea of self-discovery and actually working to change some aspect of ourselves can be scary and intimidating, and many people unconsciously shy away from the experience.

Therapists must attempt to figure out which features of an individual's thoughts, feelings, and behaviors are long-term personality traits and which features are more temporary responses to current situations.[34] Needless to say, misdiagnoses are common, especially since many clients only seek help during some serious but temporary crisis. Even therapists trained in personality assessment may only look for the more serious and diagnosable personality *disorders*, while missing the more subtle influences of milder personality *styles*. While I am all for a professional diagnosis when needed, I encourage my clients to become very educated about themselves, which will put them in a position to experience their own insights into their personality over an extended period of time. The extended time factor for self-observation is very important because only knowledgeable and non-defensive self-observations over an extended period of time will allow for the consistent inclusion of new information and new insights with ever-increasing accuracy. No therapist will ever have the consistent and comprehensive access to your personality that you possess. Continuously updating your self-awareness with your own insights and self-reflections will, over time, give you a much more accurate understanding of who you are. You will then be in a better position to tackle those problematic behaviors that may appear to have external causes, appear random, or simply have remained outside of your conscious awareness altogether.

Many personality styles are known to frequently co-occur.[6] It is common for people to have a combination of several personality styles that create patterns of thought, emotion, and behavior that make no logical sense until they recognize the multiple and divergent sources from which their personality emanates. Personality traits intermingle and blend together in a multitude of ways. It is this complexity that requires effort over time to develop greater control over ourselves and develop the ability to *choose* who we will be in life.

By identifying the specific thoughts, feelings, and behaviors in Part II that seem to reflect your personality patterns, and then reading the comprehensive descriptions of the relevant personalities in Part III, you may identify personality traits you

had not previously recognized or thought about in a serious way. You may also recognize traits you already know about but had not realized were related and stem from the same source.

Finally, no matter how well you get to know yourself and understand your behavior, you will still occasionally be a complete doofus. Behavior is much too complex for total mastery, and those who attempt to gain total mastery over their responses to life will simply present a controlled, awkward, and stilted persona—one flawed personality exchanged for another—as they struggle for self-perfection.

Please note that it can be very difficult to spot dysfunctional personality characteristics or symptoms in children and adolescents. Personality-related problems in children and adolescents may look a lot like the normal turmoil and angst that very young people typically experience. I strongly encourage the use of an experienced professional specializing in children for an accurate understanding of a child's dysfunctional behaviors.

PART II

The Search for Self-Knowledge,
Self-Understanding, and Self-Awareness

THE QUEST FOR SELF: GETTING STARTED

IN THIS BOOK, I will identify the common traits associated with commonly recognized patterns of thought, emotion, and behavior, and I will include examples of how these personalities typically play themselves out in everyday life. I will also discuss the behaviors associated with the abusive personality and the dynamics of abusive relationships.

People are very complex, and understanding ourselves and developing greater self-awareness requires an active self-interest over time. For now, read through the list of specific thoughts, feelings, and behaviors in Part II, and mark any description that rings the slightest bell about you in any way. You may find the thoughts, feelings, and behaviors you have noted fit one or more of the known personality patterns very well, or it may be less obvious. There is considerable overlap among the traits associated with various personalities, and you may find yourself uncertain as to whether you fit one or more of these patterns. Some uncertainty at this stage in the process is to be expected.

I then encourage you to go to Part III and read the full description of any personality pattern in which you recognized the slightest hint of yourself in Part II. When reading the personality descriptions in Part III, it is important to highlight any part that appears to describe you, even just a little, so that you will be able to periodically review the highlighted material. Assuming you have an active and non-defensive interest in self-discovery, your self-observations and self-reflections may require little real effort as the fascination that frequently accompanies self-discovery takes over.

The more familiar you are with the thoughts, feelings, and behaviors you seek to understand, the more likely it will be that some of your self-observations may occur outside of your conscious awareness. From time to time, you may find that some new insight about some aspect of yourself just pops into your head and brings you to a conscious self-reflection about some personal inclination that you had not previously thought much about. Over time, you may conclude that one or more personality patterns fit you very well, some not at all, and other patterns may seem to describe you only in a very mild way.

It is common that no one personality style or pattern sufficiently describes an individual's specific combination of thoughts, feelings, and behaviors.[8] Many people will find they have personality patterns stemming from several personality styles, while others may find they relate primarily to one specific personality style. At the same time, few people will have all of the traits connected to any one personality style.

Over time, you may change your mind about your connection to a given personality description as you develop greater awareness of your personality traits and characteristics. Some of those who think they may experience milder personality patterns, as well as those who recognize a more serious personality or mood disorder, may choose to seek the advice and counsel of a professional. A knowledgeable therapist may spur things along during your journey. Individuals who experience personality patterns or symptoms they do not recognize in the descriptions in this book may also extend their search by seeking the help of a knowledgeable professional. A knowledgeable professional can jump-start the process of recognition and change, and this can dramatically improve an individual's personal functioning and quality of life in general.

Any of us can initially fail to recognize aspects of our personality in the descriptions in Part II or Part III, and some of the defense mechanisms discussed at the end of this book may play a role in these blind spots. Either way, after some time and self-reflection, some of the personality descriptions may ring a stronger bell for those willing to take the time to review Part II or the descriptions in Part III. Over time, you will develop the freedom of thought and behavior that is a natural part of an accurate increase in self-awareness, but this level of self-awareness will necessarily require some effort on your part. As stated by Sheldon Kopp,[3] "To be free, first, you must choose freedom. Then the hard work begins."

SPECIFIC ASPECTS OF YOUR BASIC NATURE

YOU MAY BE *able to quickly identify some of your specific personality traits by reviewing the following 15 sets of specific thoughts, feelings, and behaviors, and mark each example in which you recognize yourself to any extent. At the end of each section, you may decide to read the full description of that personality pattern in Part III. Keep in mind that not all personality-related traits are covered in this book. If you are experiencing serious problems, consultation with a knowledgeable professional is highly recommended.*

1

Does your spouse, partner, boyfriend, girlfriend, or even a more casual friend exhibit any of these behaviors—even if there are fun times or periods of calm? Is this you?

- ☐ He is critical of your thoughts, opinions, feelings, beliefs, things you do, etc.
- ☐ He makes everything your fault. If he does something wrong, it's still your fault, e.g. "I wouldn't have done that if you hadn't (fill in the blank) ."
- ☐ You feel like you are an inadequate partner, and the problems are your fault. You think the relationship would be fine if you could just get your act together and stop upsetting him.
- ☐ When you complain about his behavior, he answers with accusations against you, possibly preventing you from fully addressing the issue you were trying to bring up.

- [ ] He seems to get in the way of or sabotage your efforts to succeed, such as your attempts to go to school, get a better job, etc.
- [ ] You have trouble following his logic during discussions or arguments. In your confusion, he usually seems to get his way.
- [ ] He controls the money and finances.
- [ ] He attempts to isolate you. This may include criticizing your family or friends and preventing you from seeing them. This may also include sabotaging your outside hobbies or activities, getting rid of your pets, etc.
- [ ] He screams, curses, rants, and raves.
- [ ] He makes you feel guilty and responsible by playing the victim. It's always your fault.
- [ ] He tells your friends that you have problems, how dysfunctional you are, or how hard it is for him to deal with you.
- [ ] He frequently asks you some variation of "Are you ok?" or "Are you all right?"
- [ ] He routinely insists on getting his way, or that his view is right, and you feel like you have not even been heard.
- [ ] You have to do most or all of the chores or child-rearing duties.
- [ ] Family possessions, cars, credit cards, the house, etc. are in his name.
- [ ] Sex is on his terms, such as waking you up for sex, forced sex, or forcing you to do things you do not want to do.
- [ ] He gets jealous and accuses you of flirting or cheating.
- [ ] He tries to control you by insisting on knowing where you are most of the time.
- [ ] He routinely uses sarcasm or humor to put you down.
- [ ] He treats you differently in public than in private.

- ☐ He points to your sadness and depression as signs that you have a problem. He fails to mention that it is the way he treats you that makes you sad and depressed.
- ☐ He denies saying what he said or doing what he did, e.g., "I never said (did) that."
- ☐ He treats you and possibly the children like his property. He thinks he owns you.
- ☐ He offers little emotional support to you or the children.
- ☐ He is authoritarian or dictatorial to you or the children.
- ☐ He ignores, or is too busy for, you or the children.
- ☐ He uses the "silent treatment" to get back at you.
- ☐ He disagrees with your parenting techniques in front of the children.
- ☐ He talks about how awful women, or an ex-wife, have treated him in the past.
- ☐ His children dislike him, but he claims his ex-wife turned the children against him.
- ☐ He lies.
- ☐ He says a man should be the head of the household.
- ☐ He has mood shifts, such as irritability or anger, for no apparent reason.
- ☐ He has been physically abusive, even once. Physically abusive behaviors include:
  - Clenched fists
  - Blocking doorways
  - Throwing things at you or near you
  - Threatening to leave you
  - Staring or glaring at you
  - Blocking your exit
  - Getting in your face or physically close in an intimidating way

- Shoving, grabbing, punching, kicking, pinching, scratching, biting
- Restraining you in any way
- Some other physically intimidating behavior

☐ He wants privileges and special treatment that you do not also receive. For example, he sleeps late while you get up to care for the children, or he watches television while you cook and wash dishes, even though you also have a full-time job.

☐ His anger outbursts are unpredictable, appearing to come out of nowhere and for no reason. You are left wondering what you did to cause his anger.

☐ He interrogates you.

☐ Periods of verbal, emotional, or physical abuse, or periods of intimidation, are followed by periods where he apologizes and becomes "Mr. Nice Guy" or "Mr. Thoughtful Husband and Father."

☐ Your parents or friends express doubts about him.

☐ Because he is nice to you when other people are present, your friends tell you how lucky you are to have found him.

☐ He has a poor credit or job history.

☐ He has few friends.

☐ He dislikes your friends.

☐ He drinks too much or has more than one DUI.

☐ He uses drugs.

If you sense yourself or another person of interest in any of these statements, you may want to read the full description of the abusive personality and abusive relationships.

2

Do any of these statements describe your thoughts, feelings, or behaviors at least some of the time?

- [ ] You are known for paying attention to every detail.
- [ ] You maintain high standards of performance for yourself.
- [ ] You are always careful to check and make sure you have not made any mistakes.
- [ ] You concentrate so much on one thing that other things get neglected—or other people say you do this.
- [ ] You miss deadlines.
- [ ] You are easily humiliated.
- [ ] You are dedicated to your work, and it is hard for you to take a day off for friends and fun activities—or other people say you do this.
- [ ] You feel a little awkward and uncomfortable when you express affection for someone.
- [ ] When you spend time with friends, it is almost always for some regularly organized event, such as a weekly dinner group or sport activity.
- [ ] It is important for you to have a clean and organized house.
- [ ] You try to be the best at everything you do—including hobbies or recreational activities.
- [ ] You postpone vacations because of work.
- [ ] It is important for your children to do things the right way, even when they are playing. For example, telling them to always color inside the lines, requiring them to make straight As in school, etc.
- [ ] You try very hard to live up to ethical, moral, or religious guidelines.

- [ ] You get upset at yourself when you make a mistake.
- [ ] You are one of those very conscientious people who always goes by the rules.
- [ ] It is hard for you to discard items because you might need them someday.
- [ ] People sometimes get tired or irritated while waiting for you to finish something.
- [ ] It is important to save money for the future. Other people may have accused you of being "thrifty," "stingy," or "cheap."
- [ ] Most vacations are working vacations.
- [ ] You are stubborn—or other people think you are stubborn.
- [ ] You usually plan things ahead in great detail.
- [ ] You hold strong opinions and find it difficult to consider the viewpoints of other people.
- [ ] You are diligent in considering every possible angle of a decision. You can be indecisive or vacillate repeatedly when there are two or more "best" options.
- [ ] You become upset or angry when things are not happening the way you want them to, and you may easily express this anger. Other times, you just hold your anger inside and ruminate about how you have been wronged.
- [ ] You get upset or angry over issues that other people consider trivial. Other people are sometimes surprised at your level of seriousness.
- [ ] You sometimes humiliate someone who has upset you or made you angry, such as criticizing or berating them in front of other people.
- [ ] It makes you uncomfortable when other people express emotions or affection in public.
- [ ] You express anger with righteous indignation. You are right; they are wrong.

- [ ] You are more reserved than most people and tend not to show your emotions, even when other people are smiling and laughing or openly expressing sadness and grief.
- [ ] You rarely compliment others, including members of your own family.
- [ ] You have a "type A" personality.
- [ ] You are easily embarrassed.
- [ ] You repeatedly perform some activity because you sense that something bad may happen if you do not perform the activity.

If you sense yourself or another person of interest in these statements, you may want to read the full descriptions of the obsessive-compulsive personalities.

3

Do any of these statements describe your thoughts, feelings, or behaviors at least some of the time?

- [ ] You worry about what other people might think of you.
- [ ] You dread social events because you think the other guests may not like you or approve of you.
- [ ] You dread social events because they have been awkward for you in the past.
- [ ] You do not talk much or express your opinions very often.
- [ ] You avoid eye contact when talking to others.
- [ ] You do not plan for the future as much as other people.
- [ ] It is more difficult for you to talk to people you are attracted to.
- [ ] You berate yourself for social mistakes.

- [ ] You think you are incompetent, boring, unattractive, weird, etc.
- [ ] Sometimes you have a brain freeze and cannot think of what to say.
- [ ] You sometimes have physical reactions in social situations, such as blushing, sweating, fast heart rate, etc.
- [ ] You avoid trying to make new friends unless you feel sure they will accept you.
- [ ] You avoid taking a new job or accepting a promotion because you think your new coworkers will not accept you.
- [ ] You just assume other people do not approve of you and will criticize you.
- [ ] You resist talking about yourself or discussing your inner feelings because you are afraid you will be ridiculed, shamed, or rejected by others.
- [ ] Your fears increase sometimes when you exaggerate the danger in a common and ordinary situation.
- [ ] You come across to other people as ill at ease, apprehensive, or uptight.
- [ ] You are a loner—or other people describe you this way.
- [ ] You have few friends, or no friends, that you can really count on.
- [ ] You do not go out much because you fear the reactions of others to your presence.

If you sense yourself or another person of interest in these statements, you may want to read the full description of the shy personality.

4

Do any of these statements describe your thoughts, feelings, or behaviors at least some of the time?

- ☐ You have feelings of inadequacy.
- ☐ You worry or brood about things.
- ☐ You are overly serious—or other people say you are overly serious.
- ☐ It is difficult for you to get interested in or take pleasure in things generally.
- ☐ You think you may have low self-esteem.
- ☐ You think you are not very interesting or just incompetent.
- ☐ It hits you pretty hard when other people reject you.
- ☐ You are socially withdrawn sometimes or much of the time.
- ☐ You sometimes feel guilt or remorse about something that happened in the past.
- ☐ You sometimes feel sad, dejected, gloomy, or unhappy.
- ☐ Sometimes you feel irritated at people or events.
- ☐ You can be pessimistic about the future or things generally.
- ☐ You frequently feel tired, fatigued, or just have low energy generally.
- ☐ You have problems at work, poor relations with your coworkers, or are frequently unemployed.
- ☐ You have a poor appetite or unwanted weight loss.
- ☐ You eat too much or gain unwanted weight.
- ☐ You sometimes abuse alcohol or drugs.
- ☐ You get too much sleep or not enough sleep.
- ☐ You have trouble concentrating or making decisions.
- ☐ You are self-critical or you blame yourself.
- ☐ You are sometimes critical or judgmental of other people.

If you sense yourself or another person of interest in these statements, you may want to read the full description of mild depression.

5

Do you experience any of these symptoms of anxiety and/or panic attack?

- [ ] Excess/chronic worry
- [ ] Sleep disorders – sleeping too much or too little
- [ ] Fast heartrate, sweating, muscle tension
- [ ] Dizziness
- [ ] Poor concentration
- [ ] Rapid breathing
- [ ] Nervousness, restlessness, jitters
- [ ] Headaches or other chronic pain
- [ ] Irrational anger/irritability
- [ ] Suicidal thoughts
- [ ] Social phobia/shy symptoms, i.e., fear of being judged or criticized, embarrassment, shame, easily intimidated
- [ ] Feelings of unreality or being detached from oneself
- [ ] Sense of doom or imminent death
- [ ] Sense of loss of control
- [ ] Irrational fears, i.e., bugs, snakes, spiders, dogs, airplanes, heights, getting shots, etc.
- [ ] Sudden feelings of intense anxiety, fear, or terror for either known or unknown reasons
- [ ] Avoiding objects, events, places, circumstances (i.e., crowds) because of apprehension or fear
- [ ] Nightmares/flashbacks/unwanted memories of some traumatic experience or event

If you sense yourself or another person of interest in these symptoms, you may want to read the full chapter on anxiety.

6

Do any of these statements describe your thoughts, feelings, or behaviors at least some of the time?

- [ ] You frequently worry about your relationship or struggle to keep your relationship from falling apart.
- [ ] You have a history of intense, chaotic, or unstable relationships.
- [ ] When you are separated from your spouse or partner, you fear the end of your relationship, even if the separation is for a short period of time.
- [ ] When your relationship seems to be falling apart, you experience serious changes in your emotions, thinking, and behavior.
- [ ] You sometimes feel like you are a bad person in some way, especially when you are not in a relationship or a relationship has just ended or is about to end.
- [ ] You dislike being alone.
- [ ] You physically hurt yourself sometimes.
- [ ] You sometimes think potential partners or lovers are just wonderful when you first meet them but soon decide the person does not really care about you or is not emotionally available.
- [ ] You feel angry, rejected, and abandoned or go into a panic if there is a change in plans, someone is late, or someone cancels an appointment.
- [ ] You can quickly change your mind about your future, such as career plans, plans for school, life goals, etc.
- [ ] Your sexual identity (what you are willing to do, how often, with whom) may change from time to time or shift very quickly.

- [ ] You sometimes change your mind about the kinds of friends you like to be around.
- [ ] You sometimes feel like you just do not matter—period. This is most likely when you are not in a relationship or a relationship has just ended or is about to end.
- [ ] You are impulsive and act without thinking things through in areas such as substance abuse, unsafe sex, irrationally spending money, reckless driving, binge eating, etc.
- [ ] You go into emotional swings or an emotional downturn if someone expects you to carry more responsibility.
- [ ] You can change your opinions about other people very quickly.
- [ ] You have a general feeling of sadness or feeling down most of the time. This may include feelings of anxiety or irritability. You rarely have feelings of satisfaction or contentment with life.
- [ ] You are easily bored and are usually looking for something to do to relieve the boredom.
- [ ] You can be sarcastic, especially when irritated or angry at someone.
- [ ] You are more comfortable having pets instead of relationships.
- [ ] You become upset and angry when you think people are not living up to their commitments to you, only to feel guilt and shame afterward.
- [ ] You quickly change your mind about what is right, what is wrong, or what is important.
- [ ] You seem to sabotage your efforts just when success is about to be achieved, such as ruining a good relationship, dropping out of school just before graduation, ending therapy just when you seem to be making progress, quitting a job just before a promotion, etc.
- [ ] You have chronic feelings of emptiness.

- [ ] You have frequent anger or recurrent temper tantrums.
- [ ] You begin to fear the worst any time you are under stress.

If you sense yourself or another person of interest in these statements, you may want to read the full description of the borderline personality.

7

Do any of these statements describe your thoughts, feelings, or behavior at least some of the time?

- [ ] You have always been somewhat uncomfortable in close relationships or found it difficult to form close relationships.
- [ ] Relationships sometimes fall apart because of some awkwardness in yourself.
- [ ] Events or occurrences seem to have some special meaning intended just for you.
- [ ] It is difficult for you to acknowledge the smiles or nods of others.
- [ ] You sometimes act in an eccentric or inappropriate manner when you interact with other people.
- [ ] People sometimes have difficulty understanding what you are saying.
- [ ] You sometimes dress in a careless or unconventional manner, e.g., clothes are worn out, dirty, do not match, do not fit, or are just out of sync with most other people at social gatherings.
- [ ] It is difficult for you to feel close to someone.
- [ ] You are interested in the paranormal, astrology, ESP, past lives, psychic abilities, etc.
- [ ] Other people consider you odd or eccentric.

- [ ] You feel anxious at social events and have difficulty with small talk.
- [ ] People notice your presence when you go to a restaurant, the mall, etc.
- [ ] People sometimes stare at you because of your odd or unusual appearance.
- [ ] You keep to yourself because you are uncomfortable around other people.
- [ ] You sometimes feel like you are different and do not fit in.
- [ ] You sometimes have poor hygiene or do not always take good care of yourself.
- [ ] You are somewhat superstitious—or other people think you are superstitious.
- [ ] You keep to yourself or remain quiet at social events.
- [ ] You have few close friends or no close friends other than close relatives.
- [ ] Other people sometimes know what you are thinking.
- [ ] You sometimes quickly and unexpectedly change topics when talking to others.
- [ ] You have some unusual mannerisms, such as difficulty making eye contact.
- [ ] You make little effort to keep in contact with friends, e.g., emails, phone calls, etc.
- [ ] You can sometimes read people's thoughts.
- [ ] You can be awkward and stiff when interacting with other people.
- [ ] People sometimes comment about the unusual way you do things.
- [ ] At social gatherings, you sometimes feel tense or suspicious of other people, only to find these feelings increase more and more the longer you stay at the event.

- [ ] As a child you had unusual ideas, thoughts, or fantasies.
- [ ] You sometimes use unusual words or language when talking to others.
- [ ] You seem to know about events before they happen.

If you sense yourself or another person of interest in these statements, you may want to read the full description of the schizotypal personality.

8

Do any of these statements describe your thoughts, feelings, or behaviors at least some of the time?

- [ ] You sometimes overstate or exaggerate your accomplishments and abilities.
- [ ] You are surprised when other people do not give you appropriate recognition.
- [ ] You sometimes see other people getting praise and recognition that they do not deserve.
- [ ] You believe you are unique, special, or even superior to others in some way.
- [ ] Most of the people you commonly associate with have their own accomplishments and higher status.
- [ ] It is important for you to have only the best lawyer, teacher, doctor, wine, the best seats at a concert, etc.
- [ ] You frequently wonder what other people are thinking about you.
- [ ] People notice you when you arrive at a party or event.
- [ ] Other people typically wish they had the things that you have.

- ☐ You become impatient and irritated with people who talk about their own lives or problems.
- ☐ You are sometimes insensitive and say things that can make another person feel hurt or sad. Examples might include talking about your wonderful possessions with an individual who is struggling financially or talking about your good health to someone who is sick.
- ☐ When other people have problems, you sometimes form a negative opinion of them and view them as weak or deficient.
- ☐ You sometimes talk about yourself without asking other people about their lives.
- ☐ After being criticized, and possibly counterattacking, you sometimes withdraw and become self-critical or less assertive.
- ☐ Sometimes you are emotionally unavailable or "cold" to other people because you have little interest in them.
- ☐ You are sometimes envious of other people and their status, accomplishments, or possessions.
- ☐ You can be a little arrogant, snobbish, or boastful, possibly without realizing it.
- ☐ Other people tell you that you can be arrogant, snobbish, or boastful.
- ☐ You are easily upset by, and sometimes ridicule, "stupid" or "dumb" service people, such as the "idiot" waiter, "birdbrained" salesperson, "half-baked" chef, "moronic" lawyer, or "simpleton" writer.
- ☐ You are sometimes humiliated or depressed by the indirect criticisms of other people, such as not being chosen for something, not being invited to something, or being recognized as having failed at some project.
- ☐ When criticized, you counterattack with defiance and anger.
- ☐ You avoid situations that involve competition with the

possibility of defeat or failure, such as avoiding academic endeavors, interviews for promotions, a new position, etc.

If you sense yourself or another person of interest in these statements, you may want to read the full description of the narcissistic personality.

9

Do any of these statements describe your thoughts, feelings, or behavior at least some of the time?

- [ ] In group situations, especially social events, people frequently focus their attention on you.
- [ ] You are sometimes openly flirtatious, or even seductive, when interacting with other people.
- [ ] You are a natural "life of the party."
- [ ] You have a tendency to be loud when in group situations—or other people think you are sometimes too loud.
- [ ] When arriving at a group situation or party, you are more likely than other people to make the rounds and greet many people individually, possibly with a hug, and possibly telling them how much you have missed them.
- [ ] You feel uncomfortable, unappreciated, or even depressed when the focus of attention is not on you.
- [ ] It is difficult for you to hold on to friends, especially same-sex friends.
- [ ] You sometimes want immediate satisfaction and become frustrated when delayed gratification is necessary.
- [ ] You sometimes try to impress others or draw attention to yourself with your appearance, e.g., dressing flamboyantly, wearing a low-cut blouse or tight jeans, etc.

- [ ] Your emotions sometimes change easily—for example, laughter to tears and back to laughter in just a few minutes.
- [ ] You sometimes fish for compliments.
- [ ] You are easily upset if someone criticizes you.
- [ ] You talk more about your general feelings and impressions about things, rather than offering specific details and facts. You might say, "That's really cool" or, "It's fantastic" but have difficulty explaining why you feel that way.
- [ ] You are sometimes expressive, theatrical, and dramatic and put on quite a display in your presentation of self to others.
- [ ] You cry easily for sentimental reasons.
- [ ] You sometimes have difficulty explaining the reasons for your opinions.
- [ ] Other people are sometimes embarrassed by your public behavior.
- [ ] Your feelings or opinions are easily influenced by the opinions of others—or by the latest fads.
- [ ] You sometimes trust other people too easily, especially those in a position of authority.
- [ ] You sometimes realize certain people or groups of people are not as intimate or close to you as you thought they were.
- [ ] It can be difficult for you to find real emotional intimacy in your romantic or sexual relationships.
- [ ] Without necessarily being aware of it, you sometimes try to turn conversations around to a discussion about you.
- [ ] You sometimes attempt to control your spouse or partner with emotional manipulation or seductiveness.
- [ ] Same-sex friends sometimes distance themselves from you because they see you as a threat to their own relationships.
- [ ] You seek excitement because you are easily bored.

If you sense yourself or another person of interest in these statements, you may want to read the full description of the histrionic personality.

10

Do any of these statements describe your thoughts, feelings, or behaviors at least some of the time?

- ☐ You allow another person—such as a parent, partner, or spouse—to make most of the decisions, such as who to be friends with, where to live, where to work, when and where to take a vacation, where to go to college, how to spend your free time, etc.
- ☐ It is difficult for you to disagree with other people, especially someone important to you.
- ☐ You agree with people even when you think they are wrong. You submit to unreasonable demands by others to avoid being rejected by them.
- ☐ You have a tendency to quickly become intimately involved with people before you know them very well.
- ☐ You rarely show even justified anger at other people out of a fear of being rejected by them.
- ☐ It is difficult for you to do things on your own because you lack self-confidence.
- ☐ You sometimes intentionally appear inept or incompetent to get other people to help you.
- ☐ You are able to function adequately and competently but only if someone else is supervising you or approves of your work.
- ☐ You tolerate verbal, physical, or sexual abuse so that your spouse or caregiver will not leave or abandon you.
- ☐ You feel uncomfortable or helpless when you are alone.

- [ ] You usually think that other people can do things better than you.
- [ ] When your relationship falls apart, you quickly find someone else.
- [ ] You worry about being abandoned by your spouse or partner, even if there are no signs that this is going to happen.
- [ ] You sometimes put yourself down or describe yourself in derogatory terms, such as calling yourself "stupid."
- [ ] You seek protection, or even dominance, from another person or group.
- [ ] You usually limit your social contacts to the person or people who take care of you.

If you sense yourself or another person of interest in these statements, you may want to read the full description of the dependent personality.

11

Do any of these statements describe your thoughts, feelings, or behaviors at least some of the time?

- [ ] You resent being asked, told, or required to do something. You routinely resist the demands of others, usually at work but possibly in relationships and social situations as well.
- [ ] You show your stubborn side through any of these responses: procrastination, forgetfulness, intentional carelessness, unproductiveness, incompetence, ineptness, ineffectiveness, laziness, etc.
- [ ] You sometimes cause problems for other people because you do not perform your share of the work.

☐ You tend to blame other people, circumstances, or society for your problems.
☐ You complain to other people because you feel unappreciated or even cheated.
☐ You are routinely upset with and complain about some authority figure, whether a teacher, boss, spouse, or parent.
☐ You experience conflict between your desire for independence and your continued dependence on others.

If you sense yourself or another person of interest in these statements, you may want to read the full description of the passive-aggressive personality.

12

Did you exhibit some of these behaviors during childhood or adolescence?

☐ Aggression toward people and animals: bullying, threatening, fighting, etc.
☐ Destruction of property: vandalism, starting fires, smashing car windows, etc.
☐ Deceitfulness or theft: breaking into houses or cars, lying, breaking promises to obtain favors or avoid debts, stealing, shoplifting, forgery, etc.
☐ Serious violation of rules: disregarding parental curfew, truancy from school, breaking other school rules, etc.

And since the age of 18, do any of these statements describe your thoughts, feelings, or behaviors at least some of the time?

☐ You have conned other people through the use of fake IDs, aliases, or other deceptions.

- [ ] You make impulsive decisions without considering the consequences for other people or yourself, such as not showing up for work, no financial planning, drunk driving, not supporting your family, not paying child support, etc.
- [ ] You can be mean to your spouse or children.
- [ ] You care little about the feelings and needs of other people, including those you say are close to you.
- [ ] You take care of what you want—other people are losers.

If you sense yourself or another person of interest in these statements, you may want to read the full description of the antisocial personality / sociopath.

13

Do any of these statements describe your thoughts, feelings, or behaviors at least some of the time?

- [ ] You sometimes think another person or group of people is going to exploit, harm, or deceive you.
- [ ] You wonder about the loyalty or truthfulness of your friends or colleagues at work.
- [ ] You think if you talk about yourself, the information you disclose might be turned around and used against you.
- [ ] You like to know where your spouse or significant other has been or what he/she has been doing.
- [ ] Events sometimes happen that make you feel like you are in danger.
- [ ] You hold grudges—or other people think you hold grudges.
- [ ] You sometimes feel like someone has attacked you or your reputation, but other people disagree with you or think you are being too sensitive.

- ☐ You counterattack when you feel like someone has criticized or insulted you.
- ☐ You suspect your spouse or partner of cheating on you.
- ☐ You are not sure anyone would help you if you were in trouble.
- ☐ People say things that make you wonder about their real motives.
- ☐ If someone asks you about something, you tell them it's none of their business.
- ☐ You sometimes interpret the humorous remarks of others as an insult or personal attack.
- ☐ It is difficult to confide in other people.
- ☐ When someone compliments you, it may sound like a veiled criticism or an attempt to manipulate you in some way.
- ☐ Some events appear to be bad omens for you.
- ☐ You get jealous.
- ☐ Sometimes you need to be in control of other people, including your spouse or partner.
- ☐ Other people cannot be trusted, so you just take care of things yourself.
- ☐ It's difficult for you to accept criticism.
- ☐ You sometimes want to take people to court.
- ☐ You form negative opinions of other groups of people who are different from yourself.

If you sense yourself or another person of interest in these statements, you may want to read the full description of the paranoid personality.

14

Do any of these statements describe your thoughts, feelings, or behaviors at least some of the time?

- [ ] You feel distant and unconnected to most people, or other people seem distant and unconnected to you.
- [ ] You prefer being alone whenever possible.
- [ ] You have little desire for a close, intimate relationship.
- [ ] You get little enjoyment from family or other group participation.
- [ ] You prefer activities and hobbies that do not involve other people.
- [ ] You have little desire for sexual contact with another person.
- [ ] You find little enjoyment from experiences, such as watching a sunset, experiencing nature, artistic beauty, etc.
- [ ] You have few close friends except maybe a close relative.
- [ ] You do not care if other people criticize you.
- [ ] You ignore other people when they nod or smile at you on the street.
- [ ] You rarely experience strong emotions, such as anger or joy.
- [ ] You seem to live day-to-day without having any specific long-term goals.
- [ ] You rarely or never go on dates.
- [ ] You work fairly well if alone or isolated but have difficulty working with other people or in groups.

If you sense yourself or another person of interest in these statements, you may want to read the full description of the schizoid personality.

15

Do any of these statements describe your thoughts, feelings, or behaviors at least some of the time?

- [ ] You sometimes think fast, with scattered thoughts and ideas.
- [ ] You go through periods when you have considerably more energy and a higher level of activity.
- [ ] You are sometimes hostile, with quick, unpredictable anger.
- [ ] You go through periods when lots of things are interesting.
- [ ] You sometimes talk too much.
- [ ] You have been diagnosed with, or it has been suggested that you may suffer from, attention deficit hyperactivity disorder (ADHD).
- [ ] You go through periods when you have a reduced need for sleep.
- [ ] Your anger can be excessive, possibly with a litany of accusations at someone.
- [ ] You go through periods when you feel really good about yourself, have more self-esteem, more self-confidence, and less shyness.
- [ ] You sometimes make impulsive decisions you have not thought through.
- [ ] You are easily distracted and frequently change the topic.
- [ ] You are easily bored.
- [ ] You sometimes talk too fast.
- [ ] You experience insomnia.
- [ ] You go on shopping sprees and spend too much.
- [ ] You are sometimes entertaining, witty, the life of the party.
- [ ] You sometimes make decisions without considering the ethics involved.

- [ ] Other people say you are sometimes hyper and energetic.
- [ ] You are sometimes sexually promiscuous.
- [ ] You are sometimes moody and easily upset.
- [ ] You become irrational when you are angry. Logic and fair play just disappear.

If you sense yourself or another person of interest in these statements, you may want to read the full description of mild bipolar (cyclothymia).

PART III

Descriptions of Specific Personalities

OFFICIAL DESCRIPTIONS OF personality styles and disorders are found in the fifth edition of the *Diagnostic and Statistical Manual of Mental Disorders (DSM-5)*.[1] The traits attributed to various personalities are the products of ongoing research, yet much is known about the patterns of behavior that people typically experience. The following personality descriptions are an easy-to-understand synthesis of current thought and research. Not all of the personality traits people may experience are covered in this book. With more serious problems, consultation with a knowledgeable professional is recommended.

THE ABUSIVE PERSONALITY / ABUSIVE RELATIONSHIPS

This description covers multiple levels of abusive patterns of thought, emotion, and behavior as experienced by both the abuser and the victim(s). Abusive traits are found in both men and women, but in relationships, they are much more common in men.

Let's start with a few facts:
- Most abusive relationships are not physically abusive—they are verbally and emotionally abusive.
- Physically abusive relationships usually begin with verbal and emotional abuse, and verbal and emotional abuse remain a part of physically abusive relationships.[46]
- The majority of abusers are men.[46] There are no shelters for battered men.
- Domestic violence will affect one in three women (American Medical Association).[12]
- More women suffer domestic violence than experience automobile accidents, muggings, and rapes combined.[2]
- Attacks by male partners are the number-one cause of injury to women between the ages of 15 and 44 (U.S. Surgeon General).[12]
- One in five teenagers has a violent experience while dating.[77]
- Five million children per year witness assaults on their mother.[12]
- According to the National Coalition Against Domestic Violence, an average of about 20 people per minute are physically abused by their intimate partner in the United States.

- Each year, the city of Dallas, Texas, receives approximately 20,000 calls concerning domestic violence.[2]
- In 2018, 137 women worldwide were killed every day by intimate partners or relatives. About 87,000 women were killed worldwide in 2017, 58 percent of them victims of domestic or family violence.[138]
- There are societies where violence against women does not exist.[52]

Many of the calls I receive for couples counseling involve some level of abuse—usually verbal and emotional abuse and usually on the part of the man. The great majority of abusers in relationships are men, the logical outcome in any male-dominated society where the man is considered to be the natural head of the household. While abuse does occur in heterosexual relationships where the woman is the perpetrator,[52] these are unusual cases. Abuse also occurs in gay and lesbian relationships. Because abusive behavior presents itself in a multitude of ways, the reader is encouraged to read this chapter in its entirety.

I initially thought the large percentage of abusive relationships walking into my office was a fluke because, through 10 years of graduate school, two masters degrees and a PhD in the behavioral sciences, I never heard even one professor so much as mention the topic of abuse. I have wondered if tenured professors avoid the topic of abuse because so many tenured professors, male and female alike, are abusive to their students, and they would be talking about themselves. Outside of relationships, such as work or academic environments, etc., I have witnessed considerable authoritarian power-trip abuse by women as well as men. The phrase "power corrupts" does describe many people. Many of us have experienced abuse at the hands of the owner or manager where we work or an instructor at school. Many abusers are equal-opportunity abusers and are somewhat abusive to almost everyone over whom they wield power. Other abusers seem to get their power-trip fix on just one or a few unfortunate victims.

Simply pointing out to the victims of abuse that people are free to get another job, change schools, or get a divorce ignores the complexities of actually doing so, and this is especially the case in abusive relationships. The longer an abusive relationship continues, and as the abuse escalates—as almost always happens—the more complex and difficult the relationship is to end,[12] and this is the case if there are no children involved. Add children to the mix, and some women find themselves mired in severely abusive relationships with no financial resources, no one who understands their plight, and no apparent way out—and the children suffer as well. It is not just the power surge and sense of dominance and control that drives the abuser, but also the privileges and special treatment they receive.[12] An abused woman's needs may be totally neglected as she caters to the needs of the abuser, justified by his assertions that she does not appreciate how difficult life is for him, how hard he works, and how tired he is. There is, however, help available for abused women who recognize the abuse and are willing to reach out. My primary goal as a therapist is to help victims of abuse begin to recognize that they are in an abusive relationship so they can begin to accept that the abuse is *not their fault*. Along with blaming her for the family's problems, it is common for an abuser to eventually accuse the abused woman of abusing him. These are manipulative attempts to counter any accusations she has made against him in the past or might make against him in the future. Only with a very clear recognition and understanding of abusive behavior can the abused woman begin to deal more effectively with the abuser and seek the help that is available if necessary.

Maintaining power and control may be done in an overt manner, with threats of retaliation or physical harm if she does not give in to his demands. But most abusers use an almost infinite variety of more subtle techniques to manipulate and control their partners. In cases of more serious verbal and emotional abuse, some level of physical abuse will likely occur in the future.[12,46] More commonly than not, the manipulated and abused woman will not recognize the abuse for what it is, and she will blame herself for the problems in the relationship and family.

WHAT ABUSERS DO

Some abusers will try to control what their girlfriend or wife thinks, believes, says, or does by immediately disagreeing with her opinion on a regular basis, regardless of the triviality of the topic. The message the woman receives is that her opinions do not matter. The abuser may act as if his partner does not even have a right to an opinion. In some cases, before the partner even finishes her sentence, it is made clear to her that she is wrong, and through words or tone of voice, she is notified that the conversation is over. She may be made to feel like she should just stop thinking, which is essentially the abuser's goal. A woman who feels totally inadequate and cannot think for herself will become less assertive and be *less capable of leaving the abusive relationship*.

This style of abuse is demonstrated in the following discussion. Watch for these abusive techniques:

- Abuser denies his obvious anger.
- Abuser insults the woman.

- The woman's opinion is completely disrespected.
- Legitimate disagreement is not allowed.
- The woman's self-esteem and self-confidence are repeatedly degraded.

She: *The new skyscraper downtown is really changing the city's quaint character.*

He: *No, its not. It's just different. You're just thinking backwards again. You always do that. You think like a child living in the Stone Age.*

She: *I was just saying that a building that tall seems…*

He: (raising his voice) *The problem is, you keep thinking. Cut out that part, and you might make at least some sense.*

She: *Why are you so angry? I was just…*

He: (Even louder) *I'm not angry. You're just telling me what to think again. You think you're so smart. You think you know everything, and when I give my opinion, you just start another argument. Try listening sometime. You might learn something, but I have my doubts.*

She: *Well, it seems to me you are angry. Maybe I say things the wrong way sometimes, but when you raise your voice and…*

He: *Yeah, it's all me, isn't it? You don't seem to notice the harassment I have to live with every day whenever you feel like dishing it out. I think you live to complain, and I'm always on the receiving end. I bust ass all day and come home, and dinner's not ready half the time, and it usually tastes like crap anyway. And then I make the slightest mistake, and you just won't let me forget it. You're a fucking shit. Remember the time you…*

In this example, the abuser angrily insults the woman while denying he is even angry, yet the woman wonders what *she* did to upset her husband. There are times when he is just so wonderful, and he never talks to other people that way. This kind of abuser may use any conversation to degrade their partner's self-esteem and self-confidence. These abusive relationships may be completely devoid of any authenticity, empathy, and honest communication. If the abused woman makes an attempt to explain to the abuser that the way he treats her is painful, the abuser angrily changes the subject to a discussion of her faults and what he does not like about her. She is now the problem, and the discussion is now about her. He is the authority, and she is now subjected to a long list of trumped-up grievances against her. His retaliation techniques make it almost impossible for her to discuss her viewpoint. If the abuser does admit to some anger, he will make it her fault that he is angry—and the woman may never even realize that she was denied the chance to discuss her unhappiness with him. In most cases involving an abusive personality, virtually all interactions, whether he is being nice or abusive, are designed to manipulate the woman's self-esteem, self-confidence, and her ability to think for herself and act on her own—all while having her stay in the relationship. There is no avenue towards a stable relationship, although the woman continues to believe she is in a committed relationship with the possibility of stability if she can just get her act together and stop upsetting him. He has convinced her that she is the problem—everything is *her* fault.

The abuser may later deny her the right to revisit the issue by simply denying that the previous discussion or abusive event ever occurred. He simply states, "I never said (did) that," possibly followed by, "You're really starting to lose it," or the seemingly milder, yet equally damaging, "Are you ok?" or, "Are you all right?" This abuse technique, if repeated often enough, may get the woman to question her own stability and sanity. Many abusers continue their denial of events right into my office, even denying severe physical abuse.

Until the abused woman recognizes the abuse for what it is, and that the abuser will probably never allow a rational meeting of the minds, she will continue to experience ever-increasing stress and pain and ever-lower self-esteem and self-confidence. Without recognizing the abuse, there is little chance the woman will have the strength to stand up to the abuser or leave him. An abuser will make sure the woman understands, at some level, that her needs and desires are less important than his needs and desires. Abusers frequently choose women who have submissive personalities. Dependent and avoidant personalities, along with those raised in strict cultural or religious environments that promote the submissiveness and subservience of women, are well represented among the spouses or partners of abusers.

UNPREDICTABILITY

The unpredictable nature of some abusers creates additional tension in the abused woman's life, as she never knows when the next round of abuse will begin or what will trigger it. After a period of relatively good times, during which some abusers come across as very loving boyfriends, husbands, or fathers, the abuser may gradually become increasingly critical of anything she does, no matter how trivial. At other times, during a seemingly normal discussion, the abuser may just explode in anger out of the blue for no apparent reason, leaving the abused woman no room to respond and, of course, wondering what *she* did to set him off.

What the abused woman does not know is that these random and unpredictable anger explosions are consciously calculated to confuse her as she struggles to figure out what *she* did to trigger his anger. The abuser knows that she will never suspect that he would treat her that badly for no reason. With repeated occurrences, an abused woman may begin to question her own stability and sanity. The sense that she is unstable increases her feelings of insecurity and incompetence. The abused woman's ever-increasing insecurity and feelings of incompetence make it much less likely that she will have the strength to leave her abusive husband—which is precisely the abuser's goal.

The tendency of some abusers to use unexpected anger and rage as a technique for ending any conversation or involvement they want to avoid may play itself out in the bedroom. One common scenario I hear involves husbands who only care about their own sexual satisfaction, not the woman's. After having his needs met, any request by the woman may draw a tirade of accusations about her selfishness and sexual inadequacy. Of course, the woman now questions her sexual adequacy as well as her emotional stability, while the abuser can get on with his day, or fall asleep, without concern for her needs.

An alternative scenario in the bedroom is the abuser who tries very hard to please the women, but in the abuser's case, it's so he can hear the woman tell him how wonderful he is. It's still about meeting his needs.[12]

MR. NICE GUY / MR. THOUGHTFUL HUSBAND AND FATHER

One of the most common techniques abusers use to keep the abused woman from leaving the relationship is to become "Mr. Nice Guy" and "Mr. Thoughtful Husband and Father" for days, weeks, or even months at a time. Typically, the longer the relationship, the shorter and less frequent the nice periods tend to be.[12] I have known several abused women who would finally decide to leave the abuser and start packing their bags only to have the abuser apologize profusely, shed some tears, and become just the nicest guy. More often than not, the abused woman forgives him and returns, convinced that he has really changed. Unfortunately, in the great majority of cases, and after a few days, weeks, or months of relative calm, the abuse begins again. The abuser becomes increasingly moody, critical, and ill-tempered at first and eventually explodes into full abuse mode, whether verbal or physical. This scenario where an abused woman starts to leave the abuser but then returns to Mr. Nice Guy may play itself out multiple times before the woman finally begins to accept that he will always abuse her again.

Unfortunately, some abused women put up with the abuse for the rest of their lives. Very few seriously abusive men do the extensive work necessary to change their abusive attitudes and behaviors on a permanent basis. Even women who recognize this fact may repeatedly convince themselves that *their* abusive man is the one who is different. They insist on believing their man will eventually recognize his abusive ways and stop his abusive behavior because it just does not make logical sense for this not to happen. I warn these women that if they decide to continue the process of breaking up and leaving the abuser after he becomes Mr. Nice Guy, to be very careful. It is at this moment, when the abuser's manipulations finely fail, that some abusers focus on *revenge* and become very dangerous.

OTHER COMMON ABUSE TECHNIQUES

The variations on abusive techniques and behaviors are endless, and abuse is usually very subtle and difficult to detect. Here is a list of the more common themes and techniques used by abusers:[12,46]

- Problems are usually her fault. Even when an abuser admits doing something reprehensible, expect him to say some variation of, "Well, you made me do it" or, "I wouldn't have done that if you hadn't ..." Unfortunately, an abused woman will likely believe the abuser's accusations and think she is the problem. She will believe she just needs to be a better wife or girlfriend and try harder not to upset him.

- The abuser may falsely accuse her of doing the same kinds of abusive things to him that he has done to her. The abuser's goal is to counter and neutralize any accusations she has made against him in the past or might make against him in the future—possibly in court. When an abused woman does react to abuse by striking back in some way, even physically, her behavior is considered defensive, not abusive.[12] Absent his abuse, the woman's response would not have occurred. But poorly trained or ignorant police officers or judges may not see it this way. It is very important that abused women not strike back physically, since this makes it possible for the abuser to call the police and have the woman arrested for domestic violence. Now the abused woman has an arrest record the abuser can hold over her head and point to when he talks about her to their friends, in divorce court, or at child-custody hearings.

- The abuser may feel threatened by the woman's job or her academic endeavors and sabotage her efforts to succeed. He may say they can no longer afford her tuition or say he can no longer watch the children while she is in class or at work. The abuser is aware that if his partner becomes educated or gets a promotion at work, she may become less dependent on him and he might lose his control over her—and she might even leave the relationship. Besides, her life should promote his needs, not her needs.

- The abuser may maintain control over the money, house, car, etc. by keeping most possessions in his name. Credit cards are in his name so he can cancel her card, or threaten to, to help

maintain his control over her. The abuser may spend much more of their income on himself than on his spouse or children.
- The abuser makes himself the victim. The abuser may actually succeed in changing the abused woman's anger at him into some level of guilt and sympathy for him. The abuser may also solicit the sympathy of friends by telling them how difficult it is to put up with her extremely emotional and irrational behavior. Most abusive behavior in relationships occurs in the home, hidden away from public scrutiny, and the abused woman may have little support from friends who believe the abuser's accusations.
- In public, the abuser will typically put on a display of Mr. Nice Guy and Mr. Thoughtful Husband and Father. Unknowing friends may tell the abused woman how lucky she is to have such a wonderful husband. When the woman's inevitable anxiety and depression are evident, the abuser points out her symptoms to their friends as confirmation that something is wrong with *her*.[12] These friends now assume the abused woman is responsible for the sadness and depression they have so often seen in her. With this technique, among others, the abuser may manipulate friends into having a low opinion of her. He may also manipulate the children into having a low opinion of their mother.
- Silent treatment: The abuser may refuse to respond to her at all. Examples include turning and walking away after rolling his eyes in disgust, refusing to return phone calls, etc. The silent treatment is an abusive response, not the lack of a response.
- Threats and Intimidation may be dished out in myriad ways, including physically threatening gestures, such as clenched fists, staring or glaring at her, screaming or cursing, blocking her exit, getting extremely close to her and in her face while

angry, threatening to leave her and the children, etc. The abuser may break or throw things, including throwing things at her or near her. The abuser views his partner and children as his *possessions* to do with as he pleases.

- The abuser may get the woman to question her stability by periodically asking, "Are you ok?" or, "Are you all right?" These questions clearly imply that something is wrong with her.
- The abuser may require his partner to take care of all chores and child-rearing tasks, leaving him free to do whatever he pleases. In some cases, the woman rarely even sees the abuser as he concentrates on other aspects of his life while ignoring her and the children.
- Jealousy: The abuser may insist on knowing her whereabouts at all times, grilling her about where she has been, who she has talked to, what took her so long at the grocery store, etc. He may repeatedly accuse her of flirting with other men or cheating.
- Isolation: The abuser may attempt to isolate the woman in any way he can, such as chasing off her friends, forbidding her to visit her family, or even getting rid of her pet. He may increase her isolation through deal-making, such as agreeing to refrain from some abusive behavior or agreeing to help her in some way if she will drop some outside activity and stay home with him. A friend of mine's abusive boyfriend said he would pay her rent if she would get rid of her dog, an obvious attempt to eliminate all of her emotional attachments except to him.
- Sarcasm is a common abuse technique and is very effective at reducing the woman's self-esteem and self-confidence. On the receiving end, the pain of sarcastic jabs can be severe, while the abuser views himself as simply having a great sense of humor. If the woman tells him she does not like the sarcasm, he may

tell her she has no sense of humor or that she is too sensitive and should just get over it.
- The abuser simply denies saying what he said or doing what he did. He may say her complaints are just another sign she is losing it. With unstable emotions from years of abuse, the abused woman may start to wonder if the abuser is right and if she is, in fact, becoming unstable.
- Confusion: While explaining his opinion, the abuser may begin to say things that are very different from, or completely the opposite of, what he said just moments earlier. Not expecting this kind of deception, the woman becomes confused and frustrated. She finally gives in assuming she is just unable to understand the complex issues involved or that it's just not worth the stress to continue arguing. The abuser gets his way—again. I am always amazed that some abusers have succeeded with this technique for so long that they walk into my office and try to pull the same confusion technique on me. I am much more likely to catch this "abuse of logic" technique because, unlike the overly trusting woman, I am watching for it.
- Abusers may use religious beliefs and the fear of God as a technique of control. Requiring strict adherence to religious beliefs, readings, or rituals, the abuser may feel secure in his abuse, knowing his wife's religious beliefs will bind her to the abusive marriage or family. Abused women may not recognize the subservient position some religion-based lifestyles may force on them.
- The abuser requires emotional support from her but offers little or no emotional support to her—or the children.
- Sexual abuse: Sexual abuse may include sex on demand, forced sex (rape), waking her for sex when she is asleep, inflicting pain during sex, or insisting on sex acts she does not want. If

the abused woman becomes pregnant, the abuse may increase, especially if it is an unwanted pregnancy.⁵²
- Criticism is the technique of choice for many abusers. A steady drip of artful criticism is all some abusers need to maintain control and dominance over the woman's thinking, emotions, behavior, and self-esteem. The compliments these abusers do offer may only be for the manipulative purpose of getting them what they want. Whether snide remarks about her clothing or cooking, or a verbal assault on her intelligence or emotions, criticism slowly chips away at the woman's self-esteem and self-confidence. The abused woman eventually internalizes his criticisms, and the abuser's presence is no longer necessary as she begins to self-criticize and doubt her own competence.¹² Lowered self-esteem and self-confidence increase the woman's dependency on the abuser. If she struggles to correct her perceived imperfections, the abuser will likely criticize her even more, triggering even more self-criticism on her part. Along with ridicule and name-calling, criticism may also have an accusatory nature. Consider these typical comments:

– *I didn't ask you what you thought. Of course, that doesn't keep you from sticking your worthless two cents into everything. I wonder how long I can put up with this crap.*

– *I can't believe you liked that movie. It sucked. If you were a little more perceptive you would know that, but you just go off into your little ozone. I hate it when you do that.*

– *You can't think, period. You get so damned emotional, and that's when you just keep going after me.*

– *The way you've done the yard looks ridiculous. The whole neighborhood will be laughing at us.*

– *You can't do anything right. You're an idiot.*

– *Blew it again, huh, dumbo?*

ABUSE OF CHILDREN

Many abusers will, directly or indirectly, abuse their children as well. Abusers may ignore or criticize their children or exhibit an authoritarian and dictatorial approach to parenting. Hidden away from public scrutiny behind the closed doors of the home, control, humiliation, and physical punishment may be the norm. There may be an absence of rational explanations for decisions and logical consequences for discipline.[45] Abuse is particularly damaging to children, since they want to pull closer to the abusing parent(s) for protection and support while simultaneously wanting to get away from the abuse. This "approach-avoidance" conflict may become the very basis of a problematic personality as the abused child grows up into adulthood.[122] When abused children with low self-esteem that is deeply ingrained reach adulthood, they may continue to allow other people, such as a spouse or boss, to abuse them as well. Abused children may sometimes grow up to be the abuser. One recent study[134] suggests children from abusive and dysfunctional homes, including physical, emotional or sexual abuse, divorce, incarceration, etc. were considerably more likely to experience cancer, depression, or attention-deficit/hyperactivity disorder in adulthood. An abusive environment may also have serious physical effects on a child's brain development. Abused children are more likely to have smaller brains as well as other brain abnormalities.[125]

Common Abuse Techniques Affecting Children:[12]
- *Criticising children:* The effect of criticism on children is hideous. After being criticized, the child will struggle to do better, only to be criticized again. The child, not understanding the parent's abusive nature, believes the parent's criticisms and concludes that he or she is just not good enough, so the

child tries even harder only to be criticized again. Believing the parent's criticisms are true, the child's self-esteem and self-confidence sink lower and lower. When the abusive parent goes through his Mr. Thoughtful Husband and Father periods, he may encourage and compliment the child, only to tear the child down again when he reenters abuse mode. The child, whose self-esteem, self-confidence, hopes, dreams, and happiness had been elevated by Mr. Thoughtful Husband and Father, is devastated—over and over again. These children may suffer depression, have problems at school, and have difficulty getting along with other children. Many of these children eventually become some of the depressed adults filling the offices of therapists and psychiatrists the world over—not to mention AA meetings. Children who are routinely criticized may not recognize their positive traits, and when successful as adults, they may be unable to give themselves the credit for their achievements. Both the child and the later adult may continue to think, consciously or unconsciously, that it is just a matter of time before everyone sees how worthless and incompetent they really are.

- ***Excessive punishment:*** Excessive punishment may be dished out for minor infractions or when the child has done nothing wrong at all. The parent/child relationship is severely damaged when the child develops hatred for, and fear of, the parent(s). Studies at the American Academy of Pediatrics and Duke University found even socially accepted spanking to increase aggression in young children.[78,79]
- ***Ignoring the children:*** When ignored, children will believe they are the problem and believe their parent would spend more time with them if they were better children. This can sabotage a child's self-esteem and self-confidence. When children are

ignored, the pain of being ignored may be worse than the pain of punishment. Children may misbehave to get attention, even if the attention comes in the form of punishment.[45]

- *Abusing the mother in front of the children:* Although some abusers may attempt to hide their abuse of the mother from the children, they are kidding themselves. Children almost always sense problems in the family, presumably because they have not developed the defense mechanisms that blind so many adults to the elephants in the room. Unfortunately, young children frequently blame themselves for the chaos in the house, with the element of guilt added to the child's fears. In some families, the children and adolescents may actually be abusive to their mother because this is the behavior they have learned from watching the abusive father. It's not lost on the children that their father always seems to get what he wants by abusing their mother, and the children may find they sometimes get what they want when they treat their mother in an abusive manner. Of course, the abusive father sides with the now abusive children if the mother complains.

- *Revenge—abusing a child or children to get back at the wife for resisting his abuse or some other perceived infraction:* Any mother will experience extreme anguish when her child is abused, and she is helpless to stop the abuse. She may submit to the man's abuse to protect the children.

- *Openly disagreeing with the mother's parenting techniques in front of the children*: This makes it much more difficult for the mother to discipline the children and enforce rules. The children may begin to view their mother as the unfair bad guy, or they may begin to manipulate their parents by playing them off against each other. It is a truism among family therapists that effective discipline requires a united front on the part of the parents.[45] It is abusive to consistently offer children the confusion of conflicting parental rules and discipline.

- *Using the children as pawns during a divorce settlement*: A common example here is the abusive father who never showed interest in, or spent quality time with, his children yet seeks full custody during the divorce to make his wife suffer for leaving him. He may also tell the children how awful or sick their mother is, and the children, having seen their mother anxious, distraught, and depressed many times, may believe it. I have witnessed abuser retaliation when the wife is leaving the relationship, or about to leave, by saying she is crazy, mentally ill, an alcoholic, having her committed to a mental institution, etc. For some abused women, it only gets worse in court, especially in situations where the man controls the money that pays the lawyers. Life may become a living hell for stay-at-home moms who may not have the financial means to fight the abuser in court. Unfortunately, many family judges and lawyers are ignorant of the dynamics of abusive relationships. Incompetent judges may believe the abuser's statements about his wife's emotional instability or incompetent parenting and even believe the abuser's statements that the mother has tried to turn the children against him. Of course, the abused mother may actually suffer emotional problems and depression, but these are symptoms caused by her husband's abuse.[12] Once the abuser has custody, he may then use the children as pawns to continue "revenge abuse" against his ex-wife for years to come, while making little effort to meet the children's needs.

AVOIDING ABUSERS
WHAT TO WATCH FOR

Most people are aware of the need to get to know someone before becoming emotionally involved, in part, to avoid the abusers. My experience as a therapist and conversations with police officers suggests there are many more abusive personalities out there than most people realize. As mentioned earlier, most abusers are very nice during the early parts of a relationship. Lundy Bancroft, in his landmark book *Why Does He Do That?*,[12] states that the abuse may begin when the abuser feels like he owns the woman. The abuser's feeling of ownership may begin when they first become sexually intimate, first move in together, or when they get married. A friend of mine got out of one abusive marriage and dated a "nice guy" for two years, only to have him refuse to sleep with her on their wedding night to get back at her for some perceived infraction. The abuse began on their wedding night. But most abusers will give off subtle signs of their abusive attitude toward women much earlier. The exceptions are the abusers who have been busted in previous couples therapy or a previous divorce and have learned to play a better game.

Here are some basic steps women can take to protect themselves.[2,12,46] Avoid a man who:

- Wants immediate, total commitment.
- Talks about how badly women have treated him in the past.
- Stares you down or looks at you in ways that intimidate you.
- Lies to you.
- Threatens to break up with you unless you (fill in the blank).
- Criticizes you—or others.
- Is emotionally unavailable. If he seems more interested in his work or hobbies than he is in you, be very careful. Of course,

he may not act this way until you have been involved with him for some time.
- Asks you for money.
- Routinely makes problems or disagreements *your fault*.
- Is overly insistent on sex on his terms, emphasizes painful or rough sex, or simply cares more about his needs than your needs.
- Is moody—his moods appear to shift for no reason.
- Even hints that the man should be the head of the household.

Many in religious communities may disagree with this, but many abusers incorporate religious beliefs into their abuse to increase their level of power, dominance, and control.

When I suspect abuse in a relationship, my first goal is for the abused woman to recognize that she is in an abusive relationship and to become educated about abuse as quickly as possible. If the abused woman has come to see me by herself, I encourage her, without the abuser's knowledge, to educate herself about abuse ASAP. I keep the amount of reading to a minimum, since many abused women must do the reading on their lunch hour at work to avoid having the reading material in a location where the abuser might see it. I ask abused women to read the following chapters in the accompanying books ASAP:

(1) *The Verbally Abusive Relationship* by Patricia Evans
Chapter: The Characteristics of Verbal Abuse
Skip the first two or three pages, and go to the list of abuse techniques and read the rest of the chapter (about 17 pages). If this is the only book you have, also read the first 58 pages while you find the second book.

(2) ***Why Does He Do That?*** by Lundy Bancroft
Chapters:
The Abusive Man in Everyday Life
The Process of Change
The Types of Abusive Men
How Abuse Begins
Abusive Men as Parents (if you have, or want to have, children)

If there has been the slightest threat of intimidation or physical abuse even once, I suggest going directly to the chapters in the second book, *Why Does He Do That?*

Even with these readings, therapy remains critical for many abused women to begin to accept that the abuse is not their fault, and that the abuser does not love her, or even desire the kind of relationship she always just assumed she was getting.[46] In my work with abused women, it is common for an abused woman to begin to recognize the reality of her husband's abusive personality, only to slide back into denial between sessions. For even extended periods of time, some abused women will begin each session with some statement to the effect of, "But he really is a good guy at heart" or, "But he must love me some." These abused women are highly resistant to accepting the fact that the abusive man is not a good guy and does not love her at all, by any reasonable definition of love.

The loving acts of kindness offered by an abuser are usually manipulations designed to get the abuser what he wants and to blind the woman to the abuse. In the abused woman's thinking, if the abuser does not love her at all, even just a little, this can only mean she is completely unlovable. I must repeatedly emphasize to these women that the abuser's lack of love for her has nothing to do with her at all. The abusive man is probably incapable of really caring about the feelings and needs of any woman, and he would have been just as abusive to, and just as incapable of loving, any other woman—not just her. With some abused women, I keep an ongoing, and growing, list of the abusive things he has said and done to her, and we review this "reality check" at the beginning of each session. Over time, repeated doses of reality can be very effective at combating deeply rooted and persistent denial—but not always.

Some abused women may suffer some level of a personality style or disorder, such as a dependent or avoidant personality, that contributes to their submissiveness and denial. Suffering from one or more of these personalities will make recognizing abuse and leaving the abuser much more difficult. In these situations, the possibility of more extreme abuse, or successive abusive relationships, becomes much more likely. Most important, the abused woman needs to accept that a serious abuser will probably never change, although he may become the nicest guy in the world for even extended periods of time as a manipulative technique to keep the abused woman from leaving the relationship.

Finally, if you seek professional help for an abusive relationship, I strongly encourage you to get a recommendation from a women's shelter or someone who understands the problem of abuse.

If possible, go see the therapist by yourself without the abuser's knowledge. Even if there has not been any physical abuse, it is best not to make assumptions about how the abuser will react to the knowledge that you are going to see a therapist who, for the abuser, represents a potential loss of control. I have met many women who were in individual or couples therapy with a therapist or minister that simply had no clue about the dynamics of abusive relationships. I've had several clients who talked about a previous therapist who just sat there while the abuser continued the abuse right there in the therapist's office.

A friend of mine was in therapy because of her abusive husband, and neither she nor her therapist recognized the abuse for what it was. My friend showed her therapist this chapter and her therapist attempted a clumsy cover by saying, "I think that's what I have been telling you all along, I just didn't use the word 'abuse.'" Poorly trained or ignorant therapists and ministers seem to have the idea that if they can just get the couple to sit down and have a calm and honest conversation, their relationship will stabilize, and they will raise their children in a peaceful and stable environment. Unfortunately, abuse doesn't work that way.

I know of many cases where an abuser has manipulated a poorly trained therapist or minister into focusing on the abused woman as the cause of the family's problems and succeeded in getting the therapist, minister, and sometimes a psychiatrist to agree that the abused woman is unstable, bipolar, an alcoholic, etc. I believe it is the norm for abused women to suffer at the hands of inadequately trained therapists as well as ignorant lawyers and judges. I have heard other therapists, and sometimes the lawyers representing an abused woman, say something to the effect of, "You know, I think a couple's problems are almost always 50/50. They're usually both at fault." This is ignorance and incompetence at its worst and reinforces the abuser's propaganda that the abused woman is the problem. Many abusers are all too happy to accept 50 percent of the blame—until they get the woman away from the therapist's office.[12] This is also abuse by incompetent graduate schools that make no attempt to adequately train their graduate students in the dynamics of abusive relationships. Just because a therapist says he or she understands abusive relationships does not make it so. Through 10 years of full-time graduate school, two masters degrees, and a PhD in the behavioral sciences, I never heard one single professor even mention the topic of abusive personalities or abusive relationships, or assign any readings on this topic. I have now encountered enough abused women who have suffered through incompetent counseling to believe the lack of training I received in graduate school is the norm.

THE OBSESSIVE-COMPULSIVE PERSONALITY

This description covers multiple levels of obsessive-compulsive patterns of thought, emotion, and behavior. Those with fewer or milder traits as well as those with the symptoms of a serious disorder may readily identify some of their thinking, as well as emotional and behavioral tendencies. A more comprehensive understanding of self usually requires an ongoing self-observation and self-reflection over time. These traits are found in both men and women.

THERE ARE TWO distinct obsessive-compulsive personalities. One personality is called obsessive-compulsive personality disorder, or OCPD, and the other is called obsessive-compulsive disorder, or OCD. Both of these personalities show up in varying degrees of severity from a minor nuisance through a serious disorder. The two personalities do have some of the same traits and symptoms, such as rituals and hoarding, but the differences between these two personalities are much greater than the similarities.

For the *OCPD*, the emphasis is on perfectionism, orderliness, the need for control, the need to be right, avoiding humiliation, and they may be quick to anger. For the OCD, the emphasis is on obsessive thoughts that produce anxiety, which are then followed by mental or behavioral rituals designed to alleviate the anxiety.

One major difference between OCPD and OCD is in the level of suffering.[65] Individuals with a more serious level of OCD experience considerable suffering and distress from a disorder they find unacceptable, and they struggle to make it go away. Individuals with a more serious level of OCPD may not even realize they have a problem because, in their struggle to be perfect, it never occurs to them that they could have a serious problem or need treatment. It is common for people discussing OCPD to mistakenly use the term OCD. I will first discuss the behaviors and symptoms related to the much more common OCPD.

OBSESSIVE-COMPULSIVE PERSONALITY DISORDER (OCPD)

The thoughts, feelings, and behaviors related to OCPD are quite common[19] and are found in varying degrees of severity. They include:

- Perfectionism: Checks and rechecks for mistakes
- Orderliness: Objects must be neatly arranged or in perfect order
- Attention to minute details
- Recurring doubt, both causing and caused by attention to minute details
- They must be right—others are wrong
- Issues are black and white—no gray areas
- Ignores new information that contradicts their opinion
- Control—both self-control and interpersonal; they must have their way
- Rigidity—in thinking, emotions, and behavior
- Rigidity—in values, morality, and religion
- Liberal use of "shoulds" and "musts" on self and others
- Angers quickly and easily
- Stubborn—refuses to listen or compromise
- Stingy with money and possessions—even with family
- Easily humiliated
- Humiliates others

- Follows strict rules and schedules
- Enforces strict rules and schedules on others
- Procrastination
- Indecisiveness
- Avoids taking risks—overly careful
- Hoarding/collecting things
- Rituals: Repeating behaviors or thoughts. May not know why they perform the ritual
- Holds grudges
- Depression
- Impulsive: May act without thinking it through
- Overly focused on details: Misses the big picture
- Unable to relax: Continuous effort toward something
- Clueless that others are unhappy with his or her behavior

VIGNETTE: Perfection, Order, Control, Righteousness, Criticism, and Anger

Todd's wife, Elise, described Todd as a control freak who orchestrated their family life in every way. Todd would become irritated if there was any clutter anywhere in the house, and as a stay-at-home mother, it was Elise's job to keep the house spotless. Elise said Todd had always pushed himself to finish one project so he could get to the next project on his list. Since Todd always seemed to be working at something, Elise suggested Todd hire outside help for repairs around the house to give him more free time, but Todd always insisted on doing the work himself because he did not trust anyone else to do a good job.

In most areas of life, Todd always wanted things done his way and would sometimes lose his temper if his instructions were not followed. Unfortunately, this attitude was applied to his children as well. The creative thinking that many parents would want to instill in their young children was thwarted in deference to doing things the right way, that is, Todd's way. The children's protestations were not tolerated unless his wife intervened. What the children usually heard from Todd was, "Because I said so."

While almost never offering compliments, Todd was very critical of the mistakes of others, including Elise and their children. Even the family's religious orientation was designed to meet the rigid views that had evolved in Todd's thinking. Elise also talked about the lack of family vacations over the years because Todd did not want to spend the money or there was some urgent project he had to finish. Elise also talked about having to "beg" Todd for enough money to run the household, and she was tired of putting up with Todd's "inquisitions" when he thought she was not being frugal enough. When Elise finally refused to postpone one family camping trip, Todd drove the family to the campsite, helped set everything up, drove back home and worked for two days, and then drove back to the campsite to retrieve his family. On other trips, Todd would stay with the family but worked out of his briefcase most of the time.

According to Elise, the weekly dinner parties held at the homes of friends were the only social event she could get her husband to go to because he always had too much work to do. Todd only attended these dinner parties because Elise forcefully insisted he go. Elise described one dinner party where Todd exploded in anger at another guest over some political discussion and berated and humiliated the surprised victim for several minutes in front of the other guests. Elise pointed out that political discussions were routine and an accepted part of these weekly get-togethers. So why Todd's extreme outburst?

After exploring the subject further, Elise thought Todd's rage may have been sparked by a previous discussion with the same guest the week before. Todd's compulsive eating had kept him obese for most of his life, and he had always been sensitive about his weight. This dinner guest may have unwittingly humiliated Todd at the previous dinner party with his story of successful weight loss, which only served to highlight Todd's inability to lose weight. Todd's attempt to humiliate his political rival in front of so many other people may have been retaliation for the humiliation Todd had experienced during the weight-loss discussion a week earlier, although Todd was probably not aware of the connection.

Whether at home, work, or social gatherings, Todd would rarely show emotion. Except when someone would say something that irritated Todd and drew his ire, he would just sit there with a blank expression on his face. Lacking outward emotional expression, Todd rarely expressed affection toward Elise in private, and never in public. Gradually, over time, the emotional connection between Todd and Elise had dissipated almost completely, to be replaced by a regimented lifestyle based on Todd's need for organized certainty in all things. For years, attempts by Elise at romance, or any emotional connection with Todd, had been awkward, and Todd would become uncomfortable and stilted. Even sex became a mechanical routine designed to meet certain requirements. The emotional coldness in their home had become unbearable for Elise, and she finally began to pull away emotionally herself and now describes her home life as simply "numb."

PERFECTIONISM

OCPD sufferers' need for a sense of control over themselves and their life may lead to some level of perfectionism. Common by-products of a perfectionistic attitude include excessive carefulness and procrastination. Perfectionism typically involves continuous self-criticism and anxiety about making mistakes, and it can be difficult for OCPDs to finish projects because of their relentless need to make sure every detail is exactly right. They may spend so much time reading and rereading material, writing yet another draft of a report, or rechecking yet again for mistakes that they never actually complete the project. They become so lost in the minute details of a project that they seem to lose sight of the overall goal.

Once they are happy with the minutia, they may still be unhappy with the overall final product and immediately commence revising the minor details again—and another deadline is missed. The forest may be missed as they concentrate on trees, branches, twigs, leaves, and seeds. Some projects may never even get started because of their extreme focus on the most trivial details of the basic preparations. Some OCPDs may also have poor time-management skills, and they may fail to complete a project because they did not leave enough time.

In work environments, if the OCPD is allowed to work independently, their intense concentration on details, along with a work ethic that emphasizes work over all other aspects of life, may get them rave reviews and promotions.[57] Otherwise the OCPD's behavior at work may be dysfunctional on several fronts. Their perfectionistic attitude may rarely offer compliments to other employees for their exceptional work. When the OCPD has no choice but to delegate work to others, intimidation may be the technique of choice to be certain the work will be done according to the OCPD's own strict guidelines.

DECISIONS, DECISIONS

Uncomfortable with decision-making, OCPDs may try to find some guiding principle or rule that helps them make the "correct" decision.[28] In this way, decisions that for most people involve a mere preference or have an emotional element are turned into a technical problem with external rules of logic or principles of tradition or morality to guide and ensure the "logical" choice. This approach may be applied to minor or inconsequential decisions with the same seriousness applied to major life decisions. Once the OCPD does finally make a decision, the decision may be written in stone with a rigid indifference to any new information that may come along.

One obvious and logical offshoot of the OCPD's perfectionism is indecisiveness.[28] In milder cases, indecisiveness may be no more than a minor irritation for the OCPD and those around him. In more serious cases, the OCPD may vacillate endlessly between two or more choices, and the indecisiveness may be incapacitating and sabotage the OCPD's efforts to lead a normal and productive life. The closer the OCPD gets to deciding on one thing, the more the alternative begins to look like the better choice—back and forth, over and over. The OCPD seems unaware that both choices might be equally suitable. The OCPD may spend a considerable amount of time just deciding what clothes to wear, only to change his mind an hour later and change clothes again. And once the OCPD has actually decided which used car to buy, and bought it, he may watch the car ads for months afterward to make sure he made the right choice.

The OCPD seems to operate on two extremes. He either has excessive doubt about something, or he has a rigid and unyielding certainty with little room for compromise.[28] It is the OCPD's inflexible emphasis on the technical or minute details that results in these two extremes. Insignificant, or even irrelevant, information may create seemingly endless doubts about the right choice, but once the required rules or principles have been met and the decision is made, then he is right, and new information may be ignored. In business and employment, the effects of indecisiveness and dysfunctional decision-making may short-circuit the OCPD's career goals.

RIGIDITY / DOESN'T LISTEN / BLAMES OTHERS

The OCPD may have a very rigid belief system that he believes is the right belief system for everyone at all times. These individuals may see their way of thinking and functioning as the right way, and everything and everyone is evaluated according to their strict standards. OCPDs do not like to be disagreed with. Completely certain of the rightness of their own opinion, the OCPDs' responses to alternative viewpoints or suggestions may range from increasing righteous indignation and criticism through extreme anger, although the anger may not be expressed in a direct manner.

Even trivial issues may be fought for and may escalate into a heated exchange, which the victim may find very difficult to gently bring to a close. The art of listening and compromise may appear foreign to the OCPD. You have the sense that he just does not hear anything you say as he simply restates his position. The OCPD does appear to be concentrating, but not on what you are saying.[28] Your views are just unacceptable interruptions. Further, this righteousness may be applied to anyone, including those the OCPD hardly knows. It's as if the small talk that new acquaintances customarily use to become comfortable with each other does not exist for the OCPD. Compromise is ruled out, as it seems to imply not only some degree of wrongness on his part, but implies some loss of control as well. Unfortunately, OCPDs are sometimes promoted to management positions by businesses and bureaucracies[57] because of the very perfectionism that makes them dictatorial bullies who will criticize and humiliate those below them. Still, the OCPD may rigidly conform to rules issued by a recognized authority or an authority they respect. At the same time, the OCPD may ignore rules issued by an authority they do not respect.

The OCPD's righteous style of discourse may cause some people to be very nice and polite in an attempt to close the conversation, which may infuriate the OCPD if the other individual has not yet conceded the correctness of the OCPD's perspective.[57] If the OCPD recognizes that you are allowing him to win a few points to settle him down because you are less serious about the topic, or just do not want to talk to him, you may be on the receiving end of the very stern lecture you were trying so delicately to avoid. On those few occasions when the OCPD does give in and change his position on some vital issue, expect his new position to be taken with the same seriousness as his previous position and defended in the same rigid manner. The OCPD's need to be right is frequently welded to his moral and ethical code. The OCPD may take his views on religion or politics very seriously, and "shoulds" and "musts" may predominate when these topics are discussed. In keeping with this attitude, the OCPD tends to blame other people or external circumstances for his problems.

Over time, the OCPD's way of responding can be very destructive to his emotions, social relationships, and employment opportunities. Unfortunately, the OCPD's rigidity, perfectionism, need to be right, and refusal to really listen to what others have to say may give them an enduring social incompetence with little opportunity for improvement. Even if they do begin to recognize their righteous or hostile communication style, the isolation they endure after driving away potential friends and acquaintances offers OCPDs fewer opportunities to practice appropriate communication.

SENSE OF EFFORT

OCPDs may feel uncomfortable when they do not have some duty or obligation they must deal with, and they may remain uncomfortable until they find some new responsibility or endeavor that requires their attention or that they can at least worry about. It is common for the OCPD to take his work with him on a vacation and avoid the idle mind so coveted by most vacationers. The OCPD may be unable to experience the freedom of thought that most people have in their thinking and decisions.

In his extraordinary book, *Neurotic Styles*,[28] David Shapiro points out that the detailed concentration of OCPDs may miss a whole range of sensual and emotional experiences as the bigger picture and spontaneity are lost to them. Allowing the mind to become spontaneously caught up in the beauty of nature, or to really hear a lyrical melody, requires a relaxation of attention that allows the mind to be available for new or unexpected stimuli. For OCPDs, unexpected or unplanned stimuli may just be irritating and distracting nuisances to be ignored, and they may lose the emotional and perceptual experiences available to a relaxed mind that can be seized by spontaneous events, thoughts, conversations, tastes, feelings, etc. Since there is always something OCPDs are concentrating on or worrying about, they rarely experience the surprise of something they just happen to notice. As Shapiro puts it, "It is not that they do not look or listen, but they are looking or listening too hard for something else." Endeavors that relax the mind, such as yoga or meditation, may be difficult for OCPDs but are exceedingly rewarding if they can stick with the process without succumbing to the sense that they are wasting time.

Shapiro also points out that the sheer effort and tension involved in the focused attention on some project may seem to be more important to OCPDs than the goal of actually completing the project. OCPDs are always "trying" to do something. This serious level of effort may be applied to all activities, including activities they have little real interest in. The continuous and intense pressure to concentrate and focus on something is a self-inflicted pressure, which OCPDs may sometimes view as a positive trait while at other times complaining about the pressure that they believe stems from outside themselves. OCPDs are not aware that it is *they* who require *themselves* to work intensely on one project and then quickly concentrate just as intensely on something else. They feel they are merely "reminding" themselves of some important necessity, especially where ethics and morals are involved.

The OCPD's emphasis on intellectual logic, with tiresome details and exact descriptions, may carry over into casual conversations with other people. The OCPD's concentration on technicalities and detailed descriptions may become time-consuming, boring, and sometimes exhausting for the listener-victim. In an electronics store I frequent, there is an extremely knowledgeable employee who always goes into an OCPD level of technical detail that is way beyond what I can possibly understand or need to know. This seems to be the only modus operandi available to her, and she never seems to notice the bewildered stares customers offer in return.

HUMILIATION

To understand the behavior of OCPDs, it is important to recognize that many OCPDs do not experience being "wrong" the way most people do. For most of us, being wrong implies a mistake to be reconsidered and corrected. Not so for some OCPDs. I have been struck by the extent to which many OCPDs experience being wrong about something, or even receiving constructive criticism, as a humiliating experience. For some OCPDs, avoiding humiliation is one of the paramount struggles in their lives and may be one of the main causes of their rigidity and intense need to be right. It is here that the need to be right, perfectionism, a rigid belief system, etc., work together, causing considerable and sometimes incapacitating procrastination and indecisiveness as OCPDs struggle to avoid the humiliating experience of being wrong. Since it is critical for OCPDs to avoid the humiliating experience of being wrong, just a suggestion or an offer of assistance by another employee may be interpreted as criticism worthy of direct or indirect retaliation. It is here that those who must deal with an OCPD may pay a high price. OCPDs may unconsciously react to their fear of being humiliated by occasionally humiliating others,[57] including their employees, their partner, and even their children. They seem to have a need to dish out that which they themselves most fear and want to avoid.

HIDES EMOTIONS / ANGERS EASILY HOLDS GRUDGES

Many OCPDs are unemotional most of the time. A restriction of emotional expression is central to OCPDs' sense of self-control.[5,28,57] When the OCPD sense of willful effort is not maintained, they may feel like they are losing control of themselves. This sense of a loss of control may occur when OCPDs allow themselves to release their controlled demeanor to spontaneous excitement and laughter or to grieve over some loss. It is extremely important to OCPDs that they not risk ridicule and humiliation from mistakes, so they strive for complete control over their emotions at all times. Connecting with OCPDs on an emotional level can be awkward at best. When they do attempt to show emotion, such as affection for a spouse or children, happiness at a family reunion, or sadness for someone's loss, the expressed emotion may appear stiff and self-conscious as they struggle to maintain some sense of control. Even in brief or casual conversations, OCPDs may seem stilted and uneasy from fear they will say the wrong thing. OCPDs may also become very uncomfortable when other people freely express their emotions, possibly because OCPDs then feel an uncomfortable and self-inflicted pressure to loosen up as well. It may be easier for OCPDs to feel displeasure at the free spirits around them than to join them. Most of the time, OCPDs may remain essentially expressionless, with little in the way of positive or negative emotions. They are just there.

So determining what emotion OCPDs are actually experiencing at any given moment may be difficult, and so it is that OCPDs may catch people by surprise with any real emotional sentiment or angry outburst. When a spontaneous show of emotion does occur, it is usually anger.[57] OCPDs get angry very quickly and easily, although they may bury their anger at someone for long periods of time, only to unload the anger on them later over some trivial or completely unrelated issue.

ORDERLINESS

Sometimes OCPDs' need for excessive control over their life is expressed through a need for everything to always be in its designated place or displayed in perfect order, and all in a perfectly clean house. Whenever things are not exactly right, OCPDs' feelings may range from a mild uneasiness through considerable distress, so they remain constantly vigilant for that which is out of place or just not quite right. Some OCPDs keep the clothes in their closet color-coded and all facing the same direction. Other sufferers feel compelled to repeatedly swipe their finger across their furniture to check for dust, and some may check for dust on the furniture in other people's homes.

RITUALS

Some OCPDs feel compelled to perform mental or behavioral rituals, such as frequent housecleaning, checking something repeatedly, mentally counting backward, reciting a prayer, never stepping on cracks in sidewalks, etc. OCPD sufferers may not be aware of any anxiety or fear of disaster that compels them to perform a ritual, whereas the OCD sufferers discussed later may experience severe anxiety or fear some disaster occurring if they do not perform some ritual.[57]

The compulsive rituals of some OCPDs may become wrapped up in a self-image that is largely based on the role or roles they play in life.[28] Performing rituals that live up to the image that OCPDs believe is expected of a certain role, such as banker, doctor, lawyer, parent, minister, etc., may become a major preoccupation. The need to act according to their "role" may give these OPCDs a demeanor that seems overly formal, forced, or contrived and may give their behavior an unnatural wooden appearance. I know a doctor who puts on a coat and tie to drive to his clinic, where he changes into scrubs for work and then changes back into a coat and tie to drive home.

HOARDING / STINGY

Some OCPDs find they are unable to throw things away because they think they may eventually find a need for them. The basements, attics, hallways, and garages of some OCPDs may simply fill up with old, useless stuff. If someone else attempts to dispose of the treasured possessions, there may be an immediate display of the OCPD trait of being quick to anger. OCPDs are also known to be very thrifty and are frequently described as "cheap." The miserly aspect of OCPDs is simply a special case of hoarding,[5] where they excessively hoard money, thinking they may need the money for some future event or disaster. OCPD misers may leave their spouse begging for money to care for the family as their savings account continues to grow.

DEPRESSION / LOW SELF-ESTEEM

Depression and low self-esteem are common among OCPDs. Not only are other people unable to live up to the rigid standards and high expectations of OCPDs, but OCPDs may be extremely self-critical when they fail to meet their own inflexible requirements. With an almost delusional self-concept of living up to the highest standards, OCPDs will inevitably and repeatedly experience their own failures, including feelings of anger when their failures involve an apparent loss of control over self or others. At the same time, OCPDs may also deal with the frequent negative reactions of other people to their behavior. As with many personality patterns, OCPDs may experience some degree of isolation as their personality drives away friends and acquaintances. This may create a vicious circle in the lives of OCPDs where isolation invariably leads to an increase in low self-esteem and depression, accompanied by ever-increasing odd or eccentric behavior that may result in even more isolation. While isolation may be the product of an individual's personality, isolation may also create the conditions that exacerbate his eccentricities, while offering fewer opportunities for the individual to practice modifying the dysfunctional behaviors. Depression and loneliness are common complaints of OCPDs who seek professional help, although they are usually not aware of the underlying problem. Individual therapy at first, with group therapy later, can be very effective at helping isolated individuals, whether they are OCPD or not, to learn to understand themselves and develop the coping and interpersonal skills they need to better relate to other struggling souls on their own journey.

THE OCPD IN RELATIONSHIPS

Although OCPDs typically have greater success staying married than individuals suffering from other personality problems, it is common for OCPDs to live alone[39] or have a history of short relationships. Even with the many OCPD characteristics that contribute to dysfunctional or failed relationships, including perfectionism, control, anger, criticism, few compliments, etc., it is frequently indecisiveness that prevents the formation of long-term relationships.

Typically when we first meet someone and enter the honeymoon stage of a relationship, everything about our potential mate is just wonderful. The new potential mate can do no wrong when viewed through the lens of a chemically induced infatuation. But with time, from just a few weeks up to a year or more later, the honeymoon stage ends, and we begin to notice minor irritants about the other person, although not necessarily about ourselves. When the OCPD begins the essentially normal process of becoming a little more realistic about the characteristics of his love interest, his tendency to have overly high expectations of others may play itself out in his relationship. Some minor flaw in the potential mate may become the only thing the OCPD notices when they are together, and other potential mates less well known to the OCPD are starting to look just so awesome. Greener grass may always grow elsewhere for some OCPDs.

If the relationship does become a long-term commitment, it may be highly dysfunctional and quite miserable for the victim/mate and children, as the OCPD's critical nature rules the house. In the home, the OCPD may want to take care of things himself because only he can do it right. The partner's attempts to help may be rejected out of hand as the OCPD emphasizes the importance of his work while negating the value of his partner's efforts. An

OCPD may even disparage the efforts and desires of his children, and the compliments that a child's self-esteem thrives on may be rare or nonexistent.

OCPDs may come across as type A personalities with their preoccupation with work, details, competitiveness, and a sense of urgency to get things done. Other areas of the OCPD's life, such as their spouse, children, vacations, home or auto maintenance, etc., may get neglected. Vacation time, so coveted by most people, may be largely ignored, postponed again and again, because of the pressure the OCPD puts on himself to get more work done. Of course, when the OCPD does not take the vacation, the spouse and children usually miss out as well. When the OCPD finally does take his family on a vacation, he may take his work with him to avoid wasting time. The OCPD works while the spouse and children play without him. The OCPD might as well not be there. If the OCPD tries to have quality time with his family during the vacation, he may still have work on his mind the whole time and soon return to his urgent duties. And the family may actually be glad he is again leaving them alone, since the OCPD typically approaches play with the same serious intensity he approaches work and dictatorially removes the element of fun for both himself and his family. For example, if the OCPD does spend time with his children, the child who just loves to throw gutter balls is ordered to "throw in a straight line." Another example is the small child who is having a blast using crayons to draw all over the pages of a coloring book but is ordered to draw only within the lines and possibly ridiculed or scolded—that is, humiliated—for any failures to do so. The real issue behind the OCPD's distaste for relaxation is that, for the OCPD, relaxation feels like a loss of control.[28,57]

The OCPD may be completely unaware of his symptoms or their impact on other people, including his family.[65] As a result of this lack of awareness, the OCPD will probably be happier in the relationship than his partner or the children. The OCPD is quite happy with his emphasis on work, dominance, and control, while the family's needs for an emotional connection, empathy, intimacy, affection, warmth, compliments, spontaneity, and fun get neglected. In some cases, the OCPD's overly strict, dictatorial approach to family life may legitimately be described as abusive. As with most abusive behavior, it is in the home, hidden from public scrutiny, that OCPD symptoms are most likely to be expressed in abusive behavior. The criticism, humiliation, and punishments the OCPD uses to control his partner and children may be severe behind the closed doors of a home. Hidden away from public scrutiny, it is control, humiliation, and severe punishment that may replace both rational explanations for decisions and logical consequences[45] for discipline. The extremely dedicated hard worker the partner knew during the early parts of their relationship may have become a controlling and punitive workaholic. In a tension-filled environment, the abusive OCPD may hold other family members responsible for most family problems. With irritation or anger quickly and easily displayed, the rest of the family may find themselves feeling uneasy when they are around the OCPD, fearing they will say or do something that sets him off. Unaware of the OCPD's underlying problem, the partner may try to figure out what it is he or she is doing that upsets the OCPD.

The partner of an OCPD may blame herself for the OCPD's emotional distance and lack of involvement in family life. The partner may also wonder why the OCPD rejects her attempts to work with him on their problems. The partner fails to recognize that the OCPD is very content with the status quo as long as he is in control. If the OCPD has rigidly held religious beliefs, the fear of God may be used as a technique of control, and rigid adherence to religious rituals, readings, etc. may be punitively enforced.[57] This, along with a lack of positive attention, encouragement, or compliments offered to children as positive reinforcements, may be severely damaging to children's self-esteem. Depression may dwell in every room of the abusive OCPD's house. An abusive personality, whether he suffers OCPD or not, desires the power, control, dominance, and privileges he experiences from being abusive to his family, employees, etc. An abusive personality combined with the symptoms of OCPD creates an extremely controlling abuser who cannot change without a willingness to commit to considerable work with a knowledgeable therapist.

CHANGE

Since OCPDs typically are not aware of the underlying cause of their problems, they may seek treatment for related complaints such as anxiety, fatigue, depression, or sexual dysfunction. Many OCPDs seek treatment only after their spouse or employer insists they do so.[19] It is frequently the spouse who brings an OCPD to my office after years of chronic marital discord, possibly threatening divorce if he does not seek help.

Even when OCPDs are aware of specific dysfunctional behaviors, such as rituals or anger outbursts, they may not have connected any dots involving their own responsibility. Whether we call it rationalization, denial, or something else, the OCPD will frequently find fault elsewhere for that which stems from within. It is the therapist's job to help OCPDs connect the dots and to enlighten them about their personality-related symptoms. With a comprehensive understanding of their personality, OCPDs can begin to work on choosing new responses and behaviors.

Unfortunately, it is common for OCPD clients to find some reason for not continuing in therapy, such as the expense or a therapist who is clearly "wrong." But those committed to the therapeutic process can learn to recognize their problematic attitudes, emotions, and behaviors and learn to respond in a way that leads to a productive life. Medications can be effective in treating OCPD.[19]

A number of problems may co-occur with OCPD, including anxiety, shyness, depression, and eating disorders, especially anorexia nervosa. Personalities found to commonly co-occur with OCPD include the paranoid, avoidant, borderline, and schizoid personalities.[19]

SIMILARITIES AND DIFFERENCES

As with the OCPD, the narcissist also seeks perfection and does not trust others to do things right, but there is one big difference. The narcissist believes he is already perfect and merely seeks affirmations to support this conviction. The OCPD does not believe he is perfect at all and may flood his brain with critical self-talk as he pushes himself toward that perfection which cannot be achieved.

OBSESSIVE–COMPULSIVE DISORDER (OCD)

The main symptoms of obsessive-compulsive disorder (OCD) involve repeating *obsessions* that are usually followed by *compulsive rituals* that are severe enough to interfere with the individual's daily activities and relationships. OCD also occurs in children, and between one-third and one-half of OCD cases in adults can be traced back to childhood symptoms. OCD exists in every country in the world.[65]

OBSESSIONS

Obsessions are recurring and persistent thoughts, feelings, mental images, impulses, or ideas that intrude into an individual's thinking, even though the individual considers them inappropriate and does not want them. Common obsessions include thoughts of contamination or being dirty, persistent doubts about something, thoughts of committing a violent act against another person or of possibly having harmed someone in the past, thoughts or images of inappropriate sex, thoughts of having offended God, etc. Individuals recognize the obsessions as originating in their own minds yet seeming to be outside of any voluntary mental process, and, therefore, they are experienced as foreign to their actual selves.[65]

COMPULSIVE RITUALS

Compulsive rituals involve the repeating performance of behaviors or mental exercises that are usually performed for any of three main purposes:

1. Reducing the anxiety or distress that accompanies an obsession
2. Preventing some terrible event or disaster
3. Relieving guilt feelings over the possibility that they may have harmed or insulted someone and avoiding the sense that they are terrible people who are capable of doing harm to others.[61]

The varieties of compulsive rituals are endless, and they can be very strange indeed. Consider the case of writer-actor-director Woody Allen:[62] Woody Allen cuts his banana for breakfast cereal into exactly seven equal pieces. He performs this ritual out of a fear—that is, an obsessional thought—that if he does not cut the banana into seven equal pieces, some disaster may befall his family, such as they may all die in a house fire. Like the great majority of OCD sufferers, Woody Allen knows very well that his thinking, and the accompanying anxiety, are completely irrational and that there is no actual connection between his cutting the banana and the possibility of some disaster. Yet, as Woody Allen points out, if he does not cut the banana into seven equal pieces and something terrible does happen to his family, "The guilt would be too much for me to bear, so its easier for me to cut the stupid banana."

Some rituals used by OCDs involve mental exercises that are not outwardly observable, such as silently reciting a phrase or prayer or mentally counting backward from 100 to zero for each unwanted thought. Concentration on mental rituals may give the individual the appearance of daydreaming.[56] Be careful not to confuse compulsive rituals with other behaviors, such as culturally based behaviors, addictions, compulsive gambling, etc. Eating disorders, however, do appear to have a strong connection to OCD.[66] All OCD sufferers have obsessions, and most OCDs will also have compulsive rituals.[56] These individuals, except for OCD children, usually recognize that their obsessive thoughts and compulsive rituals are completely irrational and may also recognize that the ritual may have no logical connection to the obsession that appears to cause it. Yet their compulsion to perform the rituals only seems to increase, taking up more and more of their time and making their lives increasingly stressful. OCD symptoms, unlike OCPD symptoms, may ebb and flow over time, which helps explain why the level of insight some OCDs have into the irrationality of their disorder may vary from time to time.[56]

While about 80 percent of OCDs recognize the irrationality of their ritualistic responses to an obsessive thought, up to half of those offer little resistance to the urge to perform rituals.[5] The other half of those afflicted may attempt to resist the ritual but usually give in to their anxiety and distress and make some ritual a part of their everyday life. In simple cases like Woody Allen's, giving in to the ritual is a reasonable accommodation. For other OCDs, their daily functioning may become seriously controlled and constricted as they perform rituals or attempt to avoid the situations that seem to trigger their OCD symptoms. The mega-wealthy aviator, industrialist, and film producer Howard Hughes became as famous for his extremely reclusive lifestyle, reportedly to avoid a germ-infested world, as for his considerable accomplishments. Obsessions, mental or behavioral rituals, or avoiding the perceived cause of an obsession may take over an OCD's life.

Interestingly, rituals may have no effect in other areas of the OCD's life.[57] The individual who washes his hands 50 times a day because he fears germs may love to race motorcycles, hang glide, skydive, climb Mt. Everest, etc. Many OCDs will have more than one symptom, and the symptoms may change over time. A fear of germs may disappear only to be replaced by a need for perfect order and symmetry.[65]

COMMON PATTERNS OF OCD

Symptoms of OCD typically show up in a gradual manner, although a sudden onset of symptoms may occur during a period of significant emotional stress, like leaving home for college, having a baby, divorce, etc. Symptoms usually present themselves in one or more of several common patterns involving obsessive thoughts and compulsive rituals.[65] Here are descriptions of the most common forms of OCD:[5]

Contamination OCD: The most common form of OCD involves an obsession with contamination by germs, dirt, viruses, etc. and is usually accompanied by rituals designed to eliminate or avoid the contamination. The obsessive thoughts may involve germ phobias such as a fear of dirty hands, a dirty body, or a dirty house. There may also be a fear of public restrooms or of the sufferer's own bodily waste products, such as sweat, urine, or feces. Habitual housecleaning, frequent showers, or repeated hand washing are common rituals performed to reduce the anxiety caused by obsessive thoughts about germs and dirt. Other rituals may be designed to avoid the contamination in the first place, such as the refusal to shake hands during greetings, staying away from trash cans, keeping bathroom doors closed, etc. OCDs may also worry that they have contracted some disease.

Doubt OCD: Having serious doubts about something is the second-most-common form of OCD. Examples of repeating thoughts involving doubt include: "Did I leave the water running?" "Did I lock the door?" "Did I buy the right car?" "Did I hurt his or her feelings?" "Have I offended God?" "Am I gay?" "Did I turn the computer off?" "Should I end my relationship?" The rituals that follow obsessive doubt may involve compulsive checking, such as checking letters or papers repeatedly for mistakes, returning to the house repeatedly to make sure all appliances and computers were turned off, doors locked, etc.

Steven Phillipson discusses a subtype of doubt OCD, referred to as "Responsibility OC."[61] Responsibility OC involves feelings of guilt caused by (1) obsessive thoughts of possibly having harmed someone or (2) guilt experienced when some ritual designed to protect others from harm, such as giving warnings or removing a dangerous object, is not carried out. Phillipson points out that the ritual of hand washing, usually connected with a fear of contamination by germs, may also reflect an OCD's sense of responsibility in not wanting to infect others when shaking hands. The fear that they may have harmed someone because of their negligence may cause OCDs to repeatedly seek assurances that they have not harmed anyone. This form of OCD has little to do with a normal sense of compassion. A Responsibility OC may take in so many stray animals that the animals and the sufferer live in unsanitary and unsafe conditions.[65]

Another element found in Responsibility OC is the low self-esteem that accompanies the guilt. In the Responsibility OC's mind, the obsessive thought of having harmed someone, or the failure to perform a ritual to protect others, seems to imply a lack of caring about other people, and the OCD sufferer's feelings of self-worth may start to crater. The protection of the sufferer's own reputation and self-esteem may actually become the major motivation for performing a ritual or attempting to avoid the obsession in the first place.

Up to 20 percent of OCDs may suffer "Hyper-responsibility hit and run OCD" and must constantly deal with the obsession that they may have hit someone with their car. Rituals then follow this obsessive thought, such as driving back by the scene where an accident may have happened or repeatedly checking police reports to see if an accident was reported.[65]

When doubt involves religious beliefs, the result may be a form of OCD referred to as "Scrupulosity OCD."[59,65] Scrupulosity OCD typically involves religious rituals, such as repeated prayers, prayers that must be spoken perfectly evenly, or frequent confessions. These rituals are designed to deal with the obsessive thought that the sufferer's thinking or behavior may have offended God or shown disrespect to some religious institution or icon. Other scrupulous rituals may involve following a strict ethical or legal regimen or a strict code of conduct. Scrupulosity OCD will usually involve overvaluation, which is the exaggerated importance given to obsessions.[56] With religious scrupulosity, the emotional involvement makes it less likely that OCDs will be fully aware of the irrationality of their obsessional thoughts and compulsive rituals.[59] Contrary to basic common sense, Scrupulosity OCD is not caused by strong religious beliefs alone, but by the combination of strong religious beliefs and a genetic predisposition to develop OCD. Religious obsessions and rituals are just how the genetic tendency toward OCD gets played out in some people.[65]

Obsessional Thoughts Only OCD (No Outward Ritual): This third-most-common form of OCD involves repeating thoughts that are not necessarily followed by a behavioral ritual. The obsessive thoughts in this form of OCD are usually about committing acts of a repulsive sexual nature or about committing a violent act, although OCDs never carry out their obsessions.

While these individuals do not respond to their obsessive thoughts with the usual behavioral performance of rituals, there may be a mental struggle within them to avoid the thought or find a solution.[60] Researchers now recognize that the internal struggle in this form of OCD may actually involve mental rituals such as the silent repetition of some prayer, phrase, counting backward, etc.[68,69] The fact that these OCDs virtually never carry out their abhorrent thoughts does not keep many of them from feeling like they could snap and do harm to another person.[65] Unfortunately, trying to resist the obsessive and unwanted thought only ensures that the thought will continue to reoccur even more frequently, and with increasing anxiety and distress. Thoughts of killing one's newborn son, shouting obscenities in public, having inappropriate sex, or thoughts that question the sufferer's sexual orientation may create extreme distress in the sufferer's mind and seem totally foreign to the sufferer's self-concept. The high level of distress then drives the obsessive thought to repeat itself.

It is important to recognize that OCDs may feel that just having the abhorrent thoughts implies that they are bad people. Believing they must be bad people, the struggle to escape the original obsessive thought and the struggle against the thought of being a bad person becomes the same struggle. Of course, everyone experiences unwanted or inappropriate thoughts from time to time, but individuals who do not suffer from OCD recognize the absurdity of the thoughts and easily shrug them off.[70] If the individual is uncertain whether a thought or idea is legitimate or stems from OCD, thoughts that are accompanied by feelings of anxiety, guilt, or a sense of urgency are probably the result of OCD.[60]

Symmetry OCD: This fourth-most-common form of OCD involves the need for symmetry, which is the need for balance, uniformity, evenness, order, or precision in certain areas of life. For example, there may be a need for objects to be in a straight line, handwriting must be perfectly even, or if one's body moves in one way—such as turning around—there is the feeling of being unbalanced unless the body is turned in the opposite direction to an equal degree. Anxiety may also occur if a daily routine is interrupted. Some OCDs may be obsessed with symmetry such that their daily showers become very slow, lasting two hours or more, as the OCD makes absolutely certain that all body parts are washed equally. Any sense of unevenness leads to the compulsion to begin the shower from scratch, yet again. Meals can become long, drawn-out ordeals for similar reasons of symmetry.

Fear of Catastrophe: There may be a compulsion to perform some ritual by exact rules to avoid some catastrophe as described earlier in the Woody Allen example. Other rituals designed to avoid some catastrophe might include never stepping on cracks in sidewalks, always touching some object in a certain way or a certain number of times when passing it, always walking through a doorway a certain number of times, turning a light switch on and off a certain number of times, etc.

Hoarding OCD: Compulsive hoarding is the extreme collecting or hoarding of useless possessions[65] to the point that it seriously affects the sufferer's life or even becomes incapacitating.

I recall years ago when an old friend of mine, a true mountain man in the high mountains of North Carolina, took me across the mountain where he lived to meet his severely OCD sister, although none of us recognized her behavior as OCD at the time. His sister owned three shacks next to her house, and if you opened the door to any one of these shacks, there was stuff piled literally to the ceiling—not stacked, just piled higher and higher. The house she lived in also consisted of endless piles of clutter. It appeared she had never thrown away anything in her life, but just opened the door to one of those shacks and threw something else on top of the pile. She was known in the area as possibly having almost anything you might need, and she was showing a bow and arrow to someone when we drove up.

Other OCDs may specialize and save clothes, junk mail, or worn-out appliances, or they may have saved every magazine they ever read. OCD hoarders may fill up so many rooms in their house that they find it difficult to live there, yet they must continue to hoard. Another example of hoarding involves money where the hoarder may become known as "cheap" or "thrifty." Hoarders feel a strong emotional or sentimental attachment to their overvalued piles of stuff, in part because of the sense of control the hoarding offers them. While they usually recognize the irrationality of their hoarding behavior, this awareness does not seem to reduce their need to hoard. Any attempts by others to clean up the mess may be met with a very angry response. Since anything can be hoarded, variations on hoarding are endless.[65]

Other Symptoms: Other symptoms that may be related to OCD include eating disorders, hair-pulling (trichotillomania), nail-biting, and excessive masturbation.[5]

TREATMENT OF OCD

The majority of OCDs experience some shame over their problem and may keep it a secret for years. With so many OCDs hiding their problems, most sufferers remain unaware of how many other people also experience OCD symptoms, so they fail to recognize that they are not alone. At the more serious and diagnosable levels of OCD, about one in 40 people suffer from the disorder. Keeping their problem to themselves, OCDs do not seek treatment for an average of more than seven years after the onset of symptoms.[67] Children are less likely to recognize the irrationality of their symptoms, or they may hide their OCD symptoms for years because of the embarrassment. This is unfortunate, because the longer treatment is delayed, the more generalized the symptoms become and the more difficult they are to treat.[71] With treatment, childhood OCD may go away or it may continue into adulthood, although the specific symptoms may change over time.[67] Keep in mind that superstitions or ritualistic behaviors are normal in young children, and the opinion of a trained professional is recommended if OCD is suspected in a child.

The treatment of choice for OCD is a form of cognitive behavioral therapy (CBT) called Exposure and Response Prevention (ERP). Antidepressant medications can also be very effective in treating OCD symptoms, and for many sufferers, it is the combination of both ERP and medication that seems to get the best results.[65]

Exposure and Response Prevention (ERP): The ERP technique, as described in *The OCD Workbook*[70] by Bruce M. Hyman, PhD, and Cherry Pedrick, RN, involves *habituation*, which is the process of becoming so accustomed to something through frequent exposure to it that it no longer holds the individual's interest and becomes boring.[65] Sufferers are asked to repeatedly expose themselves to the anxiety-producing object, such as unwashed hands, a trash can, bathroom, etc., and to try to avoid, or at least postpone, performing the usual rituals. If the anxiety-producing thought or situation cannot be enacted, as is the case with thoughts of violent or sexually inappropriate behavior, frequently imagining or visualizing the thought while accepting the accompanying anxiety rather than fighting against it usually results in the desired habituation and eventual elimination of rituals. Medications may relieve the depression and anxiety, which may allow the OCD sufferer to better concentrate on the ERP exercises.

The goal in treatment is to have the OCD accept the obsessive thought and the anxiety that accompanies it without blaming himself and without responding to the obsession with mental or behavioral rituals. The idea is to get on with other aspects of daily life while allowing the obsessional thoughts and anxiety to just be there. The acceptance of the obsessive thoughts and the resulting anxiety essentially takes away the power the obsessive thoughts have over the OCD's behavior, and only then will the obsessions occur with less frequency.

The process of acceptance may be especially difficult when obsessive thoughts involve violence toward loved ones, sexual orientation, whether to end a relationship, thoughts of having offended God, thoughts of being a bad person, or feelings of guilt. In cases where the obsessive thoughts involve religious beliefs, OCDs are less likely to even be aware of the irrational nature of the recurring thoughts or that the thoughts and religious rituals they perform may not even be related to their actual religious beliefs. The point is to "be with" the obsessions and the accompanying anxiety rather than attempting to escape them. To willingly accept the anxiety-producing thoughts rather than trying to escape them is, of course, the opposite response to what our brains are biologically designed to do when faced with anxiety and fear. The obsessional thought is not the problem. It is how the sufferer responds to the obsessional thought and the accompanying anxiety, guilt, fear, etc. that causes the problems that interrupt the individual's life.

OCD may show up any time during a person's life. About 67 percent of the more serious and diagnosable OCDs will experience major depression at some point during their lives, but effective treatments are available for depression as well.[5]

SUGGESTED READING

The OCD Workbook by Bruce M. Hyman, PhD, and Cherry Pedrick, RN. This is an excellent source of information about OCD generally and includes a chapter about OCD in children.

THE SHY PERSONALITY

This description covers multiple levels of shy and inhibited patterns of thought, emotion, and behavior. Those with fewer or milder traits as well as those with the symptoms of a serious disorder may readily identify some of their thinking, as well as emotional and behavioral tendencies. A more comprehensive understanding of self usually requires an ongoing self-observation and self-reflection over time. These traits and characteristics are found in both men and women.

THERE IS LITTLE agreement on the definitions and terminology for the various levels or subtypes of shyness.[88] Typically, definitions and descriptions of shyness involve self-conscious anxiety and a persistent fear of being scrutinized and evaluated by others and include both *shy thinking* and *feelings of anxiety*. Shyness may also have various subtypes, including performance anxieties such as public speaking, eating in public, using public restrooms, etc. The shy individual is overly sensitive to criticism, and fear and apprehension may occur in advance of an event as the individual thinks about how he will be perceived by others.

Some shy people have physical reactions in social situations, such as awkward or nervous mannerisms, including blushing, sweating, racing heartbeat, muscle twitching, or a stiff body posture with less movement. Researchers have found that the negative images and emotions experienced by shy people actually trigger the same fear responses evoked by everyone when faced with a real threat.[100] We all react to fearful thoughts. The shy person just has a greater number of irrational fears accompanied by emotional overreactions. There also may be feelings of guilt or depression, and shy people may plan less for the future. Shy people may delay leaving their family of origin until they are older, and maturing into the usual roles of marriage and career may take longer.[105] Researchers must also consider the effects of shame, anger, submissiveness, embarrassment, etc. in clarifying various subtypes of shyness. Are these different forms of shyness, or are they merely caused by different circumstances? While there appear to be both inherited and environmental, or learned, aspects of shyness,[122] considerable research remains to be done in this area. What appears certain is that the more generalized the shyness has become to multiple areas of life, the more problems the sufferer tends to experience.[88] People who actually do not care at all what other people think about them are obviously afflicted by some other problem.

Researchers have attempted to divide the concept of shyness into various categories, such as social anxiety disorder, social phobia, avoidant personality disorder, etc., yet there is no recognized point at which shyness splits into multiple and separate problems or disorders. Differences in the symptoms of shyness appear to be a matter of severity.[85,88,90,93] For the purposes of this discussion, I will consider shyness as operating on the following continuum:

- **Mild shyness**
- **Moderate to severe shyness:** Social anxiety disorder / social phobia
- **Extreme shyness:** Avoidant personality disorder

VIGNETTE: Moderate to Severe Shyness

Ian is a successful computer analyst for a large company. With considerable effort and anxiety, Ian was able to get a college degree and a good job, although he has few fond memories of his college years. Ian went all the way through high school and college without a single date, and he only goes on dates now when the stars are aligned for him to meet an accepting lady in a nonthreatening environment. There have been a few times when a more assertive lady has taken the initiative to meet Ian, which occasionally has led to a conversation but more often has failed, as Ian nervously found some excuse to flee the scene.

Ian has long recognized that he needs special circumstances to meet women, so he now volunteers for group projects at work, and he invites some of the women he meets to join him at the group dinners he organizes so he will not have to ask them out on an actual date. A few times, Ian has watched in painful frustration as the object of his fancy has begun dating another more outgoing member of the dinner group. More recently, Ian has embraced the less threatening dating technologies now available, such as Internet dating, speed dating, and singles cruises where introductions are built into scheduled activities. Ian still gets severe butterflies when he meets someone he is attracted to, but he now accepts that the woman he meets may also be shy and that if she rejects him because of his shyness, or some other reason, it does not necessarily reflect on him at all. Ian admits that he, in turn, has rejected several women over the years and that rejecting someone, or being rejected, is a natural part of the dance that can be embraced rather than feared.

Ian has also become a big fan of Seinfeld *reruns, where laughing at one's own imperfections and foibles is modeled every minute or so. When Ian speaks to groups of coworkers, he asks them up front to please forgive his nervousness, which almost everyone in his audience can relate to at some level. Mentioning his shyness up front seems to reduce the power Ian's shyness has over him, and his audiences seem to appreciate his candor. With the help of group therapy and Toastmasters meetings, talking to people is becoming easier for Ian. Ian is actually beginning to enjoy the challenge of speaking to strangers—or even a first date.*

Our relationships with other people are very important to our mental health and sense of well-being. Researchers have known for years that a lack of contact with other people can be harmful both mentally and physically, causing sickness, stress, depression, etc.[80] Most people are able to meet their social needs whether they are outwardly gregarious or more reserved. Unfortunately, for some people, this relatively normal continuum descends into feelings of inferiority, inadequacy, inhibition, and social incompetence. Shy people are not rare. Various surveys report that about half of the general population reports some shyness,[80] and up to 90 percent of the general population has experienced shyness at some point in their life.[82] Shyness covers a lot of territory, and there is considerable variation in the symptoms of shyness. Some shy individuals are merely cautious, while others are extremely self-conscious and inhibited in social situations.

By definition, the most difficult problem faced by most shy people is meeting other people and forming friendships and relationships. There are many shy people whose anxiety is limited almost exclusively to fears of social interaction. For some, shyness may increase because of the presence of another person who just happens to be near them in a restaurant, airport, elevator, etc. Shy people quickly tune in to any negative signals given off by other people and become highly aware of their own anxiety and heightened emotions. Drawing from negative social experiences from their past, they draw quick negative conclusions rather than waiting for more information.[122]

To deal with their anxiety, shy people commonly develop "safety behaviors"[96] designed to increase their sense of security. Safety behaviors may include standing on the outside of a group, talking very little and expressing fewer opinions, or avoiding eye contact, which, of course, may only increase the awkwardness of their behavior. They may also be less assertive, have fewer leadership skills, talk with less fluency, speak more softly and with a lower tone of voice, have a flat facial demeanor with less smiling, or keep a greater physical distance from those they are speaking to. With feelings of inadequacy, inferiority, and low self-esteem, the shy individual may not only seek less social contact, but may also be less approachable by others. These symptoms may be especially pronounced if they are attracted to the person they encounter. The attractiveness of the other person, their accomplishments, or their importance may also influence the degree of shyness. Some shy people experience shame and have a stream of negative thoughts about themselves.[96] They may berate themselves for any mistakes with self-talk about their obvious flaws and how awful they are. They may then come to what they believe are obvious conclusions, such as, "I'm just stupid," "She/He wouldn't like me," or "I'll be fired in no time."

Shy people may have an ongoing mental image of themselves as they think they appear to other people, such as incompetent, boring, unattractive, weird, etc. They may compare this poor self-image to their exaggerated assessment of what others expect of them. This mental self-image may be overly influenced by negative social experiences in the past, which may include reactions such as profuse sweating or blushing or freezing up from tension and not knowing what to say.[89,96] Some shy people not only criticize themselves, they find fault with and criticize other people, and they may feel some resentment toward them.[89] I have found some level of depression frequently plays a role in a shy person's negative thoughts and feelings about themselves or others (see chapter: Mild Depression).

The shy tend to think that everything they say must come out perfectly. After an event, the mental image of their performance may appear worse each time they replay the event in their mind. Research has indicated that shy people tend to underestimate their social abilities and therefore overestimate the probability of negative reactions from others.[17] Shy people may carefully and continually assess the facial expressions of other people for signs of the criticism, mockery, and rejection they expect and fear. Focused on detecting signs of imminent rejection, they lose the concentration and miss the social cues that would help them make a normal social response. This may become a self-fulfilling prophecy where anxiety causes poor social responses, which lead to even more anxiety over future responses. The tense and fearful expressions shy people project may elicit from others the very ridicule and rejection they fear. The vicious circle is now complete as the negative reactions from others only confirm their doubts about themselves with an even greater expectation of negative reactions in the future.

Shy people may *think* their way into believing a competent response or performance was highly flawed. It does not help that feedback from other people is frequently ambiguous, and the negative mind-set of the shy person will frequently project negative evaluations onto the otherwise neutral reactions of others. These negative self-evaluations then become a part of the shy person's ongoing negative self-concept.[96] At social events, shy people typically compare themselves to the more outgoing and socially competent people in the room. They fail to notice that most other people at the event are more reserved and have no desire to draw attention to themselves.

As you can see, much of the pain of shyness is over events that never take place. The shy person remains vigilant for the slightest signs of rejection and may feel rejection where there is none[90] and the fear and anxiety over what might occur takes a toll. All of this, of course, is occurring while the shy person struggles to pay attention to a conversation. Tense and mentally preoccupied, shy people become less aware of the actual content of social encounters, which makes normal conversation more difficult. Others frequently misinterpret the inhibitions, withdrawal, and awkward behavior of shy people as being something else. When shy individuals talk less, keep their distance, and do not smile, they may appear to others as aloof, uninterested, unfriendly, or snobbish. This, of course, may result in even more disapproval and rejection.

Many shy individuals attempt to maintain control over their emotions and try to hide the fact that they are unhappy to avoid criticism and rejection. Yet shyness does not always involve difficult or negative emotions or the avoidance of goals that are central to the individual's life. The outward behavior of some shy individuals may appear relatively normal.[89] It is now being recognized that some symptoms of shyness only manifest themselves under stressful conditions and are temporary, while other personality symptoms are more enduring and appear to be actual personality traits.[93] Some shy people may have fewer problems dealing with their shyness because they choose social situations and make career choices that occur in less threatening environments.[89] Shyness may no longer be a problem for shy people who finally get into a relationship.[80] Depression seems to make symptoms of shyness more likely, and the symptoms may lessen if the sufferer obtains relief from the depression.[93]

EXTREME SHYNESS (AVOIDANT PERSONALITY DISORDER)

At the extreme end of the shyness continuum is the much more severe avoidant personality disorder. Avoidants may view themselves as completely unappealing and deficient in every way and just assume negative evaluations from others are inevitable. Avoidants may avoid work, school, or social events simply because they fear they will not fit in and will be ridiculed to the amusement of everyone else. Their expectations of others are limited to criticism and disapproval, if not total rejection—a view guaranteed to create awkward encounters with strangers. Employment may be a problem for avoidants since they may turn down job interviews, or even promotions at jobs they have, out of fear of criticism and rejection by the interviewer or other employees.

Suffering the lowest of low self-esteem and with intense feelings of inadequacy, avoidants may avoid social encounters completely unless they are absolutely certain beforehand that they will be accepted and liked. Consequently, considerable coaxing, with numerous offers of support and nurturance, may be required to get an avoidant to risk attending a social event. Still, with sufficient cajoling, avoidant personalities may submit to social contact because they do desire acceptance and relationships. Avoidants may fantasize extensively about an ideal relationship, and they are able to form intimate relationships if they believe they will have uncritical acceptance. Even then, avoidants will usually remain quiet, inhibited, and somewhat invisible from a fear they will overreact emotionally, and possibly start crying, if criticized. Overreacting to ordinary situations that are blown out of proportion and avoiding new activities, avoidants live a very self-conscious and restricted lifestyle. With few friends or confidants, their lonely and isolated world may become terrifying in times of crisis when they have little support from others to help them weather the storm. Avoidant personalities are sometimes associated with obesity.[50]

EXTREME SHYNESS IN RELATIONSHIPS

Getting a relationship started with an avoidant personality is difficult at best. There is a good chance the potential partner will never meet the avoidant in the first place, since avoidants tend to avoid all social situations. Avoidants frequently form relationships with people they meet through work, since they have such difficulty meeting people anywhere else.

VIGNETTE: Extreme Fear and Anxiety

As described by Martha's fiancé: *Looking back, I'm surprised I was able to get to know Martha in the first place. I would see Martha sitting alone having lunch in a small park near my office, and I would try to start a conversation, but she quickly excused herself from my first attempts. Only with persistence on my part did Martha eventually continue our conversation. Martha later told me she started having a glass of wine before coming to the park to make it easier for her to talk to me. She later told me that our conversations were the only social life she had at the time. With the exception of work and necessary errands, Martha was unable to go almost anywhere by herself if there was any chance she would be required to interact with other people. With almost no friends, Martha would sit at home alone with her dog and read romance novels while drinking wine to numb the loneliness, sometimes into oblivion. Only when Martha was dating someone was she able to go out into the world.*

Even after Martha was comfortable with me, she was still reluctant to talk about herself in a personal way for a long time. She says she simply remained quiet to avoid saying the wrong thing and chasing me away. Unfortunately, Martha's dependency on the men she had dated before I met her had resulted in some abusive relationships that Martha found herself unable to break off regardless of how abusive they became. It seems Martha did not know the relationships were abusive until a therapist finally told her. She thought the abuse was her fault because she was such an awful girlfriend. She now recognized she was a sex toy for abusers who discarded her for days or weeks until they wanted to use their sex toy again.

Martha did finally find a way to be self-employed, which was essential because of her fear of attending job interviews. She would work hard to get a job interview and then fail to show up because she was certain she would mess up the interview anyway. With no confidence or initiative, Martha eventually lost most of the jobs that she did get. Even now, the thought of meeting new clients brings her feelings of dread back to the fore, but with the support she receives from our relationship and her group-therapy sessions, Martha is able to get through the ordeal. Martha's growing self-confidence has really helped our relationship. We are both very content with our relationship now, and we sure are glad we hung in there.

Avoidants need a partner who will give them continuous and unconditional love for the duration of their relationship, regardless of the shifting moods the avoidant may experience. Years of keeping to themselves may cause avoidants to keep some habitual emotional distance from their partner as well as other people generally. Avoidants believe it is inevitable that their partner, just like everyone else, will eventually become critical or rejecting. Even in a loving relationship, avoidants may always be somewhat timid about discussing their most private thoughts and feelings, and they may always remain somewhat untrusting with an unshakable fear of being left alone. The wrong joke, minor sarcasm, or even constructive criticism may create fear and pain and leave avoidants questioning their partner's level of commitment to the relationship. Avoidants may withdraw emotionally to an extreme degree if they believe their partner has criticized them, and attempts by partners to explain themselves and appease avoidants may initially have little impact. Recovering from a step backward with an avoidant may require an extended period of reassurance and uncritical acceptance. Even in a very loving relationship, avoidants may vacillate between periods of trust and warmth toward their partner and periods of fear, emotional distance, and rejecting behavior.

There is always the possibility avoidants will get scared and run from even a good relationship. It is critical that the avoidant's partner have a good understanding of the shifting emotions and shifting levels of trust avoidants may experience from time to time so they do not misinterpret the avoidants' behavior as rejection. As is common in relationships with difficult personalities, the avoidant may trigger the more stable partner's own insecurities. Over time, the partners of avoidants may experience their own sadness when their attempts to lift the avoidants' chronic depression are sometimes unsuccessful.

Since avoidants have a fear of going to new places and trying new things, a relationship with an avoidant may be somewhat limited and constricted. Avoidants may need considerable coaxing and encouragement before they will be willing to expand their horizons and meet new people. Simply discussing the fearful topic of increasing your social life may draw an anxious, fearful, or even angry response. When social events do occur, expect avoidants to hover near their partner and remain quiet to avoid doing something for which they might be criticized. During the early stages of a relationship, avoidants' reticence and tendency to be a chronic homebody may be more severe because of the newness of the relationship, or they may be somewhat more sociable due to the infatuation effects of honeymoon-stage brain chemistry.

During the initial honeymoon phase of a relationship, the relationship may seem very wonderful for both the avoidant and the partner. For some avoidants, though, their fears and anxiety over possible rejection may only increase as they become more emotionally attached. During the honeymoon stage, the partner may feel he is truly the white knight the avoidant needed in her life, and with the magic of their relationship, the partner expects the avoidant to move beyond the irrational fears that have ruled her life for so long. Unfortunately, the honeymoon stage with an avoidant may be relatively brief. As the brain-chemistry-induced euphoria of the honeymoon stage draws to a close, the avoidant may experience increased fears and anxiety. Instead of recognizing the normal and expected end of a chemically induced euphoria, the partner of an avoidant may feel it is his own inadequacies that have caused the avoidant to relapse into fear and anxiety. Both partners may now experience some depression and despair. As the partner's mood also begins a downward shift, the couple may find their negative moods playing off each other in an atmosphere of descending negativity, arguments, and pain. As is so common in dysfunctional relationships, each partner may blame the other for their problems.

With the remarkable antidepressant medications now on the market, I am very optimistic when working with even extreme avoidants and their relationships. Therapy with an avoidant frequently begins with couples therapy, since avoidants may feel extreme anxiety at the thought of seeing a therapist on their own. The avoidant may have never seen a therapist before coming in for couples therapy since avoidants may be unable to call a therapist on their own or show up for an appointment that was made for them. Ideally the avoidant will embrace individual therapy that eventually evolves into group therapy so the avoidant can experience other nonthreatening relationships. Having the support of other people and knowing you are not alone always helps. It will be easier for the avoidant to transfer into group therapy if the same therapist conducts both the individual and the group-therapy sessions. Couples therapy may be continued as a part of this process. I am very optimistic for avoidants who find the right therapist or support group, use medications if needed, and are committed to the process. Their lives and relationships can change dramatically.

As you can see, the biggest difference between varied levels of shyness appears to be in the level of difficulty sufferers have with life, especially in their career and social functioning. These individuals may have failed to achieve their potential in work, income, education, or social relationships. Shy children, adolescents, and adults are less popular and have fewer friends than non-shy individuals. They also tend to have fewer intimate relationships, less support from others, and may not have anyone they can confide in. Those with more severe shyness are likely to be more neurotic, socially inept, introverted, suffer negative emotions such as depression, or experience other diagnosable problems such as a personality disorder.[87]

Between 80 percent and 90 percent of people diagnosed with a serious level of shyness also suffer from at least one other disorder, with up to half of those suffering from major depression. Other disorders commonly found with more severe levels of shyness include eating disorders, agoraphobia (fear of crowds), obsessive-compulsive disorders, post-traumatic stress disorder, and bipolar disorder. Individuals with more severe shyness combined with another clinical disorder will typically suffer even greater dysfunction and a further reduced quality of life.[92] Some shy people turn to alcohol or drugs to help allay their fears or just numb the pain of isolation and loneliness. Studies have shown that many problem drinkers are shy.[80]

CAUSES OF SHYNESS

Shyness is very common and may have originally evolved as a protective behavior that allowed people to avoid negative or painful experiences.

There is very strong evidence for a genetic connection in shyness, and the conventional wisdom is that shyness is caused by some combination of biological/genetic factors[87] and psychological/social factors, including the original family environment.[93] Although some theories suggest the involvement of the brain's limbic system and the neurotransmitter dopamine, other theories emphasize dysfunctional childhoods including a low level of parental affection and nurturing,[50] critical parents, overprotective parents, and parental arguments.[17] Studies have suggested that up to 61 percent of adults with the more extreme avoidant personality disorder report excess levels of emotional abuse by their parents.[50] Bernardo Carducci, PhD, professor of psychology and director of the Shyness Research Institute at Indiana State University Southeast, does not believe shy people are born that way since a "sense of self" does not form until about 18 months of age. At the same time, Carducci points to evidence that 15 to 20 percent of infants are born with an inhibited temperament,[81] and there is research suggesting that children with a temperament involving high levels of inhibition are more likely to suffer shyness later in life.[87] The genetic predisposition exhibited by an infant may be affected by the nature of the environment in which the child is raised.[93] Children who experience rejection may become very self-conscious and begin to focus inward and blame themselves for the problems they experience. This negative thinking leads to negative emotions, including feelings of shame.[89]

Childhood shyness usually recedes as children mature. In

many cases, even severe shyness during childhood may lessen or even disappear with age,[89] although some residual shyness may remain.[23] In other cases, the shyness and fearful behavior may only increase during adolescence and the early adult years due to an increase in the awareness of the perspectives and evaluations of others. Adolescent girls must also deal with changes in their body shape.[89] Although shy adults are usually not lacking in social skills, shy children *are* lacking in social skills. As children grow into adolescence and adulthood, there is a general shift toward more shy females than males, possibly reflecting cultural values that frown on shyness in males.

Shyness may begin early in life when parents of children who are overly emotional, inhibited, or easily distressed respond to their children with overprotection, insensitivity, physical and emotional rejection and abuse, criticism, control, ridicule, shaming, or the use of considerable correcting behavior. Criticism of children may create the expectation of humiliation, failure, and a sense of foreboding that may result in a life that just doesn't seem to work.[122] Many researchers in shyness argue that the socialization process with the parents is most important in allowing a child to develop an adequate sense of self and to develop the ability to connect with others later in life.

Parents who suffer their own personality or emotional problems are more likely to respond with dysfunctional parenting.[86] Some parents may be less social themselves because of their own shyness. Self-critical parents, especially the same-sex parent, may pass their tendency toward self-criticism on to their children.[89] As the child grows, the parent(s) may continue to over control, protect, and micromanage the child's life in an authoritarian and dictatorial manner. Criticism or ridicule may continue as well. Some of these unwitting parents may then be critical of their son or daughter's shy, withdrawn behavior without recognizing the role they have played, and continue to play, in their child's insecurity, low self-esteem, loneliness, and depression.[86]

The overly protective parent may be the most potentially harmful to the shy child since this protective behavior may reinforce the child's natural inhibition and tendency to avoid new people and environments. The child's fears may elicit overprotection and isolation by the parent, or the parent's own anxieties may lead to an overprotecting parenting style.[87] Other contributors to shyness in children might include modeling by parents who view the opinions of others as more important than their own opinions; parents who use shame as a method of discipline,[87] rejection and ostracism by peers;[89,97] and being shamed by teachers in front of other students.[89]

Of course, the lack of relationships will only perpetuate the loneliness/shyness cycle. As is so often the case with personality issues, the vicious circles arising from shyness can be hideous. Many shy people have a poor self-image as they focus on the perceived negative reactions of others, which only confirm their negative self-image, sinking their low self-esteem even lower. The shy person may then mentally beat himself up with feelings and thoughts of how awful he is. At subsequent social events, the individual starts out with an even lower self-image, which may result in ever-more-fearful and eccentric behavior resulting in even more negative evaluations from others. In some cases, the shy individual may develop the more severe avoidant personality disorder and withdraw from almost all social contact.

Where poor parenting continues, healthy social encounters outside the home with teachers and friends may help mitigate some of the negative effects of inadequate parenting.[86] Needless to say, much of this unfortunate family dysfunction could be avoided if parents were more aware of their own personalities and behaviors and better able to make conscious choices about their behavior toward their children. Without some self-awareness, parents who did not receive affection and appropriate guidance from their own parents may unconsciously raise their own children in a similar fashion, even if they have always told themselves they would never, ever raise a child that way.

TREATMENT OF SHYNESS

Shyness appears to be one of the more persistent and enduring disorders,[87] yet recent research suggests the symptoms of shyness and the accompanying anxiety are very treatable for those who do not grow out of their childhood symptoms.[95] Anyone can develop the ability to form relationships with other people if they will just seek the help that is available.[80,93] Although shyness is very common in childhood and frequently becomes a chronic condition, most shy children and adolescents do not receive the treatment they need to effectively deal with the disorder. Less than five percent receive treatment within the first year after the onset of symptoms. Half of those who finally do seek treatment for shyness wait an average of 16 years before doing so. This is especially unfortunate since the treatments available today are highly effective.[94] Fortunately, poor social skills do not appear to be a major problem for shy people. Research has indicated that when shy people do not have a negative appraisal of a social situation and become less focused on themselves, their behavior may be quite skilled and appear no different from that of people who are not shy.[89,91]

Bernardo J. Carducci suggests that, initially, the shy person should work at becoming "successfully shy."[80] Successfully shy people arrange their lives to help compensate for their shyness, such as choosing a career that involves groups or teamwork, etc. Most shy people do make some attempt to attend social events and make contact with other people, but they wait for other people to start a conversation rather than taking the initiative themselves. If no one starts a conversation with them (many other people are shy too), they may feel very alone in the middle of a crowd. If a conversation is in process, listening closely to what other people say is critical to having your own conversation come across as focused and coherent. Listeners are considered cool, and they are respected, but shy people get caught up in their own thoughts and may appear absentminded and disconnected. The idea is for shy people to get caught up in what other people are saying to the same extent that they have always been caught up in their own thoughts and feelings. The long-term solution lies in focusing less on themselves and more on the people around them and what they are saying. If shy people will learn to stay in listening mode until they have more information about a conversation, this will help them develop the personality they may have so often admired in others. I encourage shy people to become highly educated about shyness, especially their own shyness, as well as learning to recognize and understand any other personality traits and characteristics they may possess. Learning to understand yourself, that is, your thoughts, emotions, and behaviors, will help you increase your self-control. Therapy with a therapist who understands personalities can be very helpful here. Along with reading about shyness and becoming an expert about themselves, I encourage my shy clients to eventually involve themselves in group counseling while exposing themselves to the situations they fear, which I call "fieldwork." Fieldwork might include conversations with others while standing in line at a grocery store, talking more to a waitress or hairdresser, going to social events, or giving lectures through a Toastmasters class. These exercises will allow individuals to gain more information about their shyness and lower their tension level by slowly becoming accustomed to threatening situations.

All of these skills can be practiced by organizing a weekly dinner group with friends, classmates, coworkers, etc., with the self-directed goal of keeping the conversation flowing. Of course, to keep the conversation flowing, you must concentrate on what your guests are saying rather than on your own thoughts. If you want to practice meeting strangers in public places, I suggest going to places where you do not usually go or hang out. The fear of rejection may be greatly reduced in locations where no one knows you. Keeping up with current events via TV news, newspapers and news magazines, seeing the best movies, etc. will allow the shy person to talk knowledgeably about current topics and events. If you have invited a shy friend to a party, ask your friend to arrive early and help you keep the conversations going by introducing the guests to each other as they arrive. Your shy friend may never realize you have helped him/her reduce their shyness by having them focus on others rather than themselves. Of course, you can practice this same exercise with yourself.

When viewed logically, rejection is rarely that disastrous. Since we all experience some rejection, the goal is to not be put off by the rejection, but to accept it as a normal part of the social dance and move on. We can only be rejected at the choice of rejectors who clearly have their own struggles with life. Although the past is the past, and change must necessarily occur in the present, it may be helpful for shy people to understand the early experiences in their lives that may have led to their pattern of negative thoughts and emotions. Understanding their past may help them understand the negative emotions that have become a major part of their self-concept and help them change the negative way they think about themselves. They may also come to understand any anger and resentment they may feel toward others. Even here, the goal is to help shy individuals stop focusing on themselves to the point that it interrupts and sabotages their communication and social behavior.[17,89]

Generally, what I have been discussing here is referred to as cognitive behavioral therapy (CBT) and involves gaining relevant knowledge and information, learning new ways of thinking about yourself and other people, and exposing yourself to feared environments. CBT has been shown to result in a higher quality of life for shy people, including improvements in their relationships, having more new experiences, greater creativity, and an increase in general playfulness.[97,98] CBT is available in individual and group formats, which appear to be equally effective. Antidepressant medications have also been found effective in treating shyness,[17] and in some cases, both CBT and medications may be combined, although some studies have shown quality CBT alone to be about as effective as CBT combined with medications. Medications may be combined with CBT when CBT appears less effective when used alone.[98] In some cases, medication may be used to reduce severe anxiety in social situations, which may reduce the fears of being judged negatively. This may allow a severely shy person to more effectively practice coping techniques in social situations. CBT has demonstrated more consistent long-term effects than medication, and symptoms of shyness are more likely to return when medication is discontinued than when CBT is discontinued.[98]

I have found there to be an unfortunate bias against the use of medications for severe shyness, and I have had severely shy clients refuse to even consider trying medications. In cases of severe shyness, I have seen medications drastically increase the sense of well-being and make it possible for the sufferer to feel less tension, worry less, and be more open to social contact with other people. I have never met a severely shy person who did not also suffer some level of depression, and the recommended medications to help with shyness are the very same antidepressant medications that help with depression. But medication without at least some exposure to the feared situations would not allow the shy person to learn that social situations are not that scary, and that rejection is usually the other person's problem. Gradual exposure to anxiety-producing situations is important whether the treatment is CBT, medication, or both.[99]

SIMILARITIES AND DIFFERENCES

It is easy to confuse the avoidant and the dependent personality since either an avoidant or a dependent personality may have feelings of inadequacy, hypersensitivity to criticism, and a constant need for reassurance. The difference is that the avoidant focuses on avoiding humiliation and rejection while the dependent personality emphasizes the need to be taken care of. When these two personalities come together, they tend to reinforce each other. It is no surprise that there is a common co-occurrence with avoidant and dependent personalities.

MILD DEPRESSION

This description covers multiple levels of depressive patterns of thought, emotion, and behavior. Those with fewer or milder traits as well as those with the symptoms of a serious disorder may readily identify some of their thinking, as well as emotional and behavioral tendencies. A more comprehensive understanding of self usually requires an ongoing self-observation and self-reflection over time. These traits are found in both men and women.

MILD OR MODERATE depression is commonly overlooked as a cause of distress and impairment in the lives of many people. What follows is a general discussion of the milder forms of depression.

Mild depression is a very common, and usually temporary, response to difficult life situations and usually resolves itself within a short period of time. For some people, though, mild depression may have been a part of the sufferer's life for many years—or most of their life. Unfortunately, most people suffering from mild depression are not aware of the problem and therefore do not seek treatment. When someone has suffered mild depression for a long time, the individual is usually accustomed to the depressed feeling, and he believes the way he feels is normal. It may not occur to the chronically depressed individual that other people do not feel the way he does. Although mild depression can make most aspects of life more difficult, mild depression typically does not prevent the sufferer from functioning well enough to get by and appear somewhat normal on a day-to-day basis.

The following is a list of commonly recognized symptoms of mild to moderate depression:

- Feelings of inadequacy
- Worries—brooding
- Sadness—dejected, gloomy, unhappy
- Overly serious
- Loss of interest or pleasure in things generally
- Low self-esteem
- Viewing oneself as not very interesting, or incompetent
- Sensitive to rejection by others
- Social withdrawal
- Feelings of guilt or remorse—brooding about the past
- Irritability / Excessive anger
- Pessimistic
- Low energy or fatigue
- Lower activity level
- Lower effectiveness and productivity
- Poor appetite / weight loss
- Overeating / weight gain
- Alcohol/drug abuse
- Too much sleep / not enough sleep
- Poor concentration / difficulty with decisions
- Feelings of hopelessness, discouragement, despair
- Self-critical / self-blame
- Critical and judgmental of others
- Problems at work / poor relationships with coworkers
- Frequent unemployment

Don't let the word *mild* fool you. Mild depression can cause severe problems in the social, family, work, or academic life of the sufferer.

VIGNETTE: Chronic Sadness

Not much in life was enjoyable for Craig, and he does not remember ever feeling really good. Craig has long known that he tends to be a loner, and he can now see very clearly that a lack of self-confidence has always played a major role in his life. Until recently, Craig never knew that the main culprit in his life was a milder, yet destabilizing, depression. Only now, at the age of 38, is Craig learning to understand the effect that his lifelong depression has had on the evolution of his personality. Craig never had many friends during his high school years, and he dropped out in the 10th grade. Craig is still single, rarely dates, and until recently would spend most of his time by himself. Craig does recall being interested in things, such as music and photography, but he never pursued these interests. Craig's basic outlook on life has always been one of chronic pessimism, which also affects his social life. When Craig would happen to meet someone he was attracted to, he would ignore her with a pessimistic expectation of guaranteed rejection, a common self-fulfilling prophecy. The more Craig worried about failing at something, the less likely he was to pursue the person, object, goal, etc. in the first place. In social situations, Craig would come across as withdrawn, awkward, and stilted because he had never routinely practiced social skills. When new acquaintances would withdraw from his negative view of the world, this would, of course, only confirm his low opinion of himself and reduce his self-confidence even further. Craig would go home more depressed than when he left—over and over again, year after year.

After dropping out of high school, Craig began a series of menial jobs during which he gained considerable weight, and his self-esteem descended to ever-lower depths. Craig never tried to promote himself or work his way up in an organization. He recalls the awful feeling from seeing so many people with good careers and raising families, while his life seemed to drift endlessly without meaning. The only times Craig thought he felt good were when he would sit in a small tavern after work and drink one beer after another until he could hardly feel anything at all. Unknown to Craig was that alcohol had become his antidepressant, and a very ineffective one at that.

Craig did eventually get his GED, and he attended night school for training as a medical technician, even though poor concentration plagued him the whole time. Even with a decent job in the medical field, Craig remained very self-critical and continued to blame himself for everything that did not go right in his life, and he rarely noticed the things that did go right. Craig was not only self-critical, but frequently criticized other people, things, situations, etc. Craig was not aware that his negative, critical side was driven by sadness, so he was unable to overrule his critical nature and consider more logical perspectives as part of a broader effort to combat his depression.

Finally Craig met a coworker who had been seeing a very knowledgeable therapist for his depression, which surprised Craig since the coworker was very outgoing and seemed to have a great social life. Craig went to see the same therapist and finally began his journey toward understanding the underlying causes of the symptoms that had plagued him for so long. With a better understanding of his parents' critical nature, and recalling stories he had heard about his grandparents, Craig now believes depression has been a part of his family history for generations, and that genetics may have played a role in his long-term depression. Craig now understands that when other people appeared to reject him, it triggered the depression and low self-esteem he had suffered while growing up with critical parents that he now believes also suffered some level of depression.

Since experiencing the relief offered by today's antidepressant medications, Craig has become involved in group therapy, developed new social skills, and found the confidence to enroll in a four-year college with plans to work toward a nursing degree. Therapy in conjunction with antidepressant medications have allowed Craig to develop his *social side, and he is now able to meet new people, join study groups, etc., and his concentration has improved dramatically. One of Craig's friends at school told Craig that she initially thought he was a snob because he always seemed to ignore other people. Craig wonders how many people in his past have thought he was stuck-up because they did not recognize his distant personality as a symptom of a depression that undermined and compromised his true self. Recognizing the sadness he has lived with all of his life. Craig is not sure if his shyness, lack of self-confidence, and low self-esteem are symptoms of his depression or vice-versa. Craig also recognizes that his parents probably never knew they suffered some level of depression accompanied by a negative, critical nature.*

Not realizing they are suffering a serious problem, mild depressives may wonder why life does not seem to work for them very well. They just cannot seem to get it right in their career, social life, or academic work, and they may be in an endless cycle of descending self-esteem. With little self-confidence and poor social skills in some cases, depressed individuals may have few social relationships. The relationships depressives do have may be dysfunctional, not only because of their role in the dysfunctional dance, but also because they attract other emotionally unstable people. For example, the depressive may attract a caretaker type of personality who will make it her job to finally bring the depressive out of his misery for all time. Some depressed individuals are overly critical and sabotage their relationships with their negative mindset. Other depressed individuals may fear the pain of rejection so much that they just remain loners who avoid relationships altogether. Another problem for depressives is that other people may misinterpret the depressive's behavior. Symptoms such as sadness, unassertiveness, irritability, etc. may be considered by others to simply be the depressive's eccentric nature, or the depressive may be viewed as a snob because she is not sociable and keeps to herself.

The conventional wisdom is that depression may be triggered by stressful events or life situations, including major life transitions, although a genetic connection where depression seems to be in the family history is common. Major events or life transitions that can trigger depression include problems at work or unemployment, having children, poor parenting skills, marital discord, divorce, physical illness, retirement, or the physical and emotional problems related to the decline from aging. Milder mood disorders, including depression, that run in families may go unrecognized for generations, although there may be family stories about the unusual or eccentric behavior of some aunt, uncle, grandparent, etc.

Depression is a serious problem for many children and adolescents, and they are seriously underdiagnosed at all socioeconomic levels, especially among minorities. In the adolescent age group, only traffic accidents cause more deaths than suicide.[54] Up to 15 percent of children and adolescents may suffer from some level of depression, and 3 to 5 percent are affected by major depression. By age 14, twice as many females as males suffer from depression.[51] Growing up with parents that are impossible to please, or with alcoholic parents, can trigger depression during childhood or adolescence. Children may react differently to depression than adults, and depression in children may be difficult to separate from the usual turmoil and angst that can be a normal part of growing up. Depression in children usually begins quietly, may come and go, and, of course, the child or adolescent does not know depression is the problem.[53] Depression in children may go unrecognized because many parents are not even aware that children can suffer from depression. More than 70 percent of children and adolescents with mood disorders, including depression, never receive an adequate diagnosis and treatment.[51]

The problem of underdiagnosis and treatment is greatest for children younger than seven years of age.[51] Common symptoms of depression in children include irritability and boredom, but children may also withdraw into a lonely existence with little desire for social involvement with other children, teachers, or even their parents. Schoolwork for these children may become a burden or a complete impossibility.[31] Children may also put themselves down, such as saying, "I'm just stupid," or they may complain about headaches, stomachaches, or other physical ailments. Depression during adolescence may show up as irritability, anger, difficulty with concentration and attention, or self-medicating with alcohol or drugs.[51]

Mild depression that is long-term—at least two years in duration, or one year for children—is called persistent depressive disorder or dysthymia. Dysthymia is sometimes the beginning stages of a much more serious major depression or bipolar disorder, which is also referred to as "manic depression." Symptoms of dysthymia appearing prior to the age of 21 are more likely to develop into a major depression, and individuals who suffered dysthymia prior to the onset of major depression are more likely to suffer recurring bouts of major depression. Individuals who suffered from dysthymia before descending into major depression are less likely to have a complete remission of depressive symptoms between bouts of major depression but will likely return to a state of dysthymia. It is common for depression to be associated with other personality problems, although it may be difficult to diagnose other personality issues since many symptoms, such as problems with relationships or low self-esteem, may be attributed to the depression.

While the big breakthroughs in depression have been the

modern antidepressant medications now available, many people find relief from depression without resorting to the use of medication. Especially with milder levels of depression, many people find relief with psychotherapy, couples therapy, or family therapy combined with lifestyle changes. Daily exercise is an excellent antidepressant in its own right and should be embraced if at all possible.

Fortunately for individuals who do not respond to other treatments, antidepressant medications may be the treatment that works. The debate about whether antidepressants are effective for depression seems very strange to those who have found such remarkable relief with the right medication. There are those who view medication as a sign of weakness, and some people believe antidepressant medications are addictive, a false but common assumption. Some depressives may simply apply their usual pessimistic view of the world to the possibility of successful treatment. Others may view our society as overly medicated, but with chronic depression, I have seen modern medications make a profound difference in the lives of many people, especially where depression seems to be a part of the family history.

MILD DEPRESSION IN RELATIONSHIPS

Since mild depression frequently goes unrecognized for years, or a lifetime in some cases, the continuing impact of depression on a relationship and family life may be severe. Depressions that are more temporary may also damage family relationships unless recognized and treated. Just as an individual suffering mild depression may appear to function somewhat normally from day to day, albeit with greater effort, relationships with a depressive may also seem to get by on a daily basis but usually with some dysfunction in the relationship and family. Neither partner may understand the underlying dynamics of their problems. The depression may go unrecognized because of its mild nature or because the family became habituated to the depressed environment as the depression emerged gradually over time.

Life with a depressed person may also be depressing for the partner and children. The depressive may have little interest in, or receive little pleasure from, things generally. If the depression goes unrecognized, the depressive will believe that there is simply nothing interesting or fun out there for him and his partner. The depressive may tend to see only the negatives in his partner and children or in their life together. Low self-esteem may have the depressive questioning his own abilities and competence, but he may also discouragingly question the competence of his loved ones without realizing it. The depressive may simply show little interest in his partner and their children, or he may criticize them, their goals and aspirations. Both partners may remain unaware that it is actually his depression that is being projected onto their relationship, their children, and the world. The couple may interpret the depressive's problem as just being one of anxiety, low energy, or chronic fatigue. If the depressive suffers from insomnia, a common symptom of depression, the insomnia may be blamed for the low energy and activity level and treated with sleeping aids rather than treating the depression directly. Some depressives sleep too much and, over time, the couple may have to deal with the tendency of the depressive to lose weight or gain weight. The couple may have to deal with chronic financial difficulties, as the depressive's mood may create problems with coworkers and management. His complaining and critical nature, combined with low energy, fatigue, and low self-esteem, may result in few promotions and frequent periods of unemployment.

The partner of a depressive may find herself to be the only driving force in the family and feel a need to constantly motivate the depressive by pretending to be upbeat—all with the additional responsibility of checking on him to see that things get done. Since opposites can attract,[3] the partner may be just the "get things done" kind of person almost designed for this caretaker role. Even with considerable effort, the partner's attempts to relieve the depressed individual's worries and uplift his sad, gloomy, and overly serious nature may fall flat as the depressive always seems to be able to explain away his discouragement and despair.

Depressives may blame their job, boss, dysfunctional childhood, or their partner for the problems in their life. The partner may remain hopeful that some change will occur or some event will happen that breaks the depressive's pessimism about the future. With longer-term depressions, the atmosphere created by the depressed individual may eventually cause the partner to also experience some level of depression. This may be the case even if the partner did not previously suffer any instability, although mutual instability is common in relationships. Needless to say, the depressive makes for a poor sounding board when the partner wishes to discuss her own personal problems or family issues.

The couple may find themselves spending considerable time alone as the depressive seems to withdraw from social activities and events. At the same time, the depressive's uninteresting and un-fun demeanor may drive away potential friends and acquaintances. Wearing depression glasses, the depressive may be highly critical and judgmental of others. With low self-esteem, the depressive may also believe people avoid her because she is not very interesting or just socially incompetent. These feelings may increase the depressive's sense of guilt about the couple's lonely existence.

It is common for depressive symptoms to show up as irritability and anger. Therapists frequently fail to recognize the depression that underlies irritability and temper tantrums and may see these couples for long periods of time to work on their "communication problems" and "anger issues." Work may be needed in these areas as well, but comprehensive treatment must include some recognition of the underlying depression and its effects. Treatment for depression is especially important in family situations, since the depressive's negative mood may misinterpret his children's behavior and he may severely punish them for minor infractions or no infraction at all. With hindsight, the partner may look back and see the red flags that were missed when first getting to know the depressive. The partner may wonder why she was initially attracted to the quiet, socially withdrawn, or irritable person she first met. Of course, the depressive's mood may have been elevated initially via honeymoon-stage brain chemistry, and there just always seemed to be some explanation for the problems and unhappiness that showed up later.

If the depressed family member is a child, the parents may not even recognize the depression. The parents may just assume the child will eventually grow out of his problem or "childish behavior." Parents may seek band-aid solutions without attempting a more comprehensive approach, including some recognition of their own role in creating the child's depression.

Finally, keep in mind that depression may have negative effects prior to the birth of a child. According to Louis Cozolino,[122] professor of psychology at Pepperdine University and author of numerous books about the neuroscience of human behavior, high levels of stress experienced during pregnancy may cause chemical imbalances that can have negative effects on a child's development. These imbalances may cause emotional problems including depression, irritability, anxiety, and problems with attachment, as well as physical problems. After birth, a stressed or depressed mother's emotionless or withdrawn expression may create distress in the infant. When mothers become depressed, their children may become depressed. The child may respond by unconsciously trying to care for the mother in a role reversal that may damage a child's normal emotional development, and the child may grow up with depression and/or a caretaker personality.

ANXIETY

Anxiety[139-147] is something we all experience from time to time, and some temporary anxiety is a normal and natural response to stress, fear, and apprehension. Some stress may even be helpful in motivating us to focus on, and tackle, the source of the stress. Many normal aspects of life, such as starting school, a new job, or public speaking may give butterflies to almost anyone. But for some people, the reaction to stress may involve a more severe negative emotional reaction about what the future may hold. When anxiety is out of proportion to the perceived threat and prevents a person from functioning normally, the anxiety is now a disorder. Anxiety may come on slowly because of some approaching event, or the stress may build up over time from multiple stressors, and this can happen to anyone at any age. If a serious level of anxiety goes untreated, it may only get worse. Fortunately, anxiety disorders are very treatable, and there are multiple treatments that have been shown to be very effective. About 30 percent of adults may be affected during their life span, and more women are diagnosed with anxiety than men.

THE SYMPTOMS OF anxiety may cause or exacerbate problems in multiple areas of life, such as relationships, work, school, social activities, etc. Symptoms of anxiety may include:
- Sleep disorders—sleeping too much or too little
- Digestive/bowel problems
- Fast heartrate, sweating, muscle tension
- Dizziness
- Poor concentration
- Rapid breathing

- Nervousness, restlessness
- Headaches or other chronic pain
- Nightmares
- Irrational anger/irritability
- Suicide ideation

Anxiety disorders are the most common of all mental disorders, and they may occur for no obvious reason, or they may be caused by a known trigger. With serious symptoms, the individual may go to the hospital out of a fear that they are coming down with a serious illness, such as a heart attack or stroke. People may try to avoid the object or event that triggers or exacerbates their anxiety, and this can make their social life, school, or job performance much more difficult. Some people may be unable to enter a place of business or even leave their house. Some individuals suffering anxiety may find some temporary relief in alcohol and/or drugs with the clear danger of becoming an addict. It may be necessary to treat an alcohol or drug addiction first before the accompanying anxiety/depression can be effectively addressed.

Anxiety and depression frequently co-occur. It is common for some level of depression to cause or contribute to some level of anxiety—or vice versa. Anxiety and depression may result in a descending spiral of ever-increasing mental instability. Fortunately, the same treatments, including counseling, medication, and lifestyle changes, may be effective for both disorders.

Children can also suffer anxiety although, as with adults, it is usually a normal part of life, and they are able to cope with it in most cases. But children may also experience the more serious levels of anxiety that may become a chronic disorder, and they may exhibit symptoms such as fearfulness, irritability, sleep issues, a sense of shame, low self-esteem, etc. But anxiety in children is treatable, although I always consider the possibility that a dysfunctional or abusive home environment is the actual cause of the child's anxiety (see chapters: Personalities in Relationships and Families, The Abusive Personality/Abusive Relationships, (and) The Family Systems of Murray Bowen.

Needless to say, anxiety in teens is to be expected with first attempts at dating, social rejection and loneliness for the less popular, tests, body image issues, etc. Many teens experience shyness that they may eventually grow out of—or not. Teens experiencing significant anxiety may also experience some level of depression. Again, I am careful to look for family dysfunction and especially dysfunction in the parents. Children and teens may not be able to make lifestyle changes without the consent and participation of parents, and it may be the parents who need to change which might include learning new parenting skills.

CAUSES OF ANXIETY

While the exact causes of anxiety are unknown, multiple causes may be involved including psychological, genetic, or environmental factors. Risk factors known to increase the likelihood of developing an anxiety disorder include:[144]

Trauma: People who have experienced some level of abuse or trauma or have witnessed others being abused or traumatized may develop an anxiety disorder at some point in their life. This can happen to children as well as adults, but with children, the anxiety disorder may be more severe and enduring.

Multiple Stressors: Multiple stressors over time which, individually, may be less significant, but together may result in considerable anxiety. For example, an individual experiencing marital and/or family discord, doesn't get along with his boss, and has financial problems caused by poor health may develop an anxiety disorder.

Personality or Mood Disorder: Individuals with some personality types, such as the obsessive-compulsive, shy, borderline, dependent, or paranoid personalities, or suffer a mood disorder such as depression or bipolar, may experience some level of stress and anxiety simply because of how they naturally view, and react to, themselves, other people, events, etc.

Blood Relatives: Anxiety disorders can run in families suggesting a genetic connection.

Drugs / Alcohol: Drug/alcohol use, abuse, or withdrawal can increase the likelihood of some level of anxiety or worsen anxiety that is already present.

Medical Condition: Anxiety disorders may be the first indication of an underlying medical condition, and a physical exam may be necessary to rule out any possible underlying causes. The known physical causes of anxiety include:

- Heart disease
- Diabetes
- Thyroid problems
- Respiratory problems such as chronic obstructive pulmonary disease or asthma
- Alcohol/drug misuse or withdrawal
- Chronic pain or irritable bowel syndrome
- Rare tumors that produce certain fight-or-flight hormones

TYPES OF ANXIETY DISORDERS

Generalized Anxiety Disorder: Generalized anxiety disorder is a sustained and unrelenting worry that prevents an individual from functioning normally on a daily basis. The sufferer may have problems with irritability, nervousness and tension, concentration, tiredness, restlessness, sleep issues, gastrointestinal problems, etc. They may worry about their family relationships, financial issues, health issues, social hurdles, etc., and they may need to avoid objects or situations that can trigger their anxiety.

Panic Disorder/ Panic Attacks: Panic disorders involve reoccurring panic attacks where the sufferer experiences sudden feelings of intense anxiety, fear, or terror which escalate quickly and leave the sufferer with feelings of extreme psychological and physical discomfort. The individual may have a sense of losing control, feelings of unreality or being detached from oneself, or feelings of doom or imminent death. Physical symptoms may include rapid heart rate, chest pain, sweating, nausea, stomach pain, chills, hot flashes, numbness, shortness of breath or choking, trembling, nausea, headaches, or dizziness. Although panic attacks are not life threatening, when the attack subsides, the individual may then experience anxiety and worry about the next attack.

Panic attacks may appear at any time and for no apparent reason, or they may be triggered by specific objects, places or events, and the individual may go to extreme lengths to avoid these circumstances. They may occur anywhere whether at home, the grocery store, a party, etc. Some people may only experience one or a few panic attacks which then just go away while others may experience recurrent attacks over longer periods of time. Some people may be more susceptible to the onset of panic attacks due to genetics, their level of stress, or they may have a temperament or personality that tends towards negative emotional reactions. Research has suggested that the body's natural "fight-or-flight" response may play a role in panic attacks. It is easy to see how the symptoms listed above might be present if an assault or being trapped in a housefire seems imminent.

Fortunately, as with other anxiety disorders, panic attacks may respond very well to medications, talk therapy, lifestyle changes, or a combination of treatments, and panic attacks may get worse without treatment. Techniques for an immediate response to a panic attack include:[143]

1: Deep breathing/meditation techniques can be very effective at reducing the stress response. In particular, practicing progressive muscle relaxation in conjunction with deep breathing techniques can be especially beneficial. There are many sources on video and online that teach deep breathing/meditation and progressive relaxation techniques.

2: Finding a quiet place that reduces the amount of stimulation can be very helpful, especially if combined with deep breathing/meditation and progressive relaxation techniques.

3: You can accurately tell yourself the attack will pass and that, with available treatments, panic attacks can be eliminated from your life completely. There is no need to struggle to make it go away. A passive attitude is more effective in the moment.

4: Regular aerobic exercise such as brisk walking, bicycling, aerobics classes, jogging, swimming, etc., can be very effective at reducing anxiety, and these kinds of exercises have been shown to have excellent antidepressant effects as well. Brisk walking is an exceptional form of exercise in that it can begin right outside your front door or happen in front of a TV with a treadmill.

Phobias: When someone has an extreme aversion to, or fear of, something that is generally harmless, this is referred to as a specific phobia. The sufferer generally knows that their fears of bugs, snakes, spiders, dogs, airplanes, heights, the sight of blood, getting shots, etc., are baseless and irrational, but their fears may remain for years or a lifetime. Their behavior may appear odd when they go to extremes to avoid the feared object or event, and they may suffer intense anxiety when the feared object or event cannot be avoided.

Agoraphobia: Agoraphobia is the fear of any situation or environment that might be difficult to get away from, including situations that might cause feelings of embarrassment, feeling trapped with no escape, or just feeling helpless. Examples include being in crowds or standing in lines, enclosed spaces, being alone in public, or using public transportation. Some sufferers may force themselves to endure the intense anxiety and fear if the situation cannot be avoided. Others may isolate themselves in their home unless they have a companion with them.

Social Anxiety Disorder/Shyness: Some people feel intense anxiety or have an outright fear of being scrutinized and evaluated by others in either social situations or situations where they must perform some task in the presence of others. Shy people experience emotional overreactions such as embarrassment, shame, submissiveness, depression, etc., and the more generalized the shyness has become to multiple areas of life, the more problems the shy person will experience (see chapter: The Shy Personality).

Posttraumatic Stress Disorder (PTSD):[146] Some people who have witnessed or been involved in a traumatic event such as war, serious accident, assault, rape, natural disasters, etc., may suffer the symptoms of PTSD for an extended period of time, even years, after the traumatic event. These symptoms may include repeating episodes of fear, anger, depression, or nightmares or flashbacks where they re-experience the event as if it were happening all over again. They may have strong reactions to reminders of the event, such as a loud noise like an auto backfire. I have had several clients who worked in positions such as emergency room nurses, ambulance medics, police officers, etc., where repeated contact with accident or assault victims eventually left them with clear symptoms of PTSD. Victims of spousal abuse or child abuse may experience the symptoms of PTSD years after leaving or being removed from the abusive environment. To be diagnosed with PTSD, the symptoms must last for more than a month although the onset of symptoms may not appear until long after the traumatic event. PTSD may co-occur with other mental disorders such as depression, problems with memory, or alcohol/drug addiction. According to the American Psychiatric Association, the symptoms of PTSD fall into four categories:[146]

1: Intrusive thoughts: flashbacks, dreams, or memories that will not go away.

2: Avoiding reminders of the traumatic event including places, people, or similar events that may trigger their symptoms. It is common for war survivors to never talk about their war experiences or refuse to watch war-based movies for the rest of their lives.

3: Negative thoughts and feelings including negative self-talk such as "I'm a loser," etc., along with negative feelings of shame, fear, guilt, etc., and there may also be feelings of isolation and separation from others. Some anxiety sufferers may get little joy from activities they used to look forward to.

4: Arousal and reactive symptoms including mood shifts such as irritability/anger, acting out in self-destructive ways, problems with concentration or sleep, or being startled when surprised by the unexpected, such as a loud noise.

There are other anxiety disorders including separation anxiety disorder, selective mutism, substance-induced anxiety disorders, and personality-based anxiety.

TREATMENT

As with many disorders, anxiety sufferers may not even know that they have a diagnosable disorder and so may not seek treatment. This is unfortunate since there are multiple treatments that have been shown to be effective in treating the symptoms of anxiety.

The most common treatments for anxiety disorders are talk therapy, including cognitive behavioral therapy (CBT) and medications, both of which have been shown to be effective in helping sufferers gain significant relief. CBT helps sufferers learn new ways of thinking and behaving allowing them to react differently to stressful or feared objects and situations.

Stress management techniques, such as deep breathing/meditation techniques including progressive relaxation can be very helpful at reducing the symptoms of anxiety. Deep breathing and progressive relaxation are sometimes used in combination with exposure therapy where the individual is gradually exposed to the feared object or situation while using relaxation techniques to help avoid emotional overreactions. Techniques for dealing with anxiety can be learned in individual counseling or group therapy settings and multiple book and online sources are available. I am a big believer in support groups where an individual can meet other people with similar problems, which may help avoid the sense of being alone as well as allow the individual to learn from the experiences of others. And, as always, becoming educated about the particular problem/symptoms an individual is experiencing may be immensely helpful in gaining control over their symptoms and eliminating self-talk about being a loser, nuts, or crazy.

For some people, lifestyle changes may be all that is necessary to obtain some relief, including:
- Changing their job
- Finding new friends
- Ending an abusive marriage (see chapter: The Abusive Personality/Abusive Relationships)
- Beginning an exercise regimen
- Cutting down or eliminating alcohol or caffeine
- Improved sleep regimen

- Improved diet
- Practicing meditation/deep breathing
- Quitting smoking

Aerobic exercises which speed up the heart are known for their antianxiety and antidepressant effects. Many people experiencing the symptoms of anxiety and/or depression find considerable relief with some form of exercise such as brisk walking, jogging, bicycling, swimming, aerobics classes, various machines such as treadmills, stair-step or elliptical machines, etc. I encourage all of my clients suffering any level of anxiety or depression to stay active on a daily basis since the beneficial effects of exercise are temporary, so a daily regimen is essential. A trial and error process of trying several forms of exercise may help you find the most enjoyable exercise for you. For people who stick with it, their exercise routine frequently becomes their favorite part of the day.

Consultation with a doctor or psychiatrist will help determine if the use of medication is warranted. I have seen many people experience considerable relief from the many effective medications now available, although a trial and error period may be necessary where different medications are tried in order to find the most effective medication for a given individual. For many people, the best results occur with some combination of medication, talk therapy, and lifestyle changes including exercise.

THE BORDERLINE PERSONALITY

This description covers multiple levels of borderline patterns of thought, emotion, and behavior. Those with fewer or milder traits, as well as those with the symptoms of a serious disorder, may readily identify some of their thinking, as well as emotional and behavioral tendencies. A more comprehensive understanding of self usually requires an ongoing self-observation and self-reflection over time. These traits are found in both men and women.

IN ITS ORIGINAL conception, the borderline personality was thought to be someone who fell somewhere on the largely hypothetical and undefined border between the neurotic personality and the psychotic personality.[36] Today the term *borderline personality* is essentiality unrelated to past descriptions. The basic characteristics of the borderline personality include:
 1) Unstable and shifting self-image
 2) Unstable feelings and emotions / difficulty with anger control
 3) A pattern of instability in their relationships
 4) Impulsive behavior

Self-image or *sense of self* has to do with beliefs about one's abilities, appearance, personality, values, and life goals. My use of the term here includes the thinking and behaviors that result from these beliefs about oneself. The unstable self-image of borderlines is subject to frequent and sometimes sudden shifts, including academic and career changes, as well as changes in their social or sexual identity or behavior. In some cases, a shift in their social identity may even cause them to choose new friends of questionable character.

Unhappy when alone, it is relationship problems that usually have the greatest effect on the borderline's self-image. Borderlines typically have the ability to form a very deep love relationship yet frequently express anger and rage at the individual to whom they feel such a strong emotional attachment. They live in fear of losing their love relationship, and the most trivial perceived slight by a loved one may be interpreted as rejection or as a sign of impending abandonment. The borderline suffers a profound sense of shame resulting from feelings of being defective, disgusting, and repulsive, and they believe they deserve to be rejected.[124] This may result in extreme changes in the borderline's thoughts, feelings, and behaviors. Changes in feelings may range from mild gloominess and irritability through inconsolable panic, anger, fear, and rage. With a simultaneous decrease in emotional inhibition and an increase in impulsivity accompanied by an inability to be comforted or appeased, they are not able to use normal thought processes to gain perspective and understand the temporary nature of the situation.[124]

In some cases, there may be threats of suicide with demands for immediate changes by the loved one. Their rage and attacks against their loved one may guarantee the eventual rejection they fear. Alternatively the borderline's reaction may involve depression and emotional withdrawal along with extreme loneliness. In more serious cases, these feelings may be accompanied by feelings of being immoral, bad, or evil. The mood shifts of the borderline may lead to impulsive behaviors, such as substance abuse, eating disorders, risky sex, reckless spending, etc.

As you can imagine, borderlines live with considerable stress, which has further consequences for their feelings and emotions. In more serious cases, feelings of paranoia or feelings of *depersonalization* may set in, but usually only for brief periods of time.

Depersonalization involves something of an unreal or dreamlike state in which sufferers feel detached from their mental or physical self or feel as if they do not even exist. In most cases, these individuals are aware of the irrational nature of their feelings, and these feelings usually lift within minutes or hours. Where these feelings are the result of the loss of a relationship, the resumption of the relationship or just the possibility of resuming the relationship may cause these symptoms to go away completely. Another characteristic of borderline individuals is their liberal use of sarcasm. Sarcasm may play a role in many personalities, but it's a specialty for borderlines.

In serious cases, borderlines may threaten suicide or intentionally hurt themselves. The sense that they are evil, and the sense that they do not really exist, may lead them to hurt or injure themselves (e.g., cutting themselves), since the pain induced by the self-injury allows them to feel like they do exist and may even relieve the sense that they are evil. The risk of suicidal behavior and self-injury is greatest during the early or young-adult years and diminishes with age, just as many other symptoms associated with the borderline personality frequently diminish with age. Of course, all threats of suicide must be taken seriously.

One of the most difficult traits for some borderlines is the tendency to repeatedly undermine their own success. After considerable effort to obtain a job or promotion, finish school, or make a relationship work, borderlines may quit the job, reject the promotion, drop out of school, or end the relationship, just when it appears their efforts are about to get positive results. Borderlines are most successful in environments that involve some structure, group effort, or a team approach, and they may function well in a leadership role. Borderlines tend to have more difficulty in environments where one-on-one relationships are required.

Dysfunctional childhoods involving hostility, neglect, physical abuse, sexual abuse, etc. are common among borderlines. Separation from one or both parents, or the permanent loss of parents during childhood, are also commonly found in the histories of borderlines.[14] According to Louis Cozolino, psychology professor at Pepperdine University and author of *The Neuroscience of Human Relationships*,[124] "Borderline personality is truly an interpersonal disorder, created in a social milieu, triggered by close relationships, and destructive to social connectedness ... the child is unable to utilize others in the development of secure attachment and to regulate overwhelming anxiety and fear. The result is that real or imagined abandonment triggers a state of terror, similar to what any young primate experiences when physically abandoned by its mother."[72]

Cozolino points out that genetics may play a role in the borderline personality and, in some cases, the genetic predisposition may overrule a stable home environment. Yet Cozolino emphasizes the "quite strong" evidence that borderline personalities are related to failures of early attachment. A possible genetic connection must be considered since a borderline personality is five times more likely to show up in families where there is a first-degree relative who is also borderline. Borderline personalities, like other personality styles and disorders, may also show up with no apparent childhood trauma or genetic connection, although the general connection between borderline personalities and a lack of nurturing during childhood is strong.[13] As children, borderlines may have repeatedly experienced emotions they did not understand and, therefore, did not learn to regulate or control. Typically there will be a pattern of instability with unstable emotions and impulsive behavior occurring at least by early adulthood. The borderline personality is sometimes found with some level of depression[14] or another co-occuring personality characteristic.

As you can see, with multiple symptoms and multiple levels of severity, the borderline personality may express itself in many ways. Fortunately for the majority of borderlines, some stability, with a reduction in emotionality, impulsivity, and unstable relationships, usually sets in during their 30s and 40s. Most borderlines may eventually experience sufficient stability to no longer warrant the label, although some problems with shifting emotions and difficult relationships may continue, especially during periods of stress.[14] A reduction in symptoms is especially likely for borderlines that have received professional help. Psychotherapy has been shown to be very effective with borderline personalities, and positive results may occur in the earliest stages of therapy. One major attempt to understand the long-term effects of the more serious borderline personality disorder was the McLean Study of Adult Development.[55] This study, funded by the National Institute of Mental Health, found that remission rates, at about 74 percent, are much higher than previously thought, and these remission rates have proven to be quite stable with few relapses. These researchers also found that some of the more severe symptoms, such as physical harm to self or suicide threats or attempts, usually resolve themselves relatively quickly. Less severe symptoms, such as anger and fear of abandonment, tend to resolve themselves more slowly. Another positive finding was that borderline patients continued to improve socially over time, eventually "achieving the milestones of young adulthood." As the most researched personality disorder,[14] further advances in the treatment of the borderline personality may be expected.

THE BORDERLINE PERSONALITY IN RELATIONSHIPS

Essentially everything about the borderline works against stability in relationships. Let's review the list: temper tantrums, chronic fear of abandonment, chronic mood shifts, impulsivity, anger and rage, sarcasm, etc.

VIGNETTE: Chaos

As described by Eddy's ex-girlfriend: *Simply put, my relationship with Eddy went fast—very fast. Eddy was very forward when I first met him. I had never had someone show so much interest in me that quickly. Unfortunately, I was flattered rather than viewing his all-consuming infatuation as a red flag. Eddy wanted to go out with me every night, and I had to start making up excuses about why I was too busy to see him that often. Eddy also appeared to be impulsive, especially with money and alcohol. Eddy was a spendthrift. He would buy me multiple gifts and take me to restaurants he could not afford to prove his love for me. Again, I was flattered rather than alarmed. Eddy obviously meant it when he said he needed me and couldn't live without me, and I made the mistake of allowing our relationship to become intimate very quickly in spite of the fact that Eddy seemed to have a history of commitment problems in most areas of life. It wasn't just his history of short relationships. Eddy had dropped out of classes so often in college that he never got a degree, and he had worked hard at several jobs that looked promising, only to quit them for trivial reasons. Still, as we became more emotionally involved, our lives became centered almost exclusively around each other. Eddy was not happy any time I was not with him.*

Over time, I began to realize the extreme extent to which Eddy was afraid I would leave him, even though I had never given him any reason to feel that way. If I was running late for a date, Eddy would become extremely upset and very sarcastic while implying that I must not really care for him as much as he cared for me. He would later apologize profusely and be very down on himself. There were times when his mood shifts would seem to come out of nowhere, and they would sometimes escalate into temper tantrums or, alternatively, descend into pessimism, self-loathing, and depression. I found myself calculating what I would say to Eddy according to how I thought he might react to what I said. Even with these efforts to sooth his fears, Eddy would still overreact emotionally.

Sometimes he thought I was the most wonderful person in the world, and other times he would vent some list of accusations about how awful I had been to him. I had heard other people refer to "chaotic" relationships, a word that now had real meaning for me. At other times, Eddy could be really critical of himself. He would sometimes suggest that I really did not even like him and then offer a list of reasons why he was, in fact, an unlikable person. When Eddy would feel this way about himself, he would, of course, feel certain that I would soon abandon him for another love. It was easy to see why Eddy had never had a long-term relationship. Needless to say, when I finally decided to leave Eddy, he would vacillate between feeling like he was so awful that he deserved to be left and demonizing me as just being a jerk like all the other women who had deserted him.

An individual involved in a relationship with a borderline may experience considerable instability and chaos in the relationship as the borderline alternately becomes hot and cold, with considerable intensity and quick turnaround time. The first few dates may go very well, as the borderline views the new relationship as just awesome in every way and exhibits a very caring and affectionate attitude. Unfortunately, this initial perspective soon reverts to skepticism, with doubts that the new Mr. Right is really serious about the relationship for the long term. The borderline may now fear losing the relationship, and the initial caring and affection may suddenly shift to a negative attitude with a fear of rejection. The borderline will expect her partner to always be available to meet her emotional needs on demand, which, of course, no partner can consistently live up to. It is a matter of time before the partner is unable to be physically or emotionally available at the moment of the borderline's need, and the partner will discover how little it takes to trigger the borderline's extreme defensive reactions. Simply forgetting some chore or being a little late for some planned event may trigger extreme emotionality, including temper tantrums and rage. The hapless partner may discover that any attempts to explain himself and his actions only increases the intensity of the borderline's emotionality and use of sarcasm to further belittle the partner's explanations. The partner may be accused of insufficient commitment to the relationship or of planning to leave her. The partner may also receive an angry review of past grievances the borderline has kept in a mental file, and the partner is found guilty on all charges.

In some cases, the borderline's response to perceived slights may be emotional withdrawal and depression. Impulsive and reckless responses by the borderline may include alcohol, drug abuse, or irrational shopping sprees. Since the borderline's self-image or self-identity may shift, there may be a change in values or life goals, including career changes, etc. If there are changes in the borderline's social or sexual identity, the borderline may seek a new circle of friends or have affairs. Some of the borderline's behavior, such as affairs, may be intended to get back at the partner for perceived slights.

As mentioned earlier, it is common for borderlines to undermine their own success, whether in a job, school, or their relationship.

This leaves the borderline's partner never knowing when the relationship will disintegrate completely. After a series of failed relationships, some borderlines may become relationship-shy and withdraw socially for an extended period of time into the security provided by pets or less intense friendships. At this point, the chronic boredom that some borderlines experience may intensify, and they may seek multiple diversions to fill their time.

SIMILARITIES AND DIFFERENCES

It is easy to confuse the borderline personality with other personalities because many personalities have symptoms in common with each other. Like borderlines, histrionic personalities also tend to be emotionally unstable, manipulative, and have a need to be the focus of attention, but borderlines will also be characterized by loneliness, fears of abandonment, and self-destructive behavior, including anger outbursts at their partner. Paranoia may be found in both the borderline and the schizotypal personalities, but borderline paranoia tends to show up in brief episodes in response to relationship dynamics. Antisocials are manipulative for personal profit, while borderlines manipulate to get someone to focus on them. Like borderlines, dependent personalities fear abandonment by their caretaker, but the dependent reacts to potential abandonment with submissive behavior, while the borderline reacts with emotional shifts, including anger, rage, demands, and feelings of emotional emptiness and loneliness. If a relationship falls apart, the dependent will immediately seek the security of a new relationship, while the borderline may withdraw from relationships. Borderlines also tend to have a greater number of unstable relationships.

THE SCHIZOTYPAL PERSONALITY

This description covers multiple levels of schizotypal patterns of thought, emotion, and behavior. Those with fewer or milder traits, as well as those with the symptoms of a serious disorder, may readily identify some of their thinking, as well as emotional and behavioral tendencies. A more comprehensive understanding of self usually requires a knowledgeable and ongoing self-observation and self-reflection over time. These traits are found in both men and women.

AN INDIVIDUAL WITH a schizotypal personality may experience:
1) Some level of discomfort in social or interpersonal relationships and may embrace a "loner" lifestyle due to a diminished ability to form close relationships.
2) Unusual or distorted perceptions and belief systems, sometimes referred to as "magical thinking."
3) An odd, eccentric, or nonconformist lifestyle, which may include unusual dress and appearance, poor hygiene, constricted or unusual emotional expressions, unusual behaviors, unrealistic or incoherent goals, poor verbal skills and odd speech. There may also be memory, attention, and learning difficulties, including poor reasoning ability.

The schizotypal personality covers a lot of territory. Only through a comprehensive understanding of the behavioral patterns involved can we understand how such disparate traits and characteristics may actually be related. Consider the following two vignettes:

VIGNETTE: The Odd and Eccentric

During my early college days, people like Jake were referred to as "street people." Jake just hangs out as much as possible, appearing to survive by doing odd jobs and basic carpentry when necessary. He only wears old and less-than-clean jeans with shirttail always on display, and his conversation always seems a little odd, even if you are not quite sure why. At times, Jake will talk about who he was in a past life, and if you broach the topic of the 9/11 attack, settle in for a lengthy diatribe about the obvious involvement of the American government in the planning and execution of the attack and the equally obvious cover-up. Jake is very intelligent and a good guitarist, and enough women are attracted to Jake for him to have occasional dates and even relationships, although no relationship has ever lasted longer than a few weeks or months. While Jake admits many women have considered him too "weird" to continue dating, he also admits frequently finding some reason why the lady is not right for him. Jake says he would rather live alone than be with someone who is not to his liking. There just never seems to be anyone to his liking—year after year. Jake doesn't know it, but as painful as his loneliness and isolation have been, he is more comfortable when he is by himself.

VIGNETTE: Extreme Weirdness

Consider the descriptions of these two individuals:

Person A: *Genius, Harvard graduate, extraordinary artist, award-winning poet, musician, former college professor.*

Person B: *Rarely bathes, body odor, dirty clothes, poor teeth, odd conversationalist with unusual laughter, usually broke, difficulty holding a job.*

It is still hard for me to believe these two individuals were actually the same person. One of the most extreme examples of the schizotypal personality I have encountered was my old friend Jerry. Jerry was a true genius and a Harvard graduate with stunning creativity with both the written word and the artist's pen and paint. His ability to capture the very essence of someone in a simple line drawing was legendary among those fortunate enough to have known him. But Jerry would never stoop to selling his art. No matter how broke Jerry was, he gave it away for free—all of it.

After a stint teaching college, although too eccentric to receive tenure, and a failed marriage, Jerry was awarded a substantial grant for his poetry by the National Endowment for the Arts. Of course, Jerry then proceeded to blow all of the money traveling Europe with a girlfriend for six months, returning home just as poor as before he received the grant. But this isn't the only Jerry people encountered. This same Jerry lived alone in a shack with no running water, food left on plates by the sink, and he shared his home with the best-fed rats in town. Jerry usually smelled like he had not bathed in weeks. Jerry rarely, if ever, saw a dentist, as evidenced by poor teeth and bad breath. Conversations with Jerry were sometimes interupted by his unusually loud laughter. I spent considerable time with Jerry when I had a little music store in a craft mall, and Jerry would come by and play his old-time banjo style. I had not studied personalities before Jerry died, so I did not know Jerry suffered from a schizotypal personality. I suspect Jerry never knew either.

One characteristic that contributes to the odd or eccentric behavior of schizotypals is that they are frequently unable to deal with all the necessary social cues and emotions for normal social interaction. Schizotypals may feel like other people notice their presence when they go out, yet normal socializing may be difficult for them due to awkwardness or limited eye contact. As the art of small talk eludes them, schizotypals tend to be anxious in social settings, especially around unfamiliar people. As a result, they may have limited interpersonal interactions, as their unusual or even bizarre behavior alienates other people who may then try to avoid the schizotypal. In some cases, the social anxiety of the schizotypal may include some paranoia and suspiciousness about the motivations of others. Whereas most people become more relaxed during social events as the evening wears on, schizotypals may only become more suspicious, tense, and awkward the longer they remain at a social event.

The schizotypal may dress in an unconventional manner with little thought given to, or awareness of, the need for an appropriate appearance at a given social setting. For some schizotypals, their appearance may be combined with some level of poor hygiene. This may include a lack of dental care with chronic bad breath, infrequent bathing, body odor, etc. Schizotypals may also have visual illusions, such as seeing their face change while they look in a mirror, or auditory illusions such as hearing critical comments in a distant conversation that are actually not loud enough to hear.[102] I must emphasize that not all schizotypals, especially milder cases, will possess all of these characteristics.

It is common for schizotypal personalities to draw inaccurate and unusual conclusions from events and circumstances. This is referred to as *magical thinking,* and schizotypals may view some incident as having some extraordinary meaning that is intended especially for them. As such, they may have odd conceptions of the paranormal or the occult, or they may believe they have unusual abilities to change other people or the environment in some way. They may be superstitious, believe they are psychic or clairvoyant, can read other people's thoughts, or have supernatural control over the behavior of others via their own thoughts or occult-based rituals. Conspiracy theories are easily embraced. Schizotypals may be drawn to unusual religious groups, cults, etc. I have wondered about the schizotypal content of those extreme right-wing militias that profess a desire to protect our country, while most people want protection from them.

Schizotypals sometimes have an unusual way of saying things in their choice of words or phrasing. Without realizing it, they may be somewhat off topic, vague, or abstract in their reasoning and discourse, with specifics offered only on request. Sometimes they even create their own altered or slang terminology and euphemisms. Other schizotypals may be overly elaborate or metaphorical, with an overemphasis on clarity and specific details. They may say the same thing in different ways to ensure correct communication. Still, even with the vague or abstract speech patterns, they are always basically coherent, and the unusual nature of their speech may not always be that noticeable.

The schizotypals' awkward mannerisms and speech patterns, poor manners, unusual clothing, poor hygiene, or peculiar thinking contribute to their odd or eccentric reputation. This may further the isolation in which the schizotypal lives. Over time, schizotypals' isolation may further reduce their self-confidence and self-esteem and make them even more eccentric and awkward, which may increase their isolation even further. Schizotypals may admit to their loneliness and a desire for more close contact with others, including relationships, yet close social interactions may be limited to their family and close relatives. Still, as painful as their isolation may be, many schizotypals feel like they do not fit in and prefer their painful isolation to the difficulty of relating to other people socially. Yet the eccentricities in the behavior of the schizotypal may, in some cases, result in a very creative personality. Schizotypal personalities are well represented among artists, poets, composers, musicians, and inventors.

Until they have seen an unusually knowledgeable therapist, schizotypals typically do not know they are schizotypal and sometimes seek treatment for other symptoms, such as anxiety or depression. Over half of the more serious and diagnosable schizotypals have suffered major depression. In many cases, schizotypals will be treated for their anxiety, depression, or other symptoms while they, and frequently their therapist, remain unaware that they possess some level of a schizotypal personality.

The schizotypal personality may show up in childhood or adolescence with solitariness, limited peer interaction, social anxiety, low grades, a highly sensitive nature, unusual thoughts and language, and unusual or even bizarre fantasies. The unusual behaviors of the schizotypal may be exacerbated by the criticism and punishments dished out by well-meaning but ignorant parents who are not aware of the personality style or disorder and its effects on their child. This, of course, will worsen the negative emotional environment for the child,[11] which may also include mockery and teasing by other children. Of course, caution must be exercised in diagnosing children or adolescents, since many of these features may reflect a child's normal and temporary emotional angst and turmoil. The involvement of an expert in child and adolescent behavior is essential for a legitimate diagnosis.

Both environmental factors and genetic factors may contribute to the formation of the schizotypal personality. Environmental factors may include stress and an emotionally dysfunctional environment involving negative emotional expressions, including criticism. While the environment may play a role, current research, including adoption and family studies, strongly suggests that schizotypal personality disorder is genetically related to schizophrenia. Individuals with schizotypal personality disorder will appear more often in families where schizophrenia is present in a blood relative. Many of the features associated with schizotypal personality disorder are now viewed as milder versions of the psychotic features associated with schizophrenia. The schizotypal's odd or unusual thoughts and ideas typically fall short of being delusional in nature. The sensory and perceptual illusions of the schizotypal usually have some basis in reality, unlike the hallucinations of the schizophrenic that have no basis in reality. Essentially, what separates schizotypal personality disorder from schizophrenia is the ability of schizotypals to question the validity and rationality of their thoughts and experiences.[102]

Detecting milder levels of various personalities can be difficult since the traits and characteristics are less severe, and there may be fewer traits and characteristics to observe. Detecting a mild level of schizotypal traits and characteristics may be especially difficult since many of these same traits and characteristics may reflect other personalities, chaotic childhood experiences, low self-esteem, shyness, peer pressure, etc.

It is important to keep in mind that many people who adopt the unusual beliefs, mannerisms, dress, etc. of some group or organization may simply be trying to fit in and feel like they are an accepted and respected member of the group. Many groups, both mainstream and otherwise, invite or require some conformity, and to conform to one group may necessarily require nonconformity with others. An individual's eccentric level of behavior, appearance, etc., may simply reflect a very natural struggle with life gone awry for any of a multitude of reasons. Jake, the individual described in the first vignette, may not be schizotypal at all. I usually look elsewhere, outside the schizotypal personality, to explain odd and eccentric behavior, because the explanations may lie elsewhere.

As you might expect, the effects of marijuana can mimic or exacerbate many schizotypal traits and symptoms. Individuals who use marijuana on a regular basis are much more likely to be disorganized, experience perceptual distortions and distortions in their thinking, and have a reduced ability to pay attention. Research does not suggest that pot smoking causes a schizotypal personality. [103]

THE SCHIZOTYPAL PERSONALITY IN RELATIONSHIPS

Since their unusual or even bizarre behavior, eccentric conversation, and odd sense of fashion drives away potential friends, schizotypals may find it difficult to form a long-term relationship. Yet as difficult as it is for schizotypals to form relationships, they do typically desire relationships. While some schizotypals may withdraw into a solitary and lonely existence, others may persevere in their attempts to find a lasting relationship.

The difficulties begin with the dating ritual. Just as the schizotypal may become increasingly tense at social gatherings, the presence of the date alone may put the schizotypal increasingly on edge. Whether alone with her date or in a larger social setting, the schizotypal may only become more tense and awkward as the evening progresses. The schizotypal may have long considered her problem to be shyness, and her difficulty with small talk and normal socializing may seem intractable and follow her into a serious relationship.

Just as schizotypals may have a history of being alone because of some level of social ineptness, their oddness and eccentricity may create a lonely relationship, as potential friends and other couples avoid the schizotypal and his significant other. Schizotypals may also bring a tendency toward some level of depression to the relationship. With a history of rejection at all levels, schizotypals may have difficulty trusting a new relationship and may periodically come across as rejecting, or even appear to run from the relationship.

As with many personalities, schizotypals may be completely

unaware that other people view their behavior as eccentric. With therapy and a patient and understanding partner, schizotypals may become more aware of the rejecting aspect of their personality and learn to consciously overrule their distancing behavior. Desiring a relationship, schizotypals may be willing participants in couples's therapy and work very hard to modify their dysfunctional behavior.

When schizotypals do form relationships, their partners may also tend toward odd and eccentric behavior. This is to be expected, since people may only recognize oddness and eccentricity that is more serious than their own oddness and eccentricity. Individuals who tend toward eccentricity, magical thinking, etc. frequently find each other. These individuals not only offer mutual support for their beliefs in the groups they join, but in their relationships as well.

SIMILARITIES AND DIFFERENCES

There is a high rate of co-occurrence between schizotypal personalities and borderline personalities, but schizotypal personalities alone do not present impulsive and manipulative behaviors like borderline personalities. Both schizotypal and schizoid personalities may suffer limited emotional expression and a lack of social skills, resulting in a loner lifestyle, but schizoids may be quite content in their isolation, while schizotypals will feel their loneliness. The magical thinking of some schizotypals is absent in the schizoid. There is also a high rate of co-occurring symptoms between the schizotypal, paranoid, and avoidant personalities.

THE NARCISSISTIC PERSONALITY

This description covers multiple levels of narcissistic patterns of thought, emotion, and behavior. Those with fewer or milder traits, as well as those with the symptoms of a serious disorder, may readily identify some of their thinking, as well as emotional and behavioral tendencies. A more comprehensive understanding of self usually requires knowledgeable and ongoing self-observations and self-reflections over time. These traits are found in both men and women.

ON A CONTINUUM from a mild inclination through a serious personality disorder, the narcissist generally has three basic characteristics:

(1) Believes himself to be superior, wonderful, awesome, the greatest, the best ever, etc., which is commonly referred to as *grandiose thinking* or *grandiosity*.

(2) Seeks attention and admiration from others to confirm his inflated opinion of himself. Bragging is common.

(3) Lacks empathy—cares little about the feelings and needs of other people.

There are many other traits associated with narcissism and they can be quite varied in their presentation. Other symptoms of narcissism include:
- A sense of entitlement and privilege
- Exaggerated self-importance
- Arrogance
- Expectation of preferential treatment
- Assumption that other people admire him

- Envying the success of others
- Exhibitionism
- Being critical
- Being manipulative
- Aggression
- Being prone to shame, humiliation, and depression when faced with failure[37]
- A controlling nature
- Being competitive / having power struggles
- In some cases, may initially come across as shy, timid, and inhibited[16]
- Sensitivity to criticism—may become enraged if criticized
- Emotional vulnerability
- Extreme neediness and shallowness below the surface

The term *narcissism* comes from the Greek myth about a boy who saw his reflection in a pond and fell in love with himself.[16] For many people, the words *narcissist* or *narcissism* imply an ego trip. This view of narcissism includes people who frequently talk about, and inflate, their accomplishments and how much people admire them. If only narcissism were this simple. Narcissistic personalities are actually much more complex than a mere ego trip and typically include an attitude that cares little about the feelings and needs of other people.

Many narcissists operate in very subtle ways and may be hard to spot initially, even by professional therapists. In some cases, the grandiosity, need for attention and admiration, sense of entitlement, and some level of arrogance may come across as simply a high level of confidence. In other cases, the narcissism may be disguised with a manipulative outward presentation of self that is sensitive, shy, inhibited, and modest. Yet, below the surface, even lower-key narcissists may possess the grandiose fantasies and self-absorption typically associated with narcissism generally.[16]

The conventional wisdom is that narcissism runs in families and may be the product of an inherited genetic makeup combined with parents who give their children excessive praise and attention. The extent to which narcissism is inherited is actually less certain, while the childhood-environment side of the cause-and-effect question is more evident.[16] When some coddled children reach adulthood, they naturally expect the praise and attention to continue and they develop a sense of entitlement. Narcissists' sense of entitlement may infect every aspect of their life on a continuum from very mild, irritating traits through a serious impairment.

Narcissists expect to be the center of attention immediately upon arrival at a social function. Narcissists may come across as conceited and boastful as they exaggerate their qualifications and personal accomplishments in their search for admiration, even as they disparage or trivialize the accomplishments of others. They may routinely complain about the incompetence of a waiter, busboy, bellhop, etc. Narcissists may be envious of the successes of other people while at the same time believing other people are envious of them. They may also surround themselves with people of professional standing or high status, since viewing their associates as exceptional not only justifies their association with them, but helps confirm their exaggerated view of themselves. Their extreme need for admiration is such that narcissists may be quite surprised when they find other people not agreeing with their excessive opinion of themselves. If denied admiration, or actually criticized, narcissists may become very angry and resentful, and they can hold grudges for extended periods of time. If you offer even constructive criticism to a narcissist, fasten your seatbelt.

Of course most people not suffering from low self-esteem,

depression, dependency, etc. will occasionally have a somewhat exaggerated opinion of their own level of competence, intelligence, importance, sexual prowess, etc.[73] A small amount of narcissism may contribute to a healthy sense of self.[64] It is also natural for us to protect our own somewhat elevated self-assessments and self-esteem with defense mechanisms that allow us to rationalize and explain our failures. It has long been recognized by therapists that the use of defense mechanisms is a healthy process that allows us to persevere in the face of difficulty or defeat and avoid the despair of low self-esteem. But most people adjust their self-concept with a somewhat reality-based self-assessment. Most of us can accept that we are not extraordinarily beautiful or a genius and survive the daydreams where we are. But with vulnerable self-esteem, the narcissist is not reality-based and is unable to make realistic self-assessments. With little awareness of his underlying motivations, the narcissist will continue to feel superior regardless of any evidence to the contrary.[73]

The most difficult trait when dealing with narcissists is their lack of empathy for other people. Narcissists' lack of empathy for others may range from a mild indifference to a complete and total insensitivity to the feelings and needs of others. Their unsypathetic and callous approach to others is interrupted only by a manipulative show of interest and caring to get them what they want. Focused on themselves, narcissists may not even notice the feelings and needs of others, including their spouse and children. Instead, the narcissistic sense of entitlement takes over, and they expect others to be attentive to their needs[16] and show irritation with those who attempt a more egalitarian relationship. In fact, the serious narcissist tends to use almost all of his personal relationships, whether romantic or otherwise, to support his own needs, self-esteem, ambitions, and goals. The severe narcissist may have little or no awareness of the negative comments he makes to, or about, other people.

At work the narcissist's sense of entitlement, and his belief that others should defer to him, will make the narcissist an unpopular team member. With little or no empathy, expect the narcissist to devalue the contributions of others as he considers his own ideas superior, and he may openly belittle his coworkers while claiming credit for their work. While being manipulative in this way, the narcissist may actually steer clear of any real competition or attempts at academic advancement to avoid the risk of criticism or a humiliating defeat. As you might expect, the narcissistic boss or manager typically has little empathy or concern for his employees, and with quick temper on call, will overwork them with few compliments for a job well done. When narcissists do cause others obvious harm, they may feel little or no remorse and see little reason to change their ways. Unfortunately, narcissists do sometimes get promoted in bureaucratic organizations because of their ambition, even as they take credit for the work done by overworked and abused employees lower on the hierarchy.

Many narcissists are very good at presenting a confident and charming persona, and almost anyone can initially buy into their sales pitch.[73] Fortunately for those who are familiar with the basics of the narcissistic personality and are not blinded by naïveté or love's denial, the narcissist can be fairly easy to spot even if he is a new acquaintance. Narcissists may have had many relationships in their past if they are anywhere past young adulthood. Their selfishness usually shows when they become bent out of shape when things do not go their way. Further, narcissists will solicit your admiration indirectly by talking about how great they are and about the admiration they receive from others.

But there is no guarantee you will recognize all of the narcissists you meet. Some may easily slip past your radar because of their superior acting ability or your own willful denial. Still, over time, the narcissist will usually give himself away with a personality that is pretentious, arrogant, disdainful, snobbish, disrespectful, and patronizing. At this point, the denial and blindness of the seduced becomes the greater problem. As with most personalities lacking in empathy and having a tendency toward abusive behavior, the narcissist is unlikely to ever change. It is much more likely that the victim of the narcissist's manipulations will wake up and change his/her attitude toward the narcissist.

Outward appearances aside, the self-esteem of narcissists is actually very fragile and is not immune to negative feelings of shame, humiliation, or even some level of depression when they are criticized or suffer a failure.[16] When this happens, narcissists may retaliate with anger and rage, or they may completely withdraw from their social life to avoid further attacks on their shaky self-esteem and inflated self-assessment. After a withdrawal into depression, even a narcissist may feel inferior and become self-critical—for a while.

Narcissism is not limited to those in the prime of life but is also found in children, adolescents, and the elderly.[16] The aging process has its ups and downs for everyone, but through a process of inevitability and acceptance, most people are able to adequately deal with the negatives while trying to enhance the positives. Not so with the narcissist. The narcissist must face the same physical and occupational limitations that we all must deal with as we get older, but as the narcissist begins to no longer match his perfect self-image, he may become prone to mood shifts and depression. Some aging narcissists may just become grumpy and unpleasant to be around, while others may withdraw socially. It is the aging process where even those narcissists whose superior talents have allowed them to obtain sufficient admiration must now deal with the inevitable and undeniable imperfections that eventually greet everyone who lives long enough.

More men are diagnosed with narcissism than women, but this is to be expected in a male-dominated society where many narcissistic traits are considered acceptable in men, such as competitiveness, less interest in intimacy, and more emphasis on self. The research on gender differences in narcissism is actually more ambiguous.[16] Narcissistic traits in women may simply be somewhat more restrained and less likely to play themselves out on the surface or in their relationships. All of this gets complicated by the fact that narcissistic personality patterns may co-occur with other personality styles or disorders, such as histrionic, antisocial, or passive-aggressive personalities,[22] and particularly the borderline personality.[16]

Therapy with a narcissist may be brief, indeed. Like the abusive, paranoid, antisocial, and obsessive-compulsive personalities, the narcissist may not show up for very many therapy sessions. Although some narcissists do respond to treatment, talking to a narcissist about his imperfections usually does not go over very well, and the therapist may soon learn that she is "wrong" or even "incompetent." In treatment, the narcissist is typically unable to admit his problems or recognize how his behavior affects others. In most cases the narcissist is in counseling for some other reason, such as depression, or his spouse insisted he seek treatment under threat of divorce. Although narcissists typically drop out of treatment, those who stick with it may experience some improvement in their symptoms.[16]

THE NARCISSISTIC PERSONALITY IN RELATIONSHIPS

With such insensitivity and their excessive sense of entitlement, narcissists have great difficulty forming true, mutually loving relationships. In some cases, the contrived confidence of narcissists gives them an image that is attractive and seductive and can draw the naïve or gullible other into a relationship, sometimes with ease. Sadly, these relationships frequently descend into abuse, where the narcissist uses his partner and children only for the purpose of maintaining his image and achieving his goals. The partner of a narcissist may spend her life taking care of most of the chores for raising children, doing housework, and managing the narcissist's business-related dinner parties, even as she works an outside full-time job equal to his. If the partner is unable to show deference to the narcissist's needs and desires, the narcissist may angrily accuse her of being selfish. I heard one obvious narcissist, impeccably groomed and dressed, say that his wife "dumped me right out of the blue, even though things were just fine, and she had been perfectly happy until she left."

VIGNETTE: Extreme Self-Centeredness
As described by Lee's ex-girlfriend: *We had a long-distance relationship at first, and Lee expected me to drive up to see him at a moment's notice, even though I had just started a new furniture business and needed to be here to keep the business afloat. But I really liked Lee, so I tried to do as he wished. When Lee wanted sex, he just assumed I would be grateful that he wanted me. Then he would fish for compliments about his performance until I learned to avoid the fishing expedition by just throwing in the praise. But Lee did seem genuinely interested in me, at least until he knew he had me locked firmly into a relationship. At that point, his intense focus on me seemed to shift to other interests. It was as if the trophy was now his, and he needed something more. The man who said he would do anything for me just expected me to show up, while offering little caring and affection in return, unless he was trying to manipulate me to get something—usually sex. But I was in denial and in love, and I made the big mistake of moving in with Lee. Soon after moving in,*

I began to notice that Lee frequently talked about how his colleagues at the law firm did not recognize how good he was at his job. He criticized his coworkers if they made a mistake, but it was their fault if he screwed up. If Lee was not criticizing his coworkers, he was criticizing the chef, the waiter, the repairman, or anyone else whose service he sought. At the end of the day, Lee might ask me how my day went, but I had not talked much before he turned the conversation around to a discussion of the wonderful things he had done or was planning to do.

And I was just gullible enough to allow Lee to talk me into spending my entire savings on a business project that he assured me could not fail. When the project failed, it was everybody's fault but his. If I complained, Lee just told me I was ungrateful and that I should appreciate how much he did for me. My opinions simply did not matter. Sometimes Lee would actually admit something was his fault and even get bummed out about it, but it was only a matter of time before he reverted back to Mr. Superiority. I finally began to wake up and smell the roses when Lee started making sarcastic jokes about my appearance, sometimes in front of other people. It seemed I was not going to the gym and working out as much as he thought I should.

When I described my life to a friend who had been married to a narcissist, she talked about how her ex-husband, a cab driver, lived in a fantasy world in which he was exceptionally brilliant and destined for greatness. She said her husband would get angry when their children did not make straight As in school in some kind of a projection of his assumed brilliance onto their children. She finally realized her husband seemed to think that an imperfect wife and imperfect children reflected poorly on him in some way. Everything was about him. My friend explained the extreme irrationality of the narcissist to me, which was later confirmed by a second therapist during another attempt at therapy with Lee. The first therapist missed the narcissism and just treated me like I was equally responsible for our problems. It was my friend who saved me from having children with a narcissist. I lost a lot, including my bank account, my self-esteem, and my dreams for the future, but Lee is gone now, and I can finally work toward getting those things back.

Predictably, most relationships involving a narcissist do not last very long—except when they do. Unfortunately, some people who become romantically involved with a narcissist have their own issues, such as a dependent, avoidant, or otherwise insecure personality, and they may endure the narcissist's abusive behavior for years or decades. Feeling like it is their own inadequacy as a partner that causes the narcissist's abusive behavior, they tell themselves they should feel lucky to be involved with such a great partner. One of the biggest mistakes the partner of a narcissist, or anyone else dealing with a narcissist, can make is expecting their influence to somehow change the narcissist into a decent human being who cares about the feelings and needs of others. The narcissist, by definition, believes he is superior to everyone and will probably never believe he needs to change. The narcissist will think it is his partner who is the problem and needs to change and recognize how wonderful he is and accept how lucky she is to have him. The narcissist will probably choose anger, rage, and grudges long before changing his attitude. Needless to say, most relationships with a narcissist will involve some level of abusive behavior. As with most abusive relationships, I frequently end up viewing the abused spouse as my real client during therapy sessions. The abused spouse is infinitely more likely to change his or her attitude and ineffective responses to the narcissistic abuse than is the narcissistic abuser to change his narcissistic and abusive ways for the long term. Most narcissists will never change.

THE HISTRIONIC PERSONALITY

This description covers multiple levels of histrionic patterns of thought, emotion, and behavior. Those with fewer or milder traits, as well as those with the symptoms of a serious disorder, may readily identify some of their thinking, as well as emotional and behavioral tendencies. A more comprehensive understanding of self usually requires an ongoing self-observation and self-reflection over time. These traits are found in both men and women.

INDIVIDUALS WITH THE histrionic personality, sometimes referred to as the "hysterical" personality, are highly emotional and typically have a need to be the center of attention most of the time. Their emotionality and need to be the center of attention may play themselves out in multiple settings, including work, social events, relationships, etc.

VIGNETTE: The Melodramatic
As described by the author: *Liza comes to the regular dinner parties in provocative dress with very loose, low-cut blouses that reveal considerable cleavage, and one expects an accident at any moment. Upon entrance, Liza goes around the room and gives everyone a big hug and expresses in a loud voice how happy she is to see them. Liza's exit strategy is the same. When Liza is leaving, she will again go around the room hugging people with a performance of true caring and intimacy, even though the other guests generally do not even like her. Those not in Liza's grasp are, once again, focused on her very audible good-byes to others. During*

the party, Liza will be exuberantly flirtatious, while manipulating the topic of conversation toward herself and what is going on in her life. Even one-on-one conversations with Liza are usually turned around to where she is the subject via stories she may have embellished considerably. Occasionally, someone will say something that upsets Liza, and her angry outburst is heard throughout the room. Liza has noticed that people distance themselves from her, but she never seems to catch on that she is the cause. As Liza sees it, her problems are the result of the way other people treat her. Of course, Liza never hears the negative conversations about her after she has left the party. As long as Liza does not learn to recognize her histrionic symptoms, she will routinely drive people away or be driven away from one social group after another, only to start over with a new group somewhere else. This pattern may repeat itself for decades. Liza remains unaware that most people do not miss her when she does not come to the weekly get-together.

When histrionics are not the focal point of interest, they tend to become uncomfortable or ill at ease and may experience some level of depression. Desiring constant attention, the histrionic's life becomes preoccupied with attempts to impress and gain the limelight through appearance or behavior. They may discuss their clothing and general appearance to elicit compliments. Their behavior may be excessively enthusiastic and animated or overly flirtatious, and their dramatic flamboyance may embarrass those who witness the display. To this end, histrionics may spend considerable amounts of money on their hair, clothes, etc., and dress in a sexually seductive way. They may carry this melodramatic flirtatiousness to embarrassing extremes, even when there is no romantic interest, or in inappropriate situations, such as a work setting. Throughout these performances, histrionics may display little or no apparent awareness of how unacceptable their behavior has become. When compliments are not forthcoming, or if they are openly criticized, histrionics may experience emotions on a continuum from mild irritation through more serious stress, anxiety, or depression.[15]

In the above example, Liza's flirtatious dress and behavior have no actual romantic content or intentions but are the way that Liza has learned to get people to focus on her. It is the same when her entrances to, or exits from, social events involve considerable volume and bear hugs, even for people she hardly knows. It is no surprise that histrionics find themselves unpopular, especially with same-sex friends who are especially put off by the sexual content of their interactions, combined with their constant need to be the center of attention. As a result of this sexualization of self, histrionics may view themselves as great lovers, although they are frequently unhappy with their actual relationships and sex life. In fact, their romantic life may involve little in the way of real intimacy. Histrionics seem unaware that their sexual flirtatiousness is designed more to gain attention than to reflect who they are as a person.

With shallow emotions being the guiding force in histrionics' lives, they tend to form "impressions" of people and things based on their emotional reactions, rather than experiencing a more logical thought process given to details and specifics.[28] The speech of the histrionic will lean toward overall impressions. For example, the histrionic may state, "It was just so wonderful," yet seem puzzled if asked for the specific reasons that led to this conclusion. With the objective details lost in the more emotional impression, the histrionic may struggle with a lack of substantiating information and finally just repeat some variation of, "It was just so wonderful." The histrionic is also prone to becoming very upset and emotional, even crying, for little reason. They may also become extremely angry over minor events. With little real depth to their emotions, histrionics may experience quick changes in their emotions whenever they are distracted by something new.

Easily bored, the usual daily routines of life may not sit well with histrionics. They may become restless with the repetitiveness of daily life and may seek stimulation from new sources. But histrionics may quickly become bored with any new pastime and impatiently renew their search for a more interesting endeavor. The shallow and fleeting nature of histrionics' emotions makes them very suggestible and subject to the manipulations of advertisers, fads, or manipulative partners. They may quickly change their opinions and emotions to meet the requirements of a significant other or a respected authority figure. It is the shallowness and changeable nature of histrionics' emotions that cause other people not to take them seriously. Fortunately for some histrionics, their symptoms may subside somewhat over time, as indicated by research that finds fewer histrionics in older populations.[15]

THE HISTRIONIC PERSONALITY IN RELATIONSHIPS

The emotionality of the histrionic does not lend itself to stability in relationships. A relationship with a histrionic may work well during the initial honeymoon stage of the relationship, stimulated by emotional intensity combined with intimate conversations. Even in the early stages of the relationship, the histrionic will be unhappy if he is not the focal point of the partner's attention at any given moment. As with Liza in the vignette, most conversations will be turned around to a discussion about some aspect of the histrionic's life, but this may initially go unnoticed by the partner's honeymoon level of infatuation and desire to please the new love interest. The tendency of histrionics to view most relationships, even casual ones, as more intimate than they actually are shows up when they quickly view a new love relationship as a deep commitment. They may just as easily become bored with a relationship and drop it to seek a new one.

The partner must be able to tolerate the histrionic's nonstop attempts to get his attention as well as the attention of others. This may include embarrassing dramatic and flirtatious performances with others as the partner stands there in embarrassed silence. The partner may have figured out that there is no actual sexual content in the histrionic's flirtatious attention-seeking behavior, and that the histrionic has little or no awareness of how unacceptable her behavior is, but this may not help the partner with his embarrassment.

The histrionic's behavior may eventually wear the partner down. The histrionic's partner may tire of the dramatic public performances and constant need for attention. Financial difficulties may occur as the histrionic spends considerable amounts of money on clothes designed specifically to get attention. Any attempt by the histrionic's partner to discuss his own needs or perspective will usually be ignored as the histrionic manipulates the conversation back to a discussion of her needs. Histrionics may use their romantic seductiveness to control a relationship for their own ends, while appearing needy and dependent at the same time. Controlling a relationship by playing the victim is a common scenario. Having watched the histrionic repeatedly become very upset or cry over insignificant events, the partner may have recognized the superficial nature of the histrionic's thinking and emotions as well as the histrionic's inability to make a deep emotional commitment. It may be a matter of time before the histrionic becomes bored with the relationship and seeks greater excitement with a new partner.

SIMILARITIES AND DIFFERENCES

While more women than men are diagnosed as histrionic, it is very likely that sex-role stereotypes skew these statistics. Descriptions of histrionic traits and characteristics might make it easier to spot the provocatively dressed woman who emphasizes how much people talk about her than the well-dressed male businessman who gets attention by talking about his power, notoriety in business or sports, or talks about his accumulated wealth and possessions, etc. These, of course, are characteristics of the narcissistic personality as well.

Like histrionics, narcissists want to be the center of attention, but the narcissist must be viewed as superior, while histrionics are actually not that concerned about how they are viewed as long as they are the center of attention. Narcissistic individuals also view their relationships as highly intimate, but unlike histrionics, they emphasize the status and importance of their spouse or partner to help support their perfect image of themselves. Differentiating between the histrionic and the borderline or dependent personality can be difficult as well. Like histrionics, borderlines have high emotionality, seek attention, and manipulate others, but borderlines may be more self-destructive with rage, demands, and chronic identity disturbances or feelings of emptiness and depersonalization. Like histrionics, individuals with a dependent personality are known to rely on others for attention and guidance, but the dependent is willing to remain in the background, whereas the histrionic goes over the top to be the center of attention.

THE DEPENDENT PERSONALITY

This description covers multiple levels of dependent patterns of thought, emotion, and behavior. Those with fewer or milder traits, as well as those with the symptoms of a serious disorder, may readily identify some of their thinking, as well as emotional and behavioral tendencies. A more comprehensive understanding of self usually requires an ongoing self-observation and self-reflection over time. These traits are found in both men and women.

TRAITS ASSOCIATED WITH the dependent personality are quite common in the general population, although most people experiencing dependent traits do not experience the more severe and sometimes incapacitating symptoms of a diagnosable disorder. Many dependents are not aware of the traits and symptoms they experience. Some dependents, especially men, may view dependency needs as indicating immaturity or weakness and may have difficulty admitting they have dependent thoughts and feelings.[27]

VIGNETTE: Insecurity and Neediness

As told by the author: *As long as Tina can remember, she has had no confidence in her ability to do anything. Growing up in a very patriarchal family, Tina recalls her brothers becoming very self-reliant, while her father just assumed she would need help with everything and usually took care of things for her. Tina's mother was an alcoholic and was usually critical of anything Tina did or wanted to do. Given this environment, it is no surprise that Tina has very low self-esteem and no confidence whatever in her ability to make either major or minor* decisions. Tina's inability to assert herself with her parents continued into her adult relationships, where she deferred all decisions to her boyfriend because she was afraid she would make the wrong decision. She rarely expressed disagreement or anger with her boyfriend about anything out of a fear that she might upset him and he might leave her. At work, Tina was quick to defer to coworkers she believed were much smarter and more competent than she was.

When Tina did not have a boyfriend, she would become desperate to find someone to help her with her extreme loneliness and feelings of inadequacy. She was always willing to date almost anyone who asked her out. With no filters to help her spot the red flags given off by abusers, Tina has been trapped in several abusive relationships. She met her last pseudo-boyfriend in a bar, and for the next five years, they would meet at a bar twice a week, have some drinks, and then go to her apartment where they would have sex, sometimes followed by physical abuse. Her pseudo-boyfriend would completely ignore her the rest of the time. Yet Tina found herself unable to leave him for five years.

When she finally did leave him, she became involved with a much nicer guy for a few months until he ended their relationship. Cratering into extreme feelings of loneliness and inadequacy, Tina picked up the phone and rekindled a relationship with the abuser for several months. Tina is less afraid of even extreme abuse than she is of feeling alone and helpless. Just a few weeks after leaving this abuser for the second time, Tina walked up to me and showed me her wedding ring. She had married another guy after knowing him for only one month. Her pseudo-husband would leave her alone in her apartment on weekdays, showing up only on weekends for sex. Tina deferred all decisions to her husband, including when to have sex, how often, and in what way. Tina said the sex seemed to be his only interest. When I asked Tina why she married him, she replied, "He asked me." Tina finally started taking an *antidepressant medication with excellent results, and said she felt good for the first time in her life. Unfortunately, Tina was still a sex slave the last time I saw her.*

At more severe levels, the dependent personality involves an extreme need to be cared for, such that the dependent is overly submissive, obedient, and will cling to others even in a relationship that is highly dysfunctional and abusive. Dependents do not believe they can manage their lives very well, even concerning everyday decisions, without excessive guidance, advice, and reassurance from other people. They may need help with minor decisions, such as what to wear, or with more important decisions, such as where they should live, which career to pursue, which school to attend, etc. Dependents may try to be with other people for protection or simply to avoid the helpless feeling they get when they are alone. Dependents try to gain the emotional support of others, and in some cases seek outright domination by rarely expressing anger and agreeing outwardly with almost anything regardless of their true feelings or beliefs. Dependent individuals may be almost paralyzed by fear of what others are thinking, so work and career problems are common, as they appear chronically helpless and unproductive to coworkers and management. Dependents tend to be very pessimistic and may be reluctant to start new projects on their own, since they are convinced others can do a better job, so why even try? Even constructive criticism may be taken as proof of their inferiority and incompetence. Dependents may even go so far as to intentionally maintain the appearance of incompetence so that the people who are helping them will not leave them alone.

In the absence of criticism from others, dependents are sure to criticize themselves with frequent thoughts about their failings and inferior status. Self-criticism, combined with their inability to take risks, learn new skills, and experience the normal failures that teach us about life, may create a vicious circle of increasing dependence that lowers their self-confidence and self-esteem even further. Ideally, those managing a dependent in a work environment will recognize that, in most cases, if the dependent individual receives the ongoing acceptance, support, and supervision they need, they will usually be able to do very competent work while demonstrating fierce loyalty to the company. In the right environment, dependency patterns may actually improve an individual's work performance via the dependent's willingness to seek support and assistance when needed, rather than produce inferior work by going it alone.[17]

The traditional view that dependents repeatedly offer the same responses to life situations has been challenged by more recent research that suggests dependent behavior is actually somewhat calculated, depending on the situation and context. The dependent may choose more passive or more assertive behavior based on their calculation of which type of response will gain them the care and nurturing they seek.[24,25,26]

THE DEPENDENT PERSONALITY IN RELATIONSHIPS

The life of a dependent may revolve almost completely around their partner or close relatives. In severe cases, dependent's social relationships may be limited almost completely to their partner or just one other person, such as a parent, that they look to for guidance. A successful relationship with a dependent may require the partner's commitment to more or less continuous guidance and interaction with the dependent. This, of course, will be to the neglect of any independence that the partner may desire. The dependent may have little or no experience at taking care of his own needs, and any progress toward greater independence may occur only gradually, although individual and couples therapy can be very effective at helping to alter the dependent's behavior. Any attempts by the partner to quickly alter the level of dependency in the relationship may be interpreted by the dependent as rejection. Feeling rejected, the dependent's needy and clingy behavior will only escalate, fueled by a desperate need to hang on to their partner to avoid being alone. Rejection in relationships is painful for anyone, but for dependents, real or imagined rejection and the thought of losing their partner may be simply terrifying. Dependents may be unaware of the destructive and self-defeating nature of their clingy and needy behavior and the increasing likelihood their behavior will drive their partner away. Not all potential partners for the dependent will be able, or willing, to sacrifice their own needs for the sake of the relationship for the long term.

Unfortunately, the excessive attempts to obtain nurturance, emotional support, or protection from others sets the dependent up to be used and abused. They may submit to the excessive demands of their partner or tolerate verbal, physical, or sexual abuse to avoid being abandoned. And when a relationship does end, dependents may immediately become involved with the very next person who shows any interest in them. In some cases, dependents' self-identity is determined more by who they are *with* than who they actually *are*. A classic example of this odd emotional crutch would be the wife of actor Spencer Tracy, who wanted very much to stay married to him for years so she could continue to be "Mrs. Spencer Tracy," all the while knowing his true love to be Katharine Hepburn.

Individual and couples therapy, especially if followed by group therapy, can be very successful with dependent personalities. This is especially the case if the dependent's partner is willing to join in the therapeutic process and participate in exercises designed to expand the dependent's level of independence and interaction with others. Do not expect a linear improvement in the dependent's symptoms. In most cases, there will be periods of improvement mixed with periods of increased fear and anxiety. Encouraging immediate changes in the dependent's behavior, or encouraging the dependent to stand up to an abusive partner, boss, etc., may only increase the dependent's fears.[5] This is especially the case when therapy first begins. A very important ingredient in these relationships is the commitment of the partner to a very supportive role for the long term. The dependent's partner needs to offer support, encouragement, compliments, etc. within a relationship that is, essentially, devoid of disapproval, criticism, and especially, humiliation. Even with constructive criticism, the partner must openly display a caring attitude, or the constructive aspect will be missed completely.

There is strong evidence for both genetic and environmental influences in dependent personalities.[18] Environmental causes of dependent traits may include overprotective parenting during which children may learn they need a powerful caretaker[18] or authoritarian/dictatorial parenting where children learn to seek and accept direction and control by others.[25] Other causes may include chronic physical illness or separation anxiety disorder during childhood or adolescence. Some studies suggest dependent personalities are more common in females, while other studies indicate a more equal prevalence. It is always possible that gender and sex-role stereotypes create a bias in researchers such that women are more likely to be viewed as weak and submissive.

SIMILARITIES AND DIFFERENCES

Many different personalities have overlapping traits and characteristics, and understanding the differences and similarities is important. To avoid confusion, it is especially important to understand the similarities and differences between the dependent and the borderline personalities. For example, individuals with borderline personalities fear abandonment just like the dependent personality. The difference is that borderlines react to abandonment with rage, demands, and emotional emptiness, whereas the dependent personality reacts with increased submissiveness and attempts to reconcile or start another relationship to regain the perceived care and support that was just lost. Borderlines may also have had a greater number of unstable relationships in their past than dependents since the dependent is usually willing to do whatever it takes to save a relationship.

Like the dependent, histrionics may be clingy in relationships with a need for constant approval, but the histrionic is also characterized by an outgoing sociability with attempts to gain attention, whereas dependents are docile and shrink from the limelight. Like dependents, individuals with an avoidant personality are hypersensitive to criticism and need continuous approval and reassurance to assuage their feelings of inadequacy. Avoidants differ from dependents in their tendency to withdraw from others to varying degrees unless they are assured of acceptance, whereas dependent individuals seek out relationships to obtain the guidance, approval, protection, and dominance they need to get through the coming day. Mood disorders, such as depression and anxiety disorders, may co-occur with dependent personalities.

THE PASSIVE-AGGRESSIVE PERSONALITY

This description covers multiple levels of passive-aggressive patterns of thought, emotion, and behavior. Those with fewer or milder traits, as well as those with the symptoms of a serious disorder, may readily identify some of their thinking, as well as emotional and behavioral tendencies. A more comprehensive understanding of self usually requires an ongoing self-observation and self-reflection over time. These traits are found in both men and women.

PASSIVE-AGGRESSIVE PERSONALITIES and their passive resistance to authority were first recognized during World War II, when it was noticed that some soldiers were antagonistic to their superiors and resistant to performing their duties.[32] The essential feature of the passive-aggressive personality involves "a pervasive pattern of negativistic attitudes and passive resistance to demands for adequate performance in social and occupational situations."[33] The passive-aggressive is routinely resentful of, and resistant to, authority such that environments where authority is the norm, such as work or the military, are the most common breeding grounds for these behaviors. Passive-aggressives may also be resistant in social situations and relationships. There has been considerable controversy among professionals as to whether the passive-aggressive personality reflects a specific personality, whether the traits and symptoms involved are caused by some other underlying problem, or simply reflect an individual who just chooses to be stubborn, self-centered, irresponsible, and contrary as a lifestyle choice. The latter appears to be the dominant view since the passive aggressive personality has been eliminated from the DSM-5. Either way, recognizable passive-aggressive personalities do exist and in severe cases may be quite striking in their presentation.

Essentially, passive-aggressive individuals are aggressive, but in a passive way, to an institution or an individual with whom they are angry and resentful because they believe they have been treated unfairly or denied the recognition they deserve. This passive resistance may involve a refusal to perform as expected through procrastination and delay, negligence, appearing absentminded or forgetful, or just general stubbornness and contrarian behavior. These are not happy people, and they tend to be pessimistic, irritable, cynical, and complaining as they routinely blame other people for their problems and behavior. They are quick to focus their anger on a specific authority figure, such as a spouse, boss, teacher, etc. The schism in their thinking may become apparent when they reverse course and try to appease those they are unhappy with by admitting their failings and promising to do better, only to drift back into a pattern of quiet resistance. Exhibiting low self-confidence and pessimism about the future, their pattern of complaining eventually becomes tiresome and frustrating for others.

THE PASSIVE-AGGRESSIVE IN RELATIONSHIPS

I have found it is the partner who is involved with a passive-aggressive that suffers the most from the passive-aggressive's manipulations and resistance. As with many personality styles and disorders, the effects of the passive-aggressive's attitudes, moods, and antics in a relationship are quite predictable. The passive-aggressive can be fired from his job, but relationships are not that simple, especially if there are children involved. The partner of a passive-aggressive may realize their relationship bears almost no resemblance to the mutually caring partnership she had expected. The passive-aggressive may view his partner as just one more authority figure to be stonewalled, and the passive-aggressive is practiced at the art of manipulation and deception. How a relationship with a passive-aggressive plays itself out may be determined, in part, by how skilled the passive-aggressive is at manipulating his partner's perceptions of his moods, behavior, and resistance. Of course, the partner's perceptions of the passive-aggressive may be influenced by the partner's own personality, including any naïveté, denial, submissiveness, etc.

VIGNETTE: Resistance and Manipulation

As described by Sean's wife: *I noticed Sean's critical side when I first met him, but his criticisms were always directed at other people, politicians, organizations, and a few of my friends who were not to his liking. Sean was big on sarcasm as part of his attempts to feel superior to those he criticized. But Sean would allow me to have my say, and early on, we had many spirited debates that were interesting and fun. Unfortunately, I moved in with Sean just a few months into our relationship, and Sean soon became negative about anything and everything. Sean never talked about his job except to say his coworkers were not carrying their share of the workload, and he was not going to bust his ass to enable their laziness. This did not quite add up for me, since Sean had changed jobs several times in three years over similar complaints. What sounded like legitimate complaints early in our relationship began to sound like the complaints of a lazy person projecting his lazy attitude onto his coworkers. I began to realize that Sean would rather be lazy and a failure at many jobs than work hard and be successful at one job.*

It seemed like Sean had "victim" tattooed across his forehead. Sean would get irritated when I asked him to do something, and then he would intentionally do it wrong or forget to do it altogether. Sean became very easy to anger, and he would hold on to his anger for extended periods of time. Sean had become increasingly critical of me over my alleged failure to do my share of the housework, which was ludicrous considering Sean's forgetful attitude and procrastination about the work he was supposed to do. When Sean did begin a project, it rarely got finished.

On one occasion, I got really angry, and Sean admitted his failure, apologized, and even shed a few tears, but the real change I had hoped for never materialized. Soon after this event, Sean made some snide remark about my appearance in front of some friends, and we had an argument right there in front of everyone. At that point, I became uncomfortable with the idea of a future that included Sean, so I enrolled in nursing school to secure a future for myself. Sean began to complain about the amount of time I needed to study for classes, and I began to sense that my schoolwork and my potential for advancement in my job had become a threat to him. When I needed Sean to do something for me so I could have more study time, he always had some excuse why he could not do it. It just seemed like he wanted me to fail or drop out of school altogether.

The more I began to understand Sean's distorted view of other people and the world, the more I began to stand up for myself and refuse to allow my opinions and feelings to be manipulated. It was the realization that the way he treated me, my friends, and his coworkers was manipulative and abusive that caused me to finally leave him. When we discussed the characteristics of the passive-aggressive personality with a therapist, Sean first denied that this was his problem, but later on, he used the diagnosis as an excuse for his behavior. He kept saying, "I can't help it."

The passive-aggressive does not openly avoid doing his share in a relationship. The goal of the passive-aggressive is to procrastinate and delay, while manipulating his partner into thinking he is either doing his share or that his failure to do his share is in no way his fault. Rather than outright stubbornness, the passive-aggressive comes across as sincere in his efforts and determination to do his best, while dealing with problems that just seem to get in his way and prevent him from doing his job. The passive-aggressive may also come across as unintentionally absentminded and forgetful, which he brushes off by pointing out that everyone forgets things. He just could not get home in time to mow the lawn, and could the partner please get up early to take the kids to school so he can get some needed sleep or get some urgent work done on his computer? It is not his fault that there is not enough money for the family because his coworkers sabotage his chances for promotions by making problems at work appear to be his fault. It is his coworkers who cause him to never get a raise or promotion, or he keeps getting fired by unfair bosses who are just out to get him. It is an act of appearing to try very hard, while just not seeming to get things done. At the same time, the passive-aggressive may dump his anger and hostility onto his partner while accusing her of not doing her share of the work. Of course, the partner has little to do with the passive-aggressive's attitude. His anger and resentment were already there before she met him.

As with some other personality styles and disorders, the behavior of the passive-aggressive can legitimately be described as abusive. The partner of a passive-aggressive may eventually become worn down by the passive-aggressive's constant negative attitude and resentment at her for expecting too much from him and not appreciating how hard he tries to do his best. The passive-aggressive's thinly veiled criticisms of his partner, possibly disguised as constructive criticism or sarcastic jokes, may seriously damage the partner's self-esteem and self-confidence. When this happens, the depressed partner is even less likely to recognize the abusive nature of the relationship. As with most abusers, the passive-aggressive's abusive side usually does not show up until the partner is firmly entrenched in the relationship. The abusive nature of the passive-aggressive's behavior eventually becomes obvious to those who know what to look for. As the passive-aggressive's criticisms and manipulations take their toll, and as the partner's self-esteem and self-confidence ebb lower and lower, the partner may sometimes wonder if she is, in fact, being unfair and expecting too much from him. Many of those who are involved with an abuser, whether he is passive-aggressive or not, will blame themselves and actually believe the abuser's criticisms, veiled or otherwise, that she is the one who needs to change her ways.

Whether passive-aggressive traits and symptoms reflect a separate personality style or disorder or are symptoms of some other underlying problem is yet to be resolved. It is important to consider the possibility that some other personality or mood issue may play a role in the passive-aggressive's behavior. Depression, in particular, is a common ingredient in the passive-aggressive personality. Help from a knowledgeable professional may be warranted. I encourage those living with a passive-aggressive to also read the chapter on the abusive personality and abusive relationships.

THE ANTISOCIAL PERSONALITY

This description covers multiple levels of antisocial patterns of thought, emotion, and behavior. Those with fewer or milder traits, as well as those with the symptoms of a serious disorder, may readily identify some of their thinking, as well as emotional and behavioral tendencies. A more comprehensive understanding of self usually requires an ongoing self-observation and self-reflection over time. These traits are found in both men and women but are much more common in men.

THE BASIC CHARACTERISTICS of the antisocial personality include "a pervasive pattern of disregard for, and violation of, the rights of others that begins in childhood or early adolescence and continues into adulthood."[1] The most common characteristics of the antisocial personality may be summed up as deceitfulness and manipulation. Antisocial personalities are much more common in men than women and are generally associated with individuals in lower income brackets. An official diagnosis of antisocial personality *disorder* requires the individual to be at least 18 years of age when diagnosed but to have a history of *conduct disorder* beginning before the age of 15 years. There are four categories of behaviors associated with childhood or adolescent conduct disorder:

1) ***Aggression toward people and animals***: bullying, threatening, fighting, rape, etc.
2) ***Destruction of property***: vandalism, starting fires, smashing car windows, etc.
3) ***Deceitfulness and/or theft***: breaking into a home or car, lying or breaking promises to obtain favors or avoid debts, stealing, shoplifting, forgery, etc.

4) ***Serious violation of rules***: disregarding parental curfew, truancy from school, breaking other school rules, etc.

VIGNETTE: The Juvenile Delinquent
As described by the author: *I knew Donny when I was about 16 years of age, and we were both high school dropouts. I dropped out of high school twice, although I finally graduated three months shy of my 21st birthday. I have always assumed Donny never finished high school. Donny was really into the drug scene, but I sold my share of marijuana and pill-like things. I used a needle with amphetamines six times. This is scary, considering one of my high school classmates died from hepatitis after using a needle just once, and three of my high school friends died decades to early from continued drug use. I used to walk down the street at 3 o'clock in the morning with friends checking for unlocked car doors. We never took the guns we found, but we took a lot of other stuff. Donny stole a car at least once. I know that because I stole it with him. Thinking big, I served probation when I was 17 for breaking into laundromat machine coin boxes with a crowbar. I ran away from home at age 16 and got caught in California after working in a car wash for six weeks. After a few days in juvey, I was airplaned home to distraught "Where did we go wrong?" parents.*

While conduct disorder usually does not result in antisocial behavior in adults,[40] I would be surprised if Donny's juvenile delinquency, which clearly ran in his family, did not eventually warrant a diagnosis of antisocial personality disorder or sociopathy (described later). In my case, the juvenile delinquency dissipated as soon as I left the severely dysfunctional home in which I was raised. It is very easy for someone like me to see why you cannot diagnose someone with antisocial personality disorder prior to the age of 18, since my behavior was juvenile and delinquent past that numerical age, and there is not an antisocial bone in my body. I have found adolescent turmoil and immaturity to last well into the 20s and even into the 30s for some people, including many who do not break the law.

When this kind of thinking and behavior continues into adulthood, there may be a broader failure to conform to the law. This may include conning others for personal pleasure, profit, or other benefits through false presentations of self, such as fake IDs, the use of aliases, etc. The antisocial may be impulsive in their decisions, with little thought of future consequences to themselves or other people. Impulsive decisions may result in not showing up for work, getting fired repeatedly, refusing to support their family, little or no financial planning, drug/alcohol abuse, drunk driving, and on and on. The antisocial may also be highly aggressive, with a record of physical assault, and they are usually abusive in relationships, which may include the abuse of children. The abuse in relationships usually plays itself out in terms of power and control, and frequent cheating and affairs are common. Through it all, the antisocial may show little remorse for anything, while rationalizing everything, and blame their victims, saying they deserved it.

Having difficulty with authority, antisocials may receive dishonorable discharges from the military, and some may eventually become destitute or homeless. As you might expect, antisocial personalities are common in the nation's prison systems. Antisocials may also have premature and sometimes violent deaths. One of the gang members that ran with Bonnie and Clyde, and survived the experience, died decades later in a bar from a shotgun blast. It is interesting that antisocials, caring so little about the rights of other people, may actually have a very close relationship with their mothers. This becomes apparent when they are imprisoned and want to have very close contact with their mother, calling her every day if possible.

To spot the antisocial, watch for someone with a lofty, pumped-up appraisal of himself that includes an arrogance that is overly opinionated and self-confident. They may be conceited and believe that ordinary work is beneath them. Antisocials are not realistic about their problems or the impact of events on their future. It is common for antisocials to complain about boredom or depression, and their impulsiveness makes them prone to addictions such as drugs, alcohol, gambling, etc. Some antisocial individuals may initially have an appealing personality, as they struggle to make themselves appear more intellectual, capable, friendly, educated, etc. than they actually are. But the surface nature of their persona becomes obvious rather quickly to those who are less gullible.

What causes some people to develop antisocial personalities, and not others, remains a mystery, but the major suspects include problems with impulse control and dysfunctional or abusive childhoods.[13] While many antisocials in prison tend to be from lower socioeconomic backgrounds, other antisocials have college degrees and engage in white-collar crimes.[122] It does appear that children from unstable homes, with inconsistent discipline or erratic parenting, and especially homes where the child experiences neglect and abuse, have a higher likelihood that childhood conduct disorder will evolve into an antisocial personality as the child grows into adulthood. The likelihood of developing an antisocial personality is greater with the appearance of conduct disorder before age 10 and accompanied by attention deficit hyperactivity disorder (ADHD).

There is evidence that more aggressive antisocial personality disorder in adults is correlated with neurobiological activity in the brain,[13] and adoption studies have shown that both genetic and environmental factors play a role in the development of antisocial personalities. Both adopted and biological children of parents who are antisocial are at greater risk for developing an antisocial personality themselves. While adopted children are more likely to turn out like their biological parents than their adoptive parents, the adoptive environment does have an influence on the outcome. Researchers are also discovering genetic markers that may explain why those suffering an antisocial personality are very likely to become substance abusers or addicts as well.[13] This, of course, reflects the "nature or nurture" debate that weaves its way throughout the behavioral sciences.

The nature-or-nurture issue arises again when we recognize that antisocial personalities are about three times more common in men than women. Explanations for this disparity center around the biological differences between men and women, the socialization process where a male-dominated society expects men to be more aggressive than women, or just a general expectation or bias that more men than women will have antisocial personalities.[13]

Antisocials may have difficulty even recognizing that they have a problem, so it is no surprise that they may never change.[41] For the antisocials who survive long enough, the disorder does tend to lessen with age and sometimes disappears completely in the later years. Criminal behavior is the most likely antisocial symptom to decrease with age, but all symptoms, including substance abuse, may decrease over time.

Antisocials usually do not seek treatment on their own, and when forced into treatment by their spouse or the courts, they will likely fake compliance rather than put forth any real effort to understand themselves and change their ways. In therapy, the antisocial may act like he is interested in the therapeutic process, while actually caring very little.[49]

It has been suggested that the antisocial personality is an extreme variant of the narcissistic personality.[43] Both of these personalities tend to be self-confident, conceited, determined to get their way and, with little empathy for others, will exploit others to get what they want. But antisocials do not need the admiration of others as much as the narcissist, while narcissists tend to not be as impulsive and aggressive as the antisocial. Narcissists also tend to not have a history of conduct disorder in childhood or criminal behavior in adulthood. Co-occurrence among personalities is common, and many personalities have traits that overlap those associated with the antisocial personality. The help of a knowledgeable professional may help to avoid confusion in some cases.

THE ANTISOCIAL PERSONALITY IN RELATIONSHIPS

The partner of the antisocial may look back and wonder what the original attraction was to someone so inconsiderate and self-centered. It is important to remember that the antisocial personality may have the same acting ability typically associated with the narcissistic personality, including an excess of self-confidence and charisma.

VIGNETTE: Uncaring Meanness

As told by Tom's ex-girlfriend: *When I first met Tom, he came across as friendly and self-confident. He was very attentive, and I sometimes had the feeling of being swept off my feet. Things were great for several months, but then Tom seemed to change. With increasing frequency, Tom would not seem very concerned about me, or anything else, for that matter. He was a crazy driver, with little concern for anyone's safety. He would sometimes just ignore me, refuse to answer his phone, and repeatedly forget about the plans we had made. He would later just casually say he* *forgot or had changed his mind. Any promises he made turned out to be for manipulative purposes only. If I pointed out to Tom that his ignoring me was painful, he would just say that he had been busy and had a lot on his mind or that I was too sensitive. If I persisted with the discussion, Tom would get angry and ask me why I was always hassling him. If he had been drinking, it was even worse. Tom had always consumed more alcohol than most men I had dated, and alcohol seemed to have a different effect on Tom. When drinking any kind of alcohol, Tom would become more and more belligerent and loud and just act like he ruled the world. Sometimes when he talked to other people, he sounded like a bully.*

It really bothered me when Tom would flirt with other women right in front of me. If I complained, he would just say that he was a naturally friendly person and that being friendly is not the same as flirting. He would tell me that just because I was not as friendly as he was, I should not expect him to change his friendly attitude. Over the next several months, Tom would disappear and not answer his phone for long periods of time. I suspected an affair, but when I would ask him where he had been, he would just say that he had been very busy with work and simply forgot to turn his phone on. I finally began to admit to myself that there were other women in Tom's life, and that he had obviously lied to me many times. I also had to admit that it was my own gullibility and denial that allowed him to treat me this way.

I made my biggest mistake when Tom said he was laid off from his job at a beer company, and I allowed him to move in with me. I later found out he was fired for stealing several cases of beer and starting a fight with his manager when he was confronted. Tom was frequently broke because he was a spendthrift and would always spend money on nonessentials, including large amounts of alcohol, but now I had to foot the bill for both of us. For the next three months, Tom said he was looking for work, but I never saw him put out much effort. When I finally put my foot down and gave Tom a deadline for getting a job, his irritable mood turned to violence, and I was slammed against a wall and held there while he raged. At this point, I checked into his background and discovered Tom had a record for domestic violence. Tom had long admitted to some lawbreaking while growing up, but he always referred to these infractions as "mistakes." Fortunately, I had developed the strength to not hang around for a second violent attack. I filed a restraining order against Tom, and he was forced to move out of my house, but he stole money from my purse and took some of my jewelry with him. I never called the police because I never wanted to see him again, even in court.

As with some other personalities, the antisocial personality virtually guarantees an abusive relationship, and probably abused children as well. Verbal and emotional abuse may play itself out in terms of power, control, and manipulation as the antisocial concentrates on getting his own needs met, with little or no concern for the feelings and needs of his partner and children. Some level of physical abuse is always a possibility. It is the partner who will probably have to take care of most of the child-rearing and housecleaning duties, even if her daytime job requires more hours than his. As an abuser, the antisocial may have chased off potential friends by virtue of his generally uncaring attitude or, more specifically, as part of the abusive technique of isolating the partner. The partner's attempts to hold on to friends by covering for the antisocial's inconsiderate attitude with explanations and revisionism will usually fail in the long run. Most of those unfortunate enough to find themselves involved with an antisocial, or any other abusive personality, may look back and recognize early signs of his abusive nature in the way he treated other people while still being very nice and considerate to her. Cheating and extramarital affairs may be the norm for the antisocial, which not only disrupts the relationship but may expose the partner to sexually transmitted diseases. Unfortunately, antisocial men frequently become involved with women who suffer from some level of a dependent or avoidant personality. These partners are submissive and will cling to the antisocial in spite of the abusive treatment he dishes out.

Planning the family finances and sticking to a budget may be difficult or impossible for the antisocial, as he impulsively quits jobs, gets fired, and spends considerable amounts of money on himself without regard for the family's present or future needs. Unpaid mortgages and bills and repossessed cars may be reoccurring events. The antisocial's poor impulse control may also play itself out in substance abuse and addictions.

It is common for those involved with antisocials or other abusive personalities to repeatedly fall for their apologies, tears, and promises to change. Like most abusers, the antisocial figures out just how much manipulation and abuse he can dish out before he must temporarily adopt a new "Mr. Nice Guy" or "Mr. Thoughtful Husband and Father" persona to keep his partner from leaving the relationship. Mr. Nice Guy and Mr. Thoughtful Husband and Father will work very hard to convince his partner that he has changed and that things will be very different in the future. But in almost all cases, it is a manipulation designed to keep his partner from leaving him and should not to be mistaken for actual regret and remorse. It is usually just a matter of time before the uncaring nature of the antisocial takes over again. Abused partners may repeatedly allow rationalization and denial to blind them to the obvious reality of the antisocial's true nature.

Desiring a partner they can manipulate in this way, the antisocial will seek out potential mates who show signs of low self-esteem and low assertiveness, such as those suffering from a dependent or an avoidant personality. These manipulative relationships may leave the unfortunate partner feeling as if she is the one with the emotional instability, which is exactly the antisocial's goal. With increasingly lower self-esteem and lower self-confidence, it only becomes more and more difficult for an abused partner to leave the abusive relationship. The longer an abusive relationship continues, and even as the abuse increases in frequency and severity, the more difficult it is for an abused partner to leave the relationship.[12] For a more comprehensive reading of abusive relationships, read the chapter, "The Abusive Personality / Abusive Relationships."

THE SOCIOPATH / PSYCHOPATH

The terms "antisocial personality disorder," and "sociopathy," are sometimes used interchangeably since the thinking and outward behavior exhibited by these individuals are very much the same. For some professionals, the antisocial personality is an individual who has his own feelings and needs, but does not care about anyone else's feelings and needs whereas the sociopath is an individual who is essentially devoid of most feelings and emotions. Without normal feelings and emotions, the sociopath has no conscience. What follows is a brief description of the sociopathic and psychopathic personalities.

AS EXTRAORDINARY AS it seems, there are people who do not experience the feelings and emotions that most people experience on a routine basis. Devoid of most feelings and emotions, sociopaths cannot love, care about, or feel empathy for another person. They are also unable to feel shame, remorse, regret, or guilt no matter what misdeeds they have committed or plan to commit in the future, or who they have harmed. Unable to experience these emotions, these people simply do not have a conscience. Conscience is a sense of right and wrong with reference to morals, values, beliefs, ethics, etc., but a sense of right and wrong is a "feeling," and for those who are devoid of feelings, there is no conscience. Sociopaths know and understand the difference between right and wrong, but there is no emotional response connected to this difference, so they do not care. They can do whatever they want regardless of the ethics involved. Sociopaths do not think they have a problem and are quite happy with how they conduct their life and will probably never see any reason to change. They rarely go to counseling on their own but may enter counseling at the insistence of someone else such as a spouse, the courts, etc. There is no treatment that can help a sociopath develop feelings and emotions. Sociopaths are one for every 25 people.[133] They are everywhere.

We sometimes hear the term "psychopath" used in cases where the worst crimes have been committed. The conventional wisdom used to be that sociopaths and psychopaths were the same thing except the term psychopath was reserved for those committing the more heinous crimes, such as serial rapists, murderers, etc. Recent research suggests sociopaths are the products of the environment in which they are raised while the thinking and behavior of psychopaths has a genetic origin.[135] This view remains theoretical, and it is recognized that the sociopath may also have a genetic predisposition towards sociopathy that must be combined with a problematic childhood, poverty, hanging out with the wrong friends, etc., to bring sociopathic thinking to fruition. Yet not all sociopaths and psychopaths come from troubled backgrounds. Many come from very good homes, and their siblings are quite normal.

It has been suggested that psychopaths may be more impulsive, reckless, and violent than sociopaths who are more likely to think things through and plan their bad deeds accordingly. Less likely to use forethought and planning, psychopaths are more likely to get caught. Thinking things through, sociopaths are less likely to get caught and are more likely to maintain stable careers and long-term relationships than psychopaths. Still, the thinking and behavior of sociopaths and psychopaths is essentially the same—a life devoid of true emotions and little or no ability to feel love, caring, empathy, shame, regret, remorse, or guilt. They live without conscience. The descriptions here apply to both sociopaths and psychopaths, so I will just use the term sociopath.

VIGNETTE: Manipulation, Deceit, and Theft.

As told by the author: *I bought a little 1910 cabin in Colorado Springs and one of my neighbors, while clearly socially awkward, was just the nicest guy. When I first met Mike, he was stooped down next to the fence between our houses and was just saying, "Hey, hey…" followed by a question about my house. It wasn't, "Hi, I'm your neighbor Mike. What's your name?" It was just, "Hey, hey…" He later mentioned his past addictions and appeared to have replaced them with all day consumptions of coffee and nicotine, although I was later told he was back into amphetamines. Mike talked about how he was a "master carpenter." He frequently offered to do remodeling work on my house free of charge since he was out of work and bored. The master carpenter I had hired to remodel my house did hire Mike to do some work, and anytime one of my carpenters would refer to Mike as a carpenter in his presence, he would correct them with something like, "I'm a top-level master carpenter." But Mike did good work except for three mistakes that needed repairs. Several times over the next few weeks, Mike said he would fix the mistakes, "in a day or two," but he never did. My own carpenter said Mike came over at eight o'clock one morning and said he would work, but wanted to go get some coffee at his house first. He didn't come back and didn't bother to inform my carpenter that he had changed his mind.*

When I backed into my sports car with my pickup truck, Mike, just the nicest guy, said he would fix the damage for free. I insisted I would pay him, and he just shrugged. I gave Mike $300.00 cash for parts and left my car in his driveway and waited. A week later I go check on things, and Mike says he hasn't had time to go get the parts from a friend of his. I tell Mike I will go get the parts for him, and he says, "I don't let friends pick up things from friends. I just don't do that." I instantly suspect my money is gone. Still, I wait a few days more when, expecting the worse, I go to Mike's house and see my car still untouched. Mike was in his shop, and I asked about my car. Mike said, "I don't owe you anything, now get *the fuck off my property." I drove my car back to my house wondering what else Mike was capable of doing. About a week later, I found out. I'm lying in bed, lights out but awake, and I hear a noise way out behind my house, but think nothing of it. In Colorado, we frequently hear noises in the night from the many animals roaming around. I went out to my shed the next day and found the lock pried off the door. Stolen were most of my tools, a guitar, some music, stereo equipment, etc. Styrofoam packing pieces covered the floor and there will probably be things I will not know were stolen until I go look for them someday in the future.*

A few days later, the first edition copy of this book that I had given to Mike was thrown behind my back door with a note inside that was printed like a second grader for disguise. The note said the music stuff would be sold after dark on the lot on the corner. The only thing that occurs to me is that the guy in the old shack on that lot could shoot me if I'm snooping around his property after dark. I call the police for the second time. The police closed the case a few weeks later saying there were no suspects.

When I would see Mike, he would give me the, "I got you," stare. His longtime girlfriend left him a month later and, without her support, Mike became homeless but still occasionally shows up in the neighborhood. A few weeks ago, someone threw a rock through my porch window. Mike wins again.

Without empathy, sociopaths are unable to form real emotional bonds with other people, and the emotions they do display may appear shallow and artificial. The expectations of society have little impact on the sociopath. They will lie to and con other people including members of their immediate family. And if they get caught, they simply deny it's their fault. Unable to experience fear about future consequences, the sociopath may be capable of horrendous deeds, and they may have a history of illegal activity. As stated by Martha

Stout,[133] "…you shred the evidence, you stab your employees and your clients in the back, marry for money, tell lethal premeditated lies to people who trust you, attempt to ruin colleagues who are powerful or eloquent, and simply steamroll over groups who are dependent and voiceless. …you can do anything at all."

As children, they may be disruptive at school, start fires, bully other kids, vandalism, etc., and they may have enjoyed torturing and killing animals. Most parents of these children are aware something is wrong early in the child's life, and the parents may wonder what they are doing wrong.

Sociopaths are easily bored. Boredom is their natural state unless stimulated by some life event and, therefore, self-stimulation is what the sociopath seeks, resulting in serious risk-taking with little fear of being caught. They may routinely attempt to self-stimulate through drug use, thrill-seeking, stealing, and attempts to gain domination over others, etc. But these are temporary fixes as they soon become bored with their current venture and search again for another source of stimulation. Sociopaths are capable of committing any act without fear, which helps them achieve the excitement they desire.

The sociopath creates a fictional persona that he offers to the world as a way of disguising who he really is. Sociopaths tend to be very good actors, and they learn to fake the emotions they see others display, such as empathy, concern, sadness, depression, shame, etc. Martha Stout[133] suggests the most reliable sign of a sociopath is their manipulative attempt to gain our pity and sympathy. Their goal is to get people to feel sorry for them. Several times I have seen an uncaring sociopathic spouse shed copious tears in an effort to keep the other spouse from leaving the relationship. Alternatively, they may be charming, charismatic, entertaining, self-confident, etc., if it gets them what they want. For many sociopaths, the main manipulation technique may be an excess of charm and flattery. The sociopath easily picks out the overly trusting person while the overly trusting will only spot the sociopath if they are already very aware of the characteristics involved. Advantage: sociopath. The sociopath views their spouse or partner as their property to be manipulated, used and exploited to meet their needs. The needs of the partner get met only if the partner's needs happen to fall in line with the needs of the sociopath.

Some sociopaths are envious and resentful of the achievements, successes, possessions, etc., of others and may find special enjoyment in causing misery in the lives of those with higher achievements than their own. They want more for themselves but, in most cases, have not achieved their own success, so they are constantly frustrated, moody, and angry over the successes of others. Sociopaths need to even the score with those whose lives appear more fortunate. Undermining or sabotaging the lives of those they envy gives them a feeling of power and control. They're on top again—the winner in the game of life. In the vignette, Mike broke into my shed to prove his superiority over me. In his mind, he won, and I lost. Sociopaths who are successful in some occupation will gain this same enjoyment from bullying those lower on the totem pole. They love a battle, and fair play is irrelevant. Any situation involving others, including their spouse and family, may be used in this way. Whatever your weakness, whether you have a caretaker personality, you are lonely, etc., the sociopath will figure this out, and flattery will get the artful sociopath everywhere. In supposedly romantic relationships, the sociopath is more interested in control and deceit than romantic feelings and emotions, although they can fake these emotions at will. Sociopaths may also cheat and manipulate people just for fun. And they will always deny responsibility for their misdeeds even when there is very clear evidence of their guilt. Rather than apologize, the sociopath will go on the attack and point the finger of blame at one or more others. It is understandable that sociopaths are attracted to gangs because they envy and desire the power held by the gang leader.

Sociopaths may be very artful and practiced at using intimidation, fear, and control to further their manipulation of others. This plays itself out differently with different sociopaths. Some are violent and may spend much of their lives in prison. Murder is easy for some sociopaths. But most sociopaths don't kill people because they don't want to spend the rest of their life in prison. When frustrated, the sociopath may respond with anger or rage, although these responses may be brief.

But some sociopaths have no desire for power over anyone, but simply want to get by in life by doing as little as possible. They're lazy and may attempt to get their spouse or others to do the chores and support them. Regardless of style, there is never a feeling of regret or embarrassment.

Anyone can be conned by a sociopath since they look like everyone else and can blend into any social situation. When our lives become difficult due to involvement with a sociopath, it rarely occurs to us that we are dealing with a sociopath since sociopathic thinking and behavior are so foreign to our own experience. Referring to psychopaths, Robert D. Hare[137] suggests one technique for spotting the psychopath. "Ask the individual about his or her friends, family, relatives, employment, place of residence, plans, and so forth. Psychopaths usually give vague, evasive, or inconsistent replies to queries about their personal lives." They may also have an awkward manner of speaking with inconsistent statements, unusual changes in topic, and other oddities of speech, and you may be creeped out by their emotionless stare. And watch for the appeal for pity and sympathy.[133]

Referring to psychopaths, Robert D. Hare,[135] states that the criminal activities of psychopaths decrease considerably at around the age of 40, especially for nonviolent offenses. But this is not the case for all psychopaths, and most of those who do change "remain egocentric, shallow, manipulative, and callous." Their behavior change does not reflect a change in their basic personality.

The sociopath may be a professional, such as doctor, psychiatrist, lawyer, police officer, minister, social worker, priest, daycare worker, teacher, politician, civil rights advocate, spouse, parent, etc. They are the abusive spouse and/or child abuser, the businessman who manipulates his coworkers, or the "friend" who is anything but. Remember, sociopaths are one out of every 25 people, and they reside in every neighborhood. They join the same groups and work in the same office buildings you do. You will encounter them. The best protection is to read Martha Stout's book, *The Sociopath Next Door: The Disturbing World of the Psychopaths Among Us,* paying special attention to the numerous examples and stories describing these people in their everyday life. It is these stories that will stick with you. They will guide you—and we all need this.

THE PARANOID PERSONALITY

This description covers multiple levels of paranoid patterns of thought, emotion, and behavior. Those with fewer or milder traits, as well as those with the symptoms of a serious disorder, may readily identify some of their thinking as well as emotional and behavioral tendencies. A more comprehensive understanding of self usually requires an ongoing self-observation and self-reflection over time. These traits are found in both men and women.

THE PARANOID PERSONALITY involves a general suspiciousness about the intentions of other people. Paranoid people just assume that other people are out to harm them via negative judgments, deception, or even a direct attack. They remain vigilant for any evidence to support their suspicions and may find evidence of ill intent even when none exists, while ignoring any evidence to the contrary. Even those they call friends are subject to the paranoid's suspicious nature and lack of trust. The paranoid may appear to be hypersensitive and on edge. They may quickly misinterpret events such that even compliments by others are viewed as insincere attempts to manipulate or con them. Mild sarcasm may be taken as an attack on their character, and the sales clerk who accidently gives back the wrong change may be publicly accused, tried, and convicted. Of course, there may be people who say negative things about the paranoid, but the paranoid fails to recognize that it is his own paranoid behavior that invites these negative responses from others. As you might expect, the negative reactions of others only confirm the paranoid's irrational suspicions.[9]

When we read about a paranoid individual in the newspaper, it usually involves a more severe paranoia or even paranoid schizophrenia. Most paranoid personalities are not that severe. While the paranoid's suspicions may be irrational, there is sometimes a slight kernel of truth that the paranoid blows out of proportion as she weaves a case that may be somewhat convincing for a time. In more serious cases, the paranoid may become delusional, especially when under stress. This mind-set may lend itself to irrational and exaggerated ideas about who they are, what they have accomplished in the past, or will accomplish in the future.

Needless to say, anyone who must deal with a paranoid, whether at home or work, will have to deal with their suspiciousness, complaints, need for control, fault-finding, hostility, detachment, and just general negativity. The paranoid may sometimes withdraw into anger and silence or, alternatively, exhibit a more-or-less rational nature on the surface, while still manipulatively finding evidence to support his suspicious and distrustful perspective. Attempts to resolve a disagreement with a paranoid may run into difficulties. Once you have made the paranoid angry, do not expect a quick resolution, as paranoids tend to hold on to their anger and hostility for extended periods of time. Legal action is common if the paranoid can afford it. Attempts to explain to the paranoid the error of his ways may draw a quick counterattack. Expect the paranoid to view your constructive criticism as further evidence of your hostile attitude toward him. Accepting their own responsibility for mistakes is not a paranoid specialty.

Paranoid personalities frequently apply their suspiciousness and intolerance to whole groups of people, as well as individuals. Convinced of the obvious rightness of their own ideas, paranoid personalities are well represented in various bigoted or racist organizations and cults.

THE PARANOID PERSONALITY IN RELATIONSHIPS

VIGNETTE: Irrational Suspicion

Toby and Jena came to see me at her insistence after Toby was fired from a good job for the third time in a year. Toby was insistent that head management at all three jobs had decided early on that they did not like him and were just waiting for a chance to fire him for some trumped-up reason. Either the managers were trying to make him uncomfortable so he would quit, or his coworkers were competitive to the point of being backstabbers, or it was something else, but he was always the loser. Toby had concluded that it is the nature of his work as a business analyst to be disliked. He just assumed all business analysts have to deal with hostile job environments. Toby admitted that he would confront his coworkers or manager any time he believed they were being unfair to him, spreading rumors about him, or if he thought he was the butt of their jokes. Toby also admitted that he had a reputation for being difficult when working on group projects, and that he was fired from his most recent job for supposedly causing trouble and being hard to get along with. Toby's view was that he was just standing up for himself. When his wife would point out that this same scenario occurred in one job after another, Toby would merely repeat that it's just the nature of the job and the kind of people that go into competitive business environments.

At this point, Jena began to point out other problems that were going on in their marriage and social life. Jena had always felt the need to soothe and placate Toby's irritable moods, which she had thought were responsible for his fears that people, including her friends, did not like him. Jena recalled that, from their earliest dating days, Toby had been reluctant to discuss his moods or anything else about himself. He would just seem to clam up, and Jena would back off and assume the role of the placating other. With almost no sense of humor, Toby always seemed to be criticizing someone for something. He had stopped talking to one neighbor that he thought was planning to break into their house when they were on vacation. Toby also tried to maintain considerable control over Jena. He wanted to know her daily itinerary and the reasons for any changes in her schedule. On one occasion, when Jena had to work late at her own job, Toby became angry and implied that she might be having an affair. This was just prior to Toby's most recent firing, and these events together were the final impetus for Jena to seek couples counseling. When Jena would make some grave mistake, such as remaining at some event too long without calling him, Toby would remain upset and hold her "problem" over her head for a long time. He seemed to keep a running tab of grievances against her, her friends, his coworkers, etc.

Jena said she could look back to when they were first dating and recall Toby exhibiting irritation at the compliments she paid him. He would fish for what she really meant, as if she was trying to gain his favor in order to manipulate him in some way. Toby would even imply that humorous remarks by friends at dinner parties were veiled insults intended to ridicule him in some way. Jena had always assumed that, with time, Toby would learn to trust her. Unfortunately, Toby's moods and distrust only seemed to worsen over time. Needless to say, Toby's negative reactions to either coworkers or friends would sometimes draw negative reactions and criticisms in return. These negative reactions from others, of course, only confirmed Toby's suspicions about them, and he would then escalate his attacks.

Over time, Toby had become very distrustful of governmental agencies, especially the IRS, and Jena had recognized Toby's increasing dislike for various minority groups and the threat they posed to the jobs and security of others, i.e., white people, although Toby was politically correct most of the time.

With his suspicious nature, rigidity, and need for control, it is easy *to see how Jena's relationship with a paranoid personality would be classified as an abusive relationship.*

Most relationships begin on high notes, with good feelings, good conversations, and good times, all fueled by brain chemicals designed to preserve the species. These chemically induced feelings and infatuations usually begin to recede after a few months to a year or more, and the realities of the personalities involved begin to show themselves. As the paranoid's suspiciousness begins to show itself, the partner may initially wonder what she is doing to trigger his lack of trust in her. Over time, the paranoid's controlling, critical, complaining, and sometimes hostile behavior toward his partner will begin to show itself, and the partner may begin to sense that she really does not know the paranoid very well. Her confusion may increase when her attempts to rekindle a sense of closeness and intimacy only elicit accusations that she is trying to manipulate him in some way. Eventually, the partner of a paranoid may recognize that she will never know him very well, since the paranoid can probably never trust the partner enough to open up and allow any real intimacy.

The suspicious and distrustful nature of the paranoid may lead to outright abuse in their relationships. Paranoids may suspect their spouse or partner of having an affair and again find supporting evidence where none exists. An abusive man who does not have a paranoid personality may still exert control by requiring his spouse to tell him where she is going, where she has been, who she has talked to, etc. Add paranoia to the mix, and the paranoid abuser may carry controlling behavior to new heights, with the goal of total control at all times. It is no surprise that this extreme level of suspiciousness and jealousy frequently results in critical and sometimes hostile behavior toward his partner. The paranoid may seek revenge against her for what he believes she has done to him or is obviously planning to do. Otherwise the spouse and children may experience little more than a cold emotional detachment. Once the paranoid is angry, he will usually remain angry for an extended period of time as he holds his partner responsible for all of the family's problems. Seldom will the paranoid recognize his role in creating the family chaos and misery.

Living with a paranoid may be a lonely experience, as the paranoid may drive away any new friends who come into the couple's life. Further, you can expect an abusive paranoid to try to get revenge if you leave him. He may use the children as pawns as he tries to get back at you, such as attempting to get full custody just to put you through the agony of a drawn-out divorce process. He may enjoy making you fearful for the safety of the children when they are not in your care.

Any kind of therapy is difficult with paranoids because of their inability to trust anyone, including the therapist. Multiple reasons to discontinue therapy may appear obvious to the paranoid personality. Yet some paranoids are able to develop some understanding of their irrational nature if they are willing to submit to a comprehensive examination of their beliefs with a knowledgeable therapist.[9]

THE SCHIZOID PERSONALITY

This description covers multiple levels of schizoid patterns of thought, emotion, and behavior. Those with fewer or milder traits, as well as those with the symptoms of a serious disorder, may readily identify some of their thinking as well as emotional and behavioral tendencies. A more comprehensive understanding of self usually requires an ongoing self-observation and self-reflection over time. These traits are found in both men and women.

THERE ARE TWO basic traits of the schizoid personality:
1: Some degree of indifference to, and detachment from, social relationships.
2: A limited range of emotional expression in the presence of other people.

Schizoids frequently have very few friends or no friends at all. Schizoids tend to keep to themselves and appear not to care what other people think about them. As with many personalities, their behavior is sometimes misinterpreted by others. Keeping their physical and emotional distance, they are sometimes viewed by others as detached and aloof, uncaring, weird, having poor social skills, etc. Schizoids may, in fact, have poor social skills because they do not pick up on the subtleties of social interaction on an emotional or nonverbal level. Schizoids may routinely fail to recognize and acknowledge a friendly smile, increasing their appearance of being aloof or disconnected. In more serious cases, they may have difficulty with most attempts at normal conversation. Schizoids may also get little or no enjoyment from a fun afternoon, a vacation, or visual experiences such as great works of art, beautiful sunsets, etc. Schizoids may also be unable to feel or express even appropriate anger. Schizoids may be handicapped at work, school, etc., as their attempts to advance are blocked by awkward conversations and relationships. Schizoids sometimes find they are happiest when they are alone, with little or no interaction with coworkers or other people generally. Many schizoids may not view their isolation as a problem,[10] while other schizoids may experience loneliness and the increasing eccentricity that usually results from ongoing isolation.

The schizoid personality may first present itself in later childhood when the child appears to prefer isolation rather than normal play with other children. The schizoid personality appears to be relatively uncommon.[10]

THE SCHIZOID PERSONALITY IN RELATIONSHIPS

With little ability to develop emotional connections with other people, relationships for the schizoid may be difficult to form and maintain. If you are in a relationship with a schizoid, it is probably a milder case, since a relationship with a serious schizoid is highly unlikely.

VIGNETTE: Distant Indifference

Erika met Ike at a party, where she had noticed that he was making no attempt to speak to anyone. He would reply if he was spoken to, but his answers were brief, and other partiers began to ignore him. Erika, having suffered from shyness her whole life, thought she saw a kindred spirit in Ike and made an attempt to have a more extended conversation with him. Besides his brief answers to the usual introductory questions, she noticed Ike would speak in a somewhat loud monotone without the usual voice inflections that accompany normal discourse.

Erika tried to ease any nervousness she thought Ike must be feeling by mentioning her own shyness in social situations. While not appearing very interested, Ike did eventually admit to Erika that he had always been something of a loner. Ike did slowly warm up to Erika enough for them to begin dating, although Erika was always the one to suggest the dates, to which Ike would offer a minimal, "Ok." Erika had thought Ike was just too shy to call her, but she sometimes wondered if Ike would even notice if she stopped calling him.

Erika continued to view Ike as an extremely shy person since Ike continued to want to avoid other people, or at least avoid talking to them. She noticed that Ike would not return the nods and smiles of passing strangers, and friends she would introduce to Ike would later ask her if Ike did not like them for some reason. Gradually Erika began to realize that Ike did not appear to even recognize the common courtesies or emotional expressions of others. He would apologize when she mentioned this to him, but even his apologies would seem mechanical and devoid of sincerity. At times, Ike's behavior was simply viewed by others as uncaring, aloof, or just plain rude. Finally, after talking to a knowledgeable therapist, Erika was able to connect Ike's lack of emotions and emotional expression with his inability to recognize and be sensitive to the emotions of others. She realized it was Ike's lack of feelings and emotions that prevented him from enjoying, or even desiring, fun experiences such as vacations, or even just appreciating Erika's involvement in his life. Ike would fail to notice the knowing touch of her hand after a difficult day or even her sexual overtures. Ike's lack of motivation appeared to run throughout his life, including a lack of career goals. With Ike's obvious indifference to praise or criticism, Erika began to recognize that Ike might never be motivated to work on his behavior, and she began to doubt that Ike could ever feel any emotional attachment to children.

Looking back to the early parts of the relationship, the partner of a schizoid may recall having interpreted the schizoid's behavior as introverted and shy. Many relationships begin with shyness and awkwardness, but these problems usually ease and dissipate with time. But schizoids' emotional distance is built into their personality. The schizoid's ongoing tendency to avoid people and not care what other people think about him may apply to his relationship as well. Even in a relationship, the schizoid may prefer being alone much of the time and may come across as uncaring, detached, and aloof. Both physical and emotional intimacy may be minimal at best, and requesting different behavior from the schizoid may fail for the long term. The schizoid may have sexual desires but prefer masturbation to sexual contact with another person.[10] The partner of a schizoid cannot necessarily expect even the minimal emotional connection of a smile or greeting.

Since the indifference of the schizoid to developing interpersonal relationships, whether with family or friends, is such an integral part of the personality itself, the schizoid may be completely unaware of his emotional distance from others, including his partner. The schizoid's emotional distance may also be exacerbated by extreme frustration after years of rejection from those the schizoid has tried to connect with, or when others have made attempts to connect with him but failed. Therapy with a schizoid is difficult and may have limited results. The schizoid cannot necessarily change his basic nature through talking and deciding to behave differently. This does not necessarily make a relationship completely impossible with a very mild schizoid, but the limitations involved and the need for an understanding partner need to be recognized.

CYCLOTHYMIA (MILD BIPOLAR)

This description covers multiple levels of cyclothymic patterns of thought, emotion, and behavior. Those with fewer or milder traits, as well as those with the symptoms of a serious disorder, may readily identify some of their thinking as well as emotional and behavioral tendencies. A more comprehensive understanding of self usually requires an ongoing self-observation and self-reflection over time. These traits are found in both men and women.

BIPOLAR DISORDER IS a *mood* disorder rather than a personality disorder and occurs at multiple levels of severity. **Bipolar Disorder, also** referred to as *manic depression*, involves mood fluctuations between a manic (hyper) state and a state of depression. *Cyclothymia* is a mild form of bipolar disorder and involves mood fluctuations, back and forth, between a mild manic state, referred to as *hypomania*, and a state of mild depression. It is important for anyone relating to this chapter in any way to also read the chapter on mild depression.

HYPOMANIA (mild mania): The symptoms of hypomania usually appear in two basic forms:

(1) Euphoria
(2) Irritability/anger

Euphoric Hypomania: Unusually cheerful or euphoric mood characterized by:

- Hyper thinking with racing and scattered thoughts and ideas
- An increase in energy or activity level
- The uninteresting becomes interesting

- Excessive talking / hyper speech
- Reduced need for sleep
- Increase in self-esteem and self-confidence / no shyness
- Impulsivity / quick decisions that are not thought out
- Easily distracted / frequent shifts in topic
- Easily bored—quickly focuses on something new
- Shopping sprees
- Entertaining / witty / life of the party
- Less emphasis on ethical decisions
- Sexually promiscuous / wants to seduce or be seduced
- Alcohol/drug abuse
- Feeling of power

Irritable/Anger Hypomania
- Easily irritated / moody
- Numerous complaints
- Quick—unpredictable anger/hostility
- Excessive anger displays / recites a litany of accusations
- Highly irrational when angry—logic may disappear completely
- No sense of fair play when angry
- You cannot talk to them—they cannot hear you

During the hypomanic phase, cyclothymics may experience either the euphoric or the irritable/anger style of hypomania, or they may alternate between these two basic styles. In some cases, there may be a mix of the euphoric and irritable styles at the same time.

In the euphoric hypomanic state, an individual may use his higher energy level to plan and work on numerous projects or hobbies but complete few of them because he gets distracted by other projects that appear more exciting, or are just new and different. Along with a higher level of energy and activity, there may also be an increase in self-esteem and self-confidence, and this may lead to an increase in occupational or social interaction with other people. In this mild euphoria, the cyclothymic may be quite entertaining, with an emphasis on nonstop wit, including jokes and one-liners. He may have a reputation as the quintessential life of the party. Impulsivity may show up in poor judgment, such as poor investments and business decisions, irrational shopping, or irrational fantasies and sexual activity. With instant decisions that have little forethought, ethical issues may take a backseat to what looks desirable, fun, or just feels good.

These behavior patterns may occur as the cyclothymic survives on only three or four hours of sleep per night. This mild euphoria may feel good to sufferers, and they may deny that anything is wrong.[54] Feeling good, a cyclothymic in the euphoric state may be resistant to treatment. I have found individuals exhibiting euphoric hypomania, as well as those presenting a more severe mania, to be similar to cocaine or methamphetamine addicts who do not want to give up the wonderful drug-induced euphoric feelings, even though the symptoms are causing severe problems in their life.

The racing mind and hyper thinking of hypomania may also show up as irrational irritability, complaining, hostility, and anger. In some cases, the anger outbursts may be severe. In the irritable state, it takes very little to upset the cyclothymic, and misunderstandings may be routine. Once a cyclothymic is pissed off, expect his logic and reasoning ability to exit the conversation—almost completely in some cases. At this point, any discussion or argument with the cyclothymic will be very one-sided as far as any exchange of information. With his mind racing, the cyclothymic may rant and rave to the exclusion of any real listening to the opposing view. Any sense of fair play in the discussion may be lost, and the chance of actual communication may require an extended breather while the cyclothymic calms down.

Some cyclothymics may function adequately during their hypomanic periods, especially those experiencing the euphoric style of hypomania. The euphoric style of hypomania may generate considerable creativity and positive social activity, with a string of witticisms, wisecracks, and general hilarity. Euphoria may also cause the hypomanic to blurt out the wrong thing and offend others or just appear awkward and eccentric. It is the unexpected shifts into irritability and anger that give the cyclothymic a reputation for being unpredictable, moody, or temperamental. Hypomania may last for hours, days, weeks, or months, but in most cases the sufferer will eventually revert back to a state of mild depression. As with personality styles and disorders, individuals with unstable and shifting moods may not even be aware that they have a problem, or there may be some denial about the severity of the symptoms. Cyclothymia usually appears gradually, beginning in childhood.

This gradual onset appears to mask the growing instability to other family members who gradually become accustomed to the cyclothymic's erratic behavior. Depression may appear first, with the child initially becoming irritable or bored since this is how depression may appear in children. Hypomanic symptoms, such as euphoria, hyperactivity, and/or anger outbursts may appear later. Children in the hypomanic state are more likely to display irritability and temper tantrums instead of euphoria. Children and adolescents may experience several mood swings in one day. These symptoms may also indicate other disorders, such as attention deficit hyperactivity disorder (ADHD), or they may just be a normal part of growing up. With children or adolescents, it frequently takes a child/adolescent specialist to tell the difference.

There is a greater frequency of mood disorders among the first-degree relatives of cyclothymic individuals. Even when there is not a clear history of mood disorders in the family, sufferers of cyclothymia may have been raised by parents with erratic behavior, such as mood swings, irrational thinking, temper tantrums, excessive criticism, etc. The cyclothymic may recall having witnessed, or heard stories about, relatives exhibiting similar behaviors. The vicious circle that is created in some extended families is obvious. The child with cyclothymia, or some other personality style or disorder, may be raised by a temperamental, critical, and irrational parent, resulting in a severely neurotic child who evolves to become a very dysfunctional parent to their own children. With its typically mild nature and similar symptoms with other personalities, cyclothymia can be difficult to spot without a good understanding of the symptoms involved. As with many difficult personalities, cyclothymics may spend a lifetime never knowing the source of their eccentric, erratic, irrational, or angry behavior. They may always blame another person, group, or something in the environment for their emotional and behavioral reactions. Some cyclothymics may never even recognize their behavior as odd or irrational. Another problem is the considerable overlap of symptoms between cyclothymia and other disorders, most notably attention deficit hyperactivity disorder (ADHD). The hyperactivity associated with ADHD may appear virtually identical to the hypomanic symptoms associated with cyclothymia or a more severe bipolar disorder.

A correct diagnosis is most important with cyclothymia or bipolar disorder. Antidepressants may precipitate or drastically increase manic symptoms in cyclothymic or bipolar individuals who begin taking them during a depression phase without recognizing they have some level of bipolar disorder. Anyone taking antidepressants and experiencing an increase in manic symptoms at any level, whether euphoria, irritability/anger, or some mix of these symptoms, should immediately consult their doctor or a mental-health professional.

CYCLOTHYMIA IN RELATIONSHIPS

The mood shifts in cyclothymia may appear in a wide variety of behavioral variations and patterns. Either the mild mania (hypomania) or the mild depression of the cyclothymic may last for hours, weeks, or months, after which the cyclothymic may then shift into the other state.

VIGNETTE: The Unpredictable and Erratic

Kyle is a 33-year-old graphic artist and has been married to Ann for six years. They have two young children. Even before they had children, Kyle would sometimes shift from being in an extremely good mood to a bad mood over trivial issues or for no apparent reason at all. Kyle's erratic behavior seemed to increase after they had children. Kyle had also cheated on Ann on one occasion, but that was not why Ann sought couples counseling. Ann finally insisted on counseling because of the severe, sometimes brutal, way her husband had punished their children, usually for minor infractions. Of course, Ann was not happy with the way Kyle sometimes treated her either, but Kyle had always told Ann that it was her emotional distance that caused their marital problems, and Ann admitted having bought into this explanation.

At the same time, Kyle admitted his unpredictable behavior was sometimes a problem. Kyle admitted that he would sometimes become distant and irritable and occasionally would go into a rage, during which it was impossible for Ann, the children, or anyone else to talk to him until he had time to calm down. Unfortunately, by the time Kyle settled down, the damage had been done. Either Ann had been irrationally criticized and, on one occasion, pushed to the floor, or the children had been severely punished or reprimanded for minor infractions. Kyle also admitted that his erratic behavior had contributed to his losing some jobs. He always seemed to do well when he was first hired, but eventually Kyle would become irritable with his coworkers or his boss. If he made it to a position of authority, Kyle would needlessly reprimand employees for minor mistakes and occasionally fire some innocent victim. What Ann never understood was how Kyle could sometimes be such a fun, energetic, and witty person, even for an extended period of time, and then quickly shift into irritability or outright hostility over nothing.

While Kyle could be the quickest wit and the life of the party, he could also be irrational during his fun, energetic periods. Kyle would typically become very impulsive during these good times, usually in terms of spending money beyond their budget on expensive toys. He would also become very talkative and more flirtatious at social gatherings. Kyle would also go through periods of constant activity, during which he would become absorbed in various unfinished projects, such as working every day on the old Volkswagen he had wanted to restore for years but just never could stick with long enough to finish the project. Most of the time, the car just took up space in the garage, while Kyle sat in front of the TV every evening drinking beer. When Kyle was not silent, he was usually criticizing some person, object, or event. Since Kyle had usually been willing to apologize for his worst behavior, Ann had hoped that Kyle's good periods would become the norm. Unfortunately, the critical and emotionally volatile Kyle would always return at some point.

Counseling sessions with Kyle and Ann seemed to go well at first, with both of them feeling good and somewhat optimistic about making changes in their family life. Unfortunately, Kyle's mood shifts began to affect his willingness to continue in therapy and do his part. Ann would come in complaining about Kyle's behavior, and Kyle would suggest that the counseling sessions were just not working and question whether they should continue spending money for therapy.

What Kyle and Ann did not know, and their previous therapists had missed, was that Kyle was cyclothymic, and the shifts in his personality and behavior were not the products of conscious choices or logical thinking.

Shifts between mild depression and hypomania may be obvious to those around the cyclothymic, or the changes may be more subtle and less noticeable. The depression stage of cyclothymia will present a whole different set of problems for the relationship and the family, as described in the chapter about mild depression. There may be periods when depression and hypomania seem to be intermixed. While unpredictability of response is the norm when living with a cyclothymic, a simultaneous mix of depression and hypomania may cause the cyclothymic to sometimes catch other family members by surprise. Within the hypomanic state alone, there may be a simultaneous mix of both the euphoric and the irritable/angry hypomanic styles. A simultaneous mix of mood states creates a chaotic household that further damages the family as a whole, especially the children. With a simultaneous mix of mood states, the partner and children can never be certain which cyclothymic will be encountered at any given moment. There may also be periods of relative normalcy when the cyclothymic is shifting between mood states and, once again, gives the family hope that a real change has come over the cyclothymic. Of course, when the cyclothymic makes a shift between mood states, the family's responses to the cyclothymic must also make a shift—without advance notice.

When euphoric, the racing mind of the cyclothymic may have thoughts and ideas scattered all over the place, and this can be difficult and tiring for other family members, especially the children. While the euphoric cyclothymic may be in a good mood and somewhat energetic and hyperactive, logic and rationality may elude her as she draws quick conclusions and makes unwise decisions with little forethought. Since anything can interest the hypomanic mind, the hypomanic's partner may be simultaneously bored and tense from endless conversations that do not appear rationally directed.

The high self-esteem and self-confidence associated with the euphoric style of hypomania may give the cyclothymic the conviction of complete certainty in thought and action. The cyclothymic may argue forcefully to win her point, with little attention paid to the partner's or children's opposing views. The cyclothymic's excessive talking and hyper speech, with little logic accompanying her complete certainty, may quickly wear down the partner's patience and leave the children with a sense that something is just not right. The children of a cyclothymic may grow up with a sense that what they think does not matter. When the cyclothymic is in the hypomanic state, there may be few periods of peace and quiet, since the cyclothymic may need very little sleep to get by. At times, the partner and children of a euphoric cyclothymic may feel neglected as the cyclothymic puts most of her energy into one project after another, with little attention paid to her partner and children. Affairs may occur due to the irrational impulsivity to which cyclothymics are prone.

There may be periods when the euphoric style of hypomania makes the cyclothymic fun to be around. The cyclothymic may be witty and entertaining, and the family may develop a circle of friends who are drawn to this interesting and humorous side of the cyclothymic. Unfortunately, it will usually be a matter of time before the cyclothymic, lacking in self-awareness, makes a serious social blunder. With little shyness or sense of decorum and a tendency to just blurt things out, there may be embarrassing moments when the cyclothymic makes inappropriate remarks to friends and acquaintances. With the cyclothymic being unpredictable and eccentric, the couple may find friends distancing themselves, while few invitations to social events arrive in the mail. Chronic financial difficulties may plague the family of the cyclothymic. Since hypomania lends itself to quick and impulsive decisions that are not thought out, there is always the danger the cyclothymic will make irrational business or investment decisions. If the cyclothymic goes on impulsive buying sprees, this may leave insufficient funds for family expenses. Of course, financial problems get much worse if the cyclothymic gets fired from his job for erratic behavior or just impulsively quits. In the hypomanic state, the racing mind of the cyclothymic is easily distracted away from important family concerns.

The cyclothymic may become moody and irritable over insignificant events, and the partner may have to listen to the cyclothymic complain about his job, boss, coworkers, the partner herself, the children, or any other aspect of life. Misunderstandings may be common, and the partner may find it difficult, if not impossible, to discuss anything with an irritable or angry cyclothymic. The partner of the cyclothymic may find her own reasoning and opinions simply have no impact on the cyclothymic's rants and raves. The partner may find it difficult to tell whether the cyclothymic has slipped into highly irrational thinking or just does not care about fair play where the partner or children are concerned. Expect the children of an irritable/angry cyclothymic to live with anxiety and a sense of foreboding of the criticisms and punishments to come.

Families with a cyclothymic member may go for years or even

decades without ever recognizing the source of the chaos that routinely invades their home. The cyclothymic may always be able to explain his erratic or eccentric behavior to his own satisfaction, and the partner and children may buy into his explanations, even when his behavior borders on abuse (see chapter: The Abusive Personality / Abusive Relationships).

PART IV

Parents Do Count

THE FAMILY SYSTEMS OF MURRAY BOWEN

Since the 1950s there has been an increasing recognition of the influence our original family environment continues to exert on our internal experience and external presentation of self throughout our lives. The conventional wisdom is that a reciprocal interaction between our genetic heritage and our environmental experiences plays the greatest part in determining who we become. Family characteristics, as well as genetically-based personality characteristics, may be handed down to subsequent generations, and the lasting effects of our upbringing are legitimately considered a basic part of our personality. This chapter emphasizes the most influential environment most of us experience—the family in which we were raised. Parents do count.

The meaning of family reaches well beyond the parents to include a multigenerational group, mostly biologically linked, of living and ghostly presences, who interact in nonrandom ways. A healthy family has four to five generations of intrapsychic family members who guide decision making, and the development of its self-image.

—David V. Keith[129]

ONE OF THE pioneers in the understanding of family functioning was Murray Bowen (1913–1990)[113,114,115,118], a psychiatrist who devoted his life to improving our understanding of families and family-therapy techniques. Murray Bowen believed excessive emotional attachment to one's family of origin to be the main obstacle to healthy individual and family functioning. Bowen found that excessive emotional attachment to one's original family, especially to the parents, prevents the development of an independent and mature self-identity. For Bowen, a mature self-identity is essential for rational thinking that is not emotionally reactive, and for the formation of healthy new relationships in the future. Many people will feel some affinity with Murray Bowen's descriptions of family functioning, although some will recognize themselves and their families to a greater degree than others. As with understanding your personality, a comprehensive understanding of your family functioning may require some ongoing observations of your family, combined with some increased awareness of the role you play in the family system.

The process of developing a mature and independent personality during childhood and adolescence is referred to as *differentiation of self*. If the process of differentiation is short-circuited due to some degree of instability in the family environment, the undifferentiated offspring may continue to have unresolved emotional attachments to their parents and family indefinitely. Even those believing they are from basically good or stable homes may recognize themselves and both their original and present family environments in this chapter. Family instability comes in degrees, and perfect parents are a total fiction. Of course, both boys and girls, and the adults they become, are equally affected by their original family environment.

Undifferentiated individuals may react in different ways to their family of origin. If children or adolescents are criticized, controlled, inappropriately punished, receive little encouragement, are offered little opportunity to develop independent creative thinking, etc., they may withdraw emotionally from their parents and family resulting in a lack of differentiation. When these undifferentiated children or adolescents are older, they may remain emotionally distant from their parents or cut them out of their lives completely. In other cases, they may become overly close to their parents and family.

Individuals with either an overly distant or overly close family history may then fail to develop a mature self-identity based on the ability to reason and think rationally while maintaining control over their emotions. They may spend their life being overly agreeable and conciliatory in their struggle for acceptance, or emotionally and/or physically distant to relieve anxiety. Some may exhibit some combination of close and distant responses in future family, social, or work relationships. Either type of response demonstrates an inability to use self-control and restraint in a way that allows them to choose logical thinking over emotional reactions. The thoughts and feelings of the undifferentiated blend together in a way that prevents the individual from thinking rationally, especially when they are in the presence of other family members or dealing with emotionally intense family situations. Just thinking about issues involving emotional family content may disrupt the logical thinking of those with lower differentiation. Their thought process becomes contaminated and distorted by the less rational emotions of the moment.

Undifferentiated people also experience a lack of differentiation between themselves and other people outside their family. With fewer thought-out opinions of their own, undifferentiated people are easily influenced by other people, and they tend to fully accept the ideas and opinions of others without thinking the issues through for themselves. In particular, they tend to accept any opinion that is expressed forcefully or with confidence, and they overreact emotionally to normal aspects of daily life, as can be seen in those with extreme religious or political views, etc. As Murray Bowen put it, "Less differentiated people are moved about like pawns by emotional tensions."[130] Undifferentiated people are much more likely to express the exact same views their parents espoused, or defensively adopt views that are the polar opposite.

Those who are able to successfully differentiate from their family will possess the individuality that comes from a mature self-identity. With greater maturity and a good self-concept, those with greater individuation are able to have more empathy and care for others in a selfless manner. They are able to maintain an objective separation between their thoughts and feelings, which drastically improves their ability to more accurately observe themselves and events and form stable relationships with others. The benefits of becoming a better observer and less emotionally reactive will pay off in many life situations. As stated by Bowen:

> *The person who acquires a little ability at becoming an observer, and at controlling some of his emotional reactiveness, acquires an ability that is useful for life in all kinds of emotional snarls. Most of the time he can live his life, reacting with appropriate and natural emotional responses, but with the knowledge that at any time he can back out of the situation, slow down his reactiveness, and make observations that help him control himself and the situation.*[132]

While some people lacking in differentiation remain overly close to their parents and family, a lack of differentiation typically results in some level of emotional distancing from the family, a process Bowen referred to as *emotional cutoff*. There are two basic methods for emotional cutoff that poorly differentiated individuals typically use for dealing with their anxiety and unstable family relationships:

(1) *Emotional Isolation:* Undifferentiated individuals may

emotionally isolate themselves from their parents even though they continue to have what appears to be normal contact with their parents or continue to live in the same house with their parents. When tension levels are high, the emotional isolation may descend into silence with little or no real communication at all.

(2) *Physical Distance:* A second form of emotional cutoff involves putting some level of physical distance between themselves and their parents. At the extreme, these individuals may move away and rarely speak to their parents for years.

Distancing responses of either the emotional-isolation or the physical-distancing types usually do not occur at extreme levels, and most undifferentiated individuals will use some combination of both emotional and physical distancing. Of course, no one is completely objective about their family, and no one can avoid all inappropriate emotional reactions. As stated by Bowen:

All things being equal, the life course of people is determined by the amount of unresolved emotional attachment, the amount of anxiety that comes from it, and the way they deal with this anxiety.[117]

Murray Bowen pointed out that the individual who physically distances himself from his family under a false premise of achieving independence is just as emotionally attached to his family as the individual who maintains an emotional distance while keeping a physical presence within the home. The latter simply uses different emotional cutoff techniques to achieve a comfortable level of emotional distance, such as an unwillingness to fully communicate or even a more serious silent treatment. The more threatened and insecure family members feel, the more serious these symptoms will be. Emotionally distant individuals remain in denial about their continuing emotional attachment to their parents, which allows them to delude themselves into believing they have achieved emotional independence from their parents when this is far from the case. When emotions interfere with more logical and rational thinking, these individuals usually rationalize their behavior and do not recognize the role their emotions play in recreating a similar dysfunction in their later relationships, marriage, and family life.

Without a normal process of differentiation during adolescence, continuing unresolved emotional attachment to the parents and family causes many adolescents to exhibit extreme behaviors in their attempts to appear mature and grown up. As stated by Bowen:

The intensity of the denial and the pretending in adolescence is a remarkably accurate index of the degree of unresolved emotional attachment to the parents.[131]

Where a family is seriously disengaged, the parents may not even notice when a family member is experiencing even serious levels of stress, depression, problems at school, drugs, alcohol, or involvement in gang activity, etc.

Most important, the undifferentiated will also experience a lack of differentiation in their future relationships and family life. Individuals raised in either emotionally distant and disengaged families or in overly close families may have difficulty developing stable relationships with others later on. These individuals unconsciously create an emotional atmosphere in their new family that is similar to the emotional atmosphere in which they were raised. If there was emotional distance in their original family, they will probably be critical and emotionally distant to their spouse and/or children. Without realizing it, the individual raised in an emotionally distant family will eventually become very distant to the spouse and/or children, preventing the forming of a relationship based on love, caring, sharing, trust, empathy, etc. A common example of this is the stereotypical *emotionally uninvolved father*. In the same way these individuals distanced themselves from their parents, they will distance themselves from their spouse and children after essentially normal or even trivial disagreements. If there was a very close emotional attachment to their parents, they may smother their spouse and/or children with neediness in their struggle to recreate the sense of security and acceptance they unconsciously assume is normal for everyone. Of course, smothering one's spouse and children with an overabundance of affection may achieve the opposite of the intended effect and create an emotional distance within the family. In a new relationship, each spouse or partner unconsciously attempts to create a relationship that feels familiar and, therefore, comfortable to them, which is essentially a recreation of the environment in which they were raised.

Individuals with a more severe emotional cutoff from their parents are likely to create a more severe emotional cutoff in their future relationships. As strange as it seems, even people raised in extremely chaotic or abusive environments may unconsciously attempt to re-create this same painful environment in their new family. As parents, they may project their problems onto one or more of the children and view the child or children as the cause of the family's problems. When one spouse has an extremely close attachment to one or both parents, this undifferentiated spouse may allow his or her parent(s) to repeatedly exercise some control over the couple by interfering in the couple's life with excess affection, criticisms, suggestions, guilt trips, etc. Emotional cutoff or needy smothering may occur repeatedly through multiple relationships or marriages.

A lack of differentiation and a history of emotional cutoff may play havoc with all aspects of an individual's life. Individuals with a more severe cutoff and little contact with their family of origin are more likely to suffer multiple symptoms, such as marital problems, more stress and higher anxiety, difficulties with friends, problems at work, financial problems, or experience dysfunctional behavior on the part of their children. Without some increase in their self-understanding, self-awareness, and level of differentiation, the immature behavior they were unable to grow out of within their original family may stay with them for life. This will eventually impact virtually everything they do, and all family members may suffer, especially the children.

If you are involved with someone who is unable to maintain objective control over his or her emotions when interacting with their family of origin, or even when they are just talking about them, do not expect this individual to remain objective and control his or her emotions in a new relationship with you or any children involved. Of course, it may take some time for the dysfunctional nature to display itself. Everyone is more vigilant and on their best behavior when they first form a relationship. The ultimate test for differentiation is whether an individual can repeatedly maintain some level of maturity, individuality, and independence of thought without experiencing excess emotionality, while remaining in the physical presence of other members of his/her original family. I encourage anyone who begins to take a new relationship seriously to go with their love interest to visit his/her family several times. You may gain some very useful information, and extended visits may gain you extended information.

Murray Bowen's research led him to conclude that the great majority of people have some level of unresolved emotional attachments to their parents and fail to develop a mature sense of self based on a mature relationship with their parents. Compounding the problem is that people tend to choose mates whose level of differentiation is similar to their own. When two undifferentiated individuals come together in a relationship, a healthy and stable relationship is highly unlikely. These couples may experience severe emotional withdrawal and cutoffs between themselves, or they may smother each other with neediness, and jealous responses may be the norm. Each spouse may be blind to their own instability while remaining critical of the other spouse's failings. Each feels the other is the cause of their problems. Quarreling is common among couples in which one or both spouses remain undifferentiated and lack a good self-identity. Blaming the partner, these couples may argue incessantly in a way guaranteed only to generate more arguments. Some couples never get beyond their constant bickering and quarreling.

Family-systems therapists typically do not view any given member of a dysfunctional family as responsible for the family's problems. Systems therapists believe family problems are a reflection of the interactions within the dysfunctional family as a whole rather than reflecting on any specific member of the family, no matter how obvious it seems to the family that one particular person is the problem. Systems therapists believe the way to help individual family members is to treat the family as a whole. In part, this view stems from the idea that family problems and a lack of differentiation usually reflect a multigenerational process where the lack of differentiation and immaturity gets passed down from grandparents to parents to children to grandchildren—ad infinitum. How the parents in any given family respond to their own lack of differentiation, especially in their marriage and parenting duties, is a major determinant in their children's level of differentiation. Unless parents work on their own unresolved emotional attachment to their own parents and family, the emotional structure of the parents will likely be accurately handed down to the children, give or take some variation based on how the parents handle anxiety and stress in their marriage and parenting duties.

Whether talking about personalities or family systems, I have found it very difficult to get people to stop thinking in terms of people always "choosing" their thoughts, feelings, and behaviors, whether dysfunctional or not. Both our past and present environments, as well as our personalities, may have an overpowering influence on who we are at any given moment unless we very consciously contemplate every thought, emotion, action, and reaction—and none of us can do that all of the time. The alternative is to use knowledgeable self-observations and self-reflections within the guidelines suggested by Murray Bowen in the next section.

MURRAY BOWEN'S TRIANGLES

Central to the revolutionary ideas of Murray Bowen were his descriptions of *triangles*, the three-way relationships we all form with other people, things, events, etc. [113,114,115,118,111,119] Murray Bowen recognized that two-person relationships are inherently unstable to some degree and that some emotional tension, criticisms, arguments, etc. are an inevitable part of all relationships. Whenever a couple experiences difficulties, some feelings of unfairness, hurt, and rejection may result. Feeling wronged, one or both partners may attempt to reduce their stress and anxiety by seeking the comfort and support of a third entity in their relationship. The triangulated third entity is usually a parent, child, or an outside friend, but not always. A job, hobby, or a substance such as drugs or alcohol may also be triangulated into a relationship. For example, with enough tension in a relationship, one or both spouses may:

- Complain to a parent
- Complain to a friend or coworker
- Seek consolation by spending more time with the children
- Increase discipline of children / kick the dog / fire an employee
- Have an extramarital affair
- Watch television by the hour
- Become a workaholic
- Begin or increase the use of alcohol or drugs
- Increase time at a health club, volunteer work, or other activity

While triangulating these third entities into their life, the problems within the relationship are not dealt with in a productive way and the couple's or family's dysfunction will likely worsen over time. Feeling some support and comfort from the triangulated entity, some people unconsciously hang on to their triangles for years or decades as the emotional distance between the couple only increases. The greater the stress and anxiety in the relationship, the stronger the triangulation tends to be.

When children are present in a dysfunctional relationship, one spouse/partner may become closer to the children, that is, triangulated, while the other parent emotionally and/or physically withdraws and becomes an outsider. Some parents may helicopter over their child's every move with overprotection, while other parents may smother their children with attention and affection. Children also become triangulated when parents blame the child or children for the problems in their relationship or family life, and the punishment level of a triangulated child may increase to abusive levels.

Whether children are smothered with affection or punished for perceived infractions, they may develop their own problems and symptoms as a result. It is the triangulation of children by parents that prevents children from growing into differentiated and mature adults who can take care of themselves in a mature fashion and form stable relationships in the future. Triangulation with a child may cause the child to develop symptoms such as behavioral problems, problems at school, physical illness, juvenile delinquency, use of drugs or alcohol, gang activity, inability to leave home for college or begin a career, etc. When the triangulated child or adolescent develops symptoms, the symptoms may then draw further criticism and punishment from parents, school personnel, etc. It is very common for couples with a dysfunctional marriage, possibly combined with poor parenting skills, to bring their difficult child or adolescent to a counselor while clearly unaware of the extent to which it is they who are the actual cause of the child's or adolescent's difficulties.

Furthermore, the problems the parents are experiencing in their relationship may simultaneously encompass other triangles involving their own parents, in-laws, their job, an ex-spouse, school personnel, the police, alcohol, drugs, etc. Triangles frequently overlap with other triangles. In work settings, triangles naturally form among various employees, since it takes considerable effort and a serious level of awareness of both self and triangles to avoid becoming caught up in them. Everyone becomes involved in some triangles, and triangles may not be so obvious when emotions are calm. It is when anxiety, stress, and tension increase that less-differentiated individuals become more emotionally reactive within their various triangulated relationships as well as creating new triangles.

The process of detriangulation and avoiding unhealthy triangles in the future is an art requiring some awareness of the dynamics of family functioning combined with an increase in self-awareness and differentiation. The process of dealing with triangles and the process of increasing one's level of differentiation are the same process. The most difficult aspect of reconnecting with an emotionally distant or cut-off family is that the work primarily needs to be done on an individual, one-on-one, basis. Speaking individually with family members will avoid family cliques and gossip and reduce the likelihood of emotional overreactions. The greater the number of family members present, the greater the power the family's history will have over the emotions, thoughts, and behaviors of the gathering. The idea is to have conversations about your family relationships, including emotional issues, with each member of the family without blaming, getting angry, taking sides, being defensive or confrontational, and without drawing (triangulating) others into the conversation/relationship. It is important to resist the very natural tendency to allow the conversation to veer to irrelevant topics in an attempt to relieve the anxiety and tension of the moment. Ideally, an emotional issue will arise naturally rather than being intentionally inserted into a conversation, although this can be done if necessary at the risk of appearing aggressive.

As hard as families work to maintain the family myths about how they interact and not see the elephants in the room, even as they feed the elephants on a regular basis, it is inevitable that some event or disagreement will bring a family's emotions to the fore if you hang around long enough. If you are attacked, recognize this as a natural part of the process, and do not counterattack. Responding with silence is also inappropriate. Bowen points out that the silence itself is an emotional response, and this may draw an emotional response in return. As these conversations progress over time, family members may begin to sense that something is different, although it is unlikely this will be openly acknowledged.

It is important that you not explain your goals and the individuation/differentiation process to other family members so as not to trigger a negative defensive reaction. An explanation to other family members that reconnecting with your extended family will help you increase your own level of individuation and maturity might be taken as a criticism or accusation against them, e.g., "Oh, so your problems are our fault. Is that what you're saying?" Members of your family may unconsciously try very hard to get you to change back to your old self as an equal contributor to the tension-filled family system. It's as if the other family members take it personally when they cannot get an emotional reaction out of the more differentiated family member—and up the ante. At times you may wonder if they are intentionally trying to rile you up. Of course, this is not at all the case, since other family members are not consciously aware of the dynamics of what is occurring in their midst. Observing the reactions of a family system from a knowledgeable perspective is an experience most people never have. In this situation, it is important to respond in a rational manner, which must include the willingness to calmly listen to any accusations that come your way and respond in a calm manner. With parents, one-on-one conversations can be especially informative. As Bowen puts it:

> *Person to person relationships with their parents will reveal all the emotional problems the parents have had in their relationship, and that they [the parents] had in their own families of origin.*[120]

If you become triangulated with your arguing parents, avoid taking sides unless one of your parents is an abuser (see chapter: The Abusive Personality / Abusive Relationships). With parents who are extremely locked into their thinking, whose defenses and denial are simply so great that they cannot hear what anyone else is saying, Bowen suggests beginning the differentiation process via siblings, aunts, uncles, grandparents, etc. Of course, some families with strong defenses will create roadblocks no matter where you go. In families with severe roadblocks stemming from the most extreme denial, or where the parents and/or other family members are deceased, the bulk of the differentiation work may involve a comprehensive understanding of the extended family history combined with a considerable increase in self-understanding and self-awareness. Therapy with an experienced—and differentiated—therapist may greatly improve this process. Bowen suggests that it is beneficial if individuals have some understanding of how their extended family has functioned as far back as the grandparents. If forgiveness needs to play a role, forgiving a family system is easier if you understand the system and easier still if you recognize the dysfunction has been unconsciously handed down for generations. In highly volatile and chaotic families, it may be necessary to keep your visits short until those you contact begin to accept the different relationship they have encountered and, consciously or unconsciously, adjust their emotional reactions accordingly.

Remaining calm and rational while in the presence of family members can be a difficult process and, of course, the greater the number of family members present, such as a family reunion, the more difficult it may be to maintain a calm, differentiated state. If you feel yourself becoming a part of the emotional triangles in your family, end the visit until you have had time to plan more rational responses. Improvising calm, rational responses while in an emotionally intense family conversation is always a lost cause. It is important that an individual thoroughly understand how they wish to interact differently with other family members and to *plan in advance* how to respond should emotional tensions increase during the conversation. Only with a detailed plan for reacting to an undifferentiated family can there be any chance of not getting caught up in the emotional tension and turmoil of old. The unconscious tendency to respond to emotional family content with the same emotional and behavioral patterns from the past is too strong to resist without detailed advance planning. If an early exit from the conversation appears necessary, it is essential that you make leaving a calm, logical choice rather than storming out in anger. Bowen points out that these conversations have nothing to do with the friendly and agreeable conversations people have with their parents and family during more tranquil periods and that are mistaken for healthy relationships. A very cool side effect of this process is that, if you consistently change your reactions to the emotional family system, other family members may unconsciously make their own positive changes to adapt to the calmer and more rational environment you have created.

It can be very helpful for couples, or anyone beginning the detriangulation/differentiation process, to form a new triangle with an experienced—and differentiated—therapist. Some triangles are healthy. A therapeutic atmosphere can help individuals, couples, or whole families improve on their responses and communication, while increasing their level of differentiation.

Murray Bowen believed therapy should emphasize both the couple's immediate issues as well as their lack of differentiation with their own parents, although he emphasized the latter. For Bowen, the main goal of therapy is to increase one's level of differentiation rather than focus on individual symptoms. A dysfunctional couple must be willing to lower the temperature and stop discussing their problems with their parents or friends while working to change the nature of their own relationship and their relationships with parents and family. Bowen went so far as to suggest that it may be more productive for a couple experiencing marital problems to use counseling sessions to concentrate on their relationships with their own parents rather than attempting to break through their own relationship and family problems. When spouses increase their level of differentiation from their original family, their relationship to each other begins to change. This, in turn, will change their relationship with other family members including their children. Bowen frequently witnessed considerable change in couples' relationships when the only therapy involved emphasized the relationship of each spouse to his or her family of origin.

With sufficiently motivated clients, I see no reason not to emphasize both ends of the extended family by encouraging simultaneous work on both current and past family functioning. Murray Bowen suggests it might be difficult to find a therapist who is skilled in working with family systems and has also worked on his relationship with his own parents, which Bowen considered a requirement for any therapist hoping to help other couples achieve true stability. An undifferentiated therapist might have difficulty controlling his/her own emotions when caught up in the emotional reactivity of his clients.

Bowen recognized that some couples are reluctant to commit to their own differentiation work and reconnecting with their parents and family. These clients always seem to have some reason for not following through, frequently blaming other family members for any failure to reconnect. Of course, in most cases, it is their own inner foreboding that sabotages their efforts. This is not surprising, since therapy from this perspective requires an active effort to learn about the dynamics of their family's functioning along with some recognition of one's own emotional reactivity within the family.

The differentiation process, of course, will increase the objectivity with which one can observe events in one's family. When more objective family observations are combined with an increased number of visits to the family, the individual can begin to differentiate from the "myths, images, distortions, and triangles" that may have been a part of the family history for generations. For Bowen, learning about one's family, becoming a better observer of one's family, and reducing a person's emotional reactivity to that family are all a part of the same process. To improve in one area is to improve in the others as well. It is unfortunate that most people never recognize that they can discover themselves and their original family in this way—including many people who have invested significant amounts of time and money on various forms of therapy and/or self-help books.

If you want a more comprehensive reading of Murray Bowen's work, his most influential papers have conveniently been brought together in one book:

Family Therapy in Clinical Practice[113]
by Murray Bowen

PART V

Continuing the Journey Into the Self

COUNSELING / THERAPY

Though the patient enters therapy insisting that he wants to change, more often than not, what he really wants is to remain the same . . . (but) to feel better. He prefers the security of known misery to the misery of unfamiliar insecurity.

—Sheldon Kopp[3]

COUNSELING WITH A knowledgeable and experienced therapist can vastly increase the rate and amount of progress you make in your journey of self-discovery and change. It has been suggested that as little as six months of therapy may result in the equivalent of 20 years of gradual personality change without intervention.[108] Depending on the situation and level of motivation, I have found just a few therapy sessions can transform the lives of many people, whether individuals, couples, or family life as a whole. For some people, even very brief counseling works quite well if they gain the information and insights they need. Effective counseling will help keep you focused and give you new ideas to work with as you work toward your goals. Even with longer-term issues, most people do not need weekly therapy for months or years on end although I am a serious believer in periodic brief therapy to help maintain momentum and counter the defense mechanisms that come so naturally to us all (see last chapter).

Although emotional problems are routinely treated with medications, problems that develop throughout childhood and have their roots in a dysfunctional family history are rarely resolved through medication alone. In some cases, though, medication can be very helpful at reducing symptoms and allowing therapy to be more acceptable and effective. Treating long-term emotional problems with medications alone may limit the discussion to "the disease," and continuing problems may be attributed to the medication's ineffectiveness rather than the ongoing relationship problems[12] or unrecognized personality characteristics. In dysfunctional families, a diagnosis of "chemical imbalance" or "neurological disorder" may interrupt and reduce a family's desire to change the nature or structure of their dysfunctional relationships.[127] Unfortunately, many doctors have little training in personalities or the dynamics of family functioning.

If you are unhappy in your relationship or family life, you may wonder whether you are the problem or if the problem resides in your spouse or other family circumstances. A doctor or therapist must attempt to determine if dysfunctional family relationships are the result of an environment created by the symptoms of one particular family member or if the symptoms exhibited by specific family members are caused by the dysfunctional family as a whole.[126] Family members who are worn out, frustrated, and depressed after dealing with the emotional and behavioral problems of a dysfunctional family member may eventually begin to exhibit their own symptoms. In some cases, it may be impossible to tell whether the problems originate in family relationships or in a specific family member. In these cases, some intervention into the family's relationships and functioning, via family therapy, may be helpful. In some cases, individual, couples, or family therapy, or some combination of these, may reduce the need for medications.

Couples counseling where two people disagree about the cause and nature of their problems requires a counselor with considerable training and experience. The therapist must be able to recognize when problems in a relationship or family stem primarily from the thoughts, emotions, and behavior of one spouse or are the products of interactions between both spouses. The therapist must be able to avoid becoming "sucked in" by the accusations of a manipulative or abusive spouse intent on making the other spouse, and/or one or more of their children, the cause of family problems. It is important for couples to learn to understand both their own personality and their partner's personality. Depending on the nature of the couple's relationship, it may be extremely helpful for the couple to learn to participate in constructive and nondefensive *mutual* criticism in the presence of a supportive therapist. Even people who have a good understanding of their personality will sometimes fail to recognize or maintain an ongoing awareness of some of the irrational emotions and behaviors they exhibit. Family therapy involving the whole family may be extremely helpful to children or adolescents who are confused or even afraid of events occurring in the home. The children or adolescents may have been treated harshly in the past whenever they expressed an opinion, and the sense that they are finally being heard may give them a sense of security and a new willingness to express themselves. But in many cases, the benefits of family therapy for children and adolescents come from a different place altogether.

Without realizing it, children and adolescents may misbehave, get sick, have poor performance or behavioral problems at school, become a juvenile delinquent, get into drugs, etc., to give their dysfunctional parents something to concentrate on besides their dysfunctional marital relationship.[111] Children, including very young children, and adolescents are almost always aware at some level of the dysfunction in the family regardless of the extent to which the parents believe they have hidden their marital strife from the children. Sensing the difficulties his/her parents are experiencing, the child or adolescent unconsciously develops problems as a diversion for his dysfunctional parents. The parents now concentrate on their "problem child" or "difficult adolescent" instead of their own dysfunctional relationship.[111] I cannot count the times I have had parents bring their problem child or adolescent to me for treatment when, during family therapy, it was just a matter of time before the parents' own problems began to show themselves. When this happens, and it happens a lot, I am then able to turn my attention to the parents during subsequent sessions. When the problem child or adolescent sees his parents receiving therapeutic help for their own relationship problems, the child or adolescent unconsciously recognizes that there is no longer any reason to "help" their parents by misbehaving, remaining sick, breaking the law, doing drugs, causing trouble at school, etc. Of course, once the parents' own problems have been exposed, this approach cannot work if one or both of the parents are so defensive or abusive that they make up some reason why they cannot continue in therapy.

> ***I now consider myself to be at the beginning of the beginning of making something serious.***
> ***—Vincent van Gogh***

If you want to give counseling a try, look for a therapist with many years of experience. There are many good therapists who are well worth their fee and would love to assist you in your journey. But even a competent therapist may not be the right therapist for your particular issues. I am convinced there are multitudes of therapists out there whose education and training were totally inadequate. As extraordinary as it seems, I went through 10 years of graduate school in the behavioral sciences, including two masters and a PhD, without hearing one single professor even mention the topics of personalities or abusive relationships. Do not assume an experienced and licensed therapist knows beans about your particular issues or personality. Unfortunately, therapists, like everyone else, are not always aware of what they don't know. A part of this problem is the "knowledge explosion" that requires graduate students and professionals to focus their time on very narrow areas of knowledge and research, and a broader view of personality and family difficulties gets lost in the forest.[126] In some cases, therapists may not need any particular expertise to help clients deal with their particular issues. In these instances, it is the therapist's personality and style that is more important in determining the therapy's effectiveness. It is accepted practice among therapists to refer a client to another therapist when the therapist's own knowledge base is deficient or something else simply creates a poor fit between client and therapist. This norm notwithstanding, I believe it is common for people to remain in expensive therapy with the wrong therapist for extended periods of time. Many people spend considerable time and money on therapy that deals with surface symptoms only and never obtain the information about themselves or their family that is necessary for them to begin working on important underlying issues. I have found most people with sufficient motivation can make rapid progress in therapy when they finally begin to understand their most basic self and the dynamics of their relationship and family functioning.

It has always seemed to me that long-term therapy with the same therapist can actually impede progress by reducing the flow of new ideas, new information, and different approaches for dealing with problems. If you have been seeing the same therapist for a considerable length of time, you might benefit from a different perspective provided by a different therapist. This does not mean your present therapist is not a good therapist, but rather that you may have already learned what you can from that therapist's knowledge or approach to your particular issues. In cases where the client remains in continuous therapy for years, it may be the therapist who is holding on to the client for money, while clearly offering inadequate therapy. I have had several clients who were told by a previous therapist during the very first session that they would need weekly therapy for at least a year or more to resolve their issues. This is a manipulative money grab by therapists whose crystal balls are fake. In cases where it is the client who seems overly attached to therapy as some kind of ongoing crutch, this is an issue the therapist should address as part of the therapy.

In some cases, clients "feel better" after each session, so they think the therapist is just great, even though little real progress occurs over time. Of course, feeling better is sometimes all the client really wants. There are people who think they want to change and will say they want to change but would drop out of therapy if the therapist pointed out their lack of real effort and suggested they actually do some serious work. But some therapists will not confront their clients. Their goal is to keep the cash cow coming back each week as long as they can, regardless of any real progress in their client's life.

Also, watch out for the therapist who claims to be an expert in a whole slew of therapeutic techniques. The jack-of-all-trades therapists always seem to have $$$ stamped on their foreheads, as far as I can tell. Taking a three-hour workshop in some therapeutic technique and being an expert in that technique are not the same thing. In some cases, a therapist may claim to have discovered a new and miraculous breakthrough therapeutic technique that actually makes them some money until the next breakthrough technique comes along. Of course, these kinds of problems increase exponentially when the therapist's training is massively dumbed down as occurs with coaching, schools of hypnotherapy, fake degrees, including fake PhDs from nonaccredited correspondence courses, etc. While I encourage you to seek recommendations when searching for a therapist, you still need to put more stock in your own gut feelings after you begin therapy. If you have discovered a part of yourself in this book, you are now in a better position to spot the wrong therapist.

WITH PERSEVERANCE, EXPECT SUCCESS

You look at people who have aged successfully, and they all seem to have the same characteristics. They try new things, they're adventurous, they're into cooking, woodworking, or something else that uses all their faculties.

      — **Lawrence C. Katz (1957–2005)**
      Professor of neurobiology
      Duke University Medical School

THE IDEA OF actually making changes in our personality can be intimidating, and many people shy away from the experience of personal change. Some people simply may not be aware that they can learn to understand themselves in a comprehensive way, while others may run from the inevitable decisions and anxiety that might be involved. Some people may not want to change because they do not want to give up the rewards and perks they get with the status quo. Yet for those who would like to change some aspect of their basic self, there are techniques anyone can actively use to avoid becoming "stuck," although the specific path you continue down will necessarily be your own. While your journey may involve ideas and information you gather from therapists or psychology and self-help books, your journey will still reflect the unique individuality with which you approach life. Know that you can make the changes you desire. We all have the capacity to do this. With an increase in self-understanding and self-awareness, you can make serious progress toward becoming the person you want to be. Increased self-understanding and

self-awareness can have a major impact in many areas of life. Would you like to become:
- **Less worried**
- **More understanding and considerate**
- **More independent**
- **More outgoing**
- **Less gullible**
- **Less angry**
- **A better spouse or parent**
- **More knowledgeable about something**
- **Less shy**
- **Less stressed and more relaxed**
- **A better listener**
- **More friendly**
- **Less isolated**
- **More interesting and less boring**
- **Less self-absorbed, with more empathy for others**
- **Better able to understand your reactions to others**
- **(You fill this one in)** _____

Your journey into your basic self is clearly under way, but how far you travel is a choice that must be reaffirmed from time to time. As you continue your intellectual journey into self-understanding and self-awareness, it is important that you actively make changes toward the life you desire. Waiting for opportunities that may or may not present themselves is not a sound game plan. As one saying goes, "You will miss 100 percent of the shots you don't take." Do not confuse what I am saying with the statements of those farcical self-help gurus who swell their bank accounts by telling their readers some variation of, "You can do or be anything you want to do or be if you will just buy my book/CD collection," etc. This is false. We all have limitations, and your extended journey may involve a search for some combination of that which you can excel at best, and that which you will continue to enjoy for the long term.

Success is sometimes the outcome of a whole string of failures.
—Vincent van Gogh

Even where we have little natural ability, we may find we enjoy something enough to be willing to work at it harder than other people or, like my banjo and guitar picking, just settle for doing it badly. Of course, your desires and goals may change over time as a natural part of the process of self-discovery. Giving up on something is fine as long as you try something else. Many of the decisions you make along the way will be informed by the crashes and ashes of previous decisions. The word *failure* is false terminology when used to describe the very natural trial-and-error process of self-discovery. We can all experience the adventure of the search as long as we become aware of, and consciously overrule, those personality characteristics that get in our way and block our willingness to struggle, persevere, or simply start over again—repeatedly if necessary. This is the stuff of a successful life.

Reading this book is the first step toward getting to know and understand yourself. Simply put, people are complex, which is why a comprehensive self-understanding and self-awareness requires knowledgeable self-observations and self-reflections over an extended period of time. For example, a person who constantly wonders what his girlfriend or spouse is doing may have an obsessive-compulsive personality, or he may have a controlling personality with an abusive sense of entitlement that views the woman as his property, etc.

And many people deal with multiple issues. Consider the unhappy mother who cannot get along with her distraught daughter, but also has problems in her marriage, at work, physical-health issues, etc. She may also suffer some level of depression that may contribute to her other problems, or were caused by her other problems, but plays an integral role in her life either way. Maybe her distraught daughter has an undiagnosed personality or mood disorder missed by the school counselor or family therapist, or maybe the daughter is acting out in an unconscious attempt to stop the family chaos by giving her bickering parents something else to concentrate on besides themselves. While a knowledgeable therapist may be immensely helpful for information, guidance, and advice, only you can have the ongoing observations, self-reflections, and insights necessary for acquiring self-control. An increase in self-control arises naturally when you finally understand your personality and your interactions with other people and the outside world.

> *I'll start with small things.*
> —Vincent van Gogh

As you continue to develop a more in-depth understanding of your personality, think about further changes you would like to make. Make a conscious effort to ignore or overrule the little voices left over from critical parents, other critical or judgmental people, negative past experiences, or your pessimistic side from wherever it arises. If you read Part IV and think a lack of differentiation plays some role in your life, I strongly encourage you to work with an experienced therapist while reconnecting with your original family. If you have to speak with several therapists to find the right one, it will be worth the effort. Depending on your goals, the process of change may involve intellectually, emotionally, or physically going places you have never been or trying out new things you find interesting. You may decide to drop the couch-potato thing and watch only the best TV so you can use the rest of your free time on more interesting endeavors, which will inevitably make you a more interesting person. Even if you decide to drop a new activity that doesn't grab you, you will know you tried it, and you will be more interesting as a person for having made the attempt. Every new experience in life, even the unsuccessful ones, changes us a little bit. With each new experience, you will become a more interesting conversationalist around others, and you will enjoy keeping your own company more as well.

> *I'm drawing a great deal and I think its getting better.*
> —Vincent van Gogh

Look for those niches in life where you sense the best fit and think you will gain the most enjoyment. Our negative symptoms tend to show up more in those environments in which we feel unhappy, awkward, tense, anxious, depressed, etc. For most of us, positive niches that feel right don't just fall into our lap, although that does seem to happen for some people by virtue of the environment, timing, talent, or luck. The great majority of us must conduct an extensive search for the meaningful life we desire. In the world of work, few of us get to make a ton of money doing what we want to do anyway and would do for free if we had to. But you can still work to be great at whatever it is you do and to improve your skills at life.

For example, the most complex job anyone can have is to be a parent. The most competent rocket scientist can be an incompetent parent. Even working in the most mundane job, if you succeed at being a competent spouse and parent, you have done well. People are not born with great parenting skills built into their genes, so I recommend all present and future parents take a parenting-skills course, or at least do some reading and *create* the great parent they want to be. For some, a major part of becoming unstuck simply means spending more quality time with the family they have neglected. As psychologist and Auschwitz survivor Victor Frankl[4] pointed out, it is up to each one of us to search for and create the meaning in our lives. It may be our job, our family, something we produce, or volunteer work at an animal shelter. True meaning in life is available to everyone. The trick is to adopt an *attitude* that allows you to seek out that meaning. The choice is yours alone. As Victor Frankl put it, "The last of the human freedoms is to choose one's attitudes."

I would now wish you the best of luck, but with sufficient motivation, a sense of adventure, counseling if needed, and perseverance in your desire to apply some self-understanding and self-awareness to life's opportunities and choices, luck becomes an unnecessary ingredient.

PART VI

Defense Mechanisms

One major problem we all have in forming an accurate assessment of our own personality, aside from the self-ignorant starting point I have been discussing, is that we must view ourselves through the prism of the very personality we are trying to figure out.[76] Defense mechanisms are unconscious psychological techniques that help all of us to avoid the anxiety, depression, and lowered self-esteem that might otherwise accompany our reactions to some of our more uncomfortable thoughts, emotions, impulses, desires, conflicts, or to other people or life circumstances. I encourage you to conduct a brief review of the more common defense mechanisms to see if you recognize some of your reactions to anxiety-causing thoughts, things, people, events, etc.

Without realizing it, most of us have defenses that operate on a continuum from a mild bias through extreme denial. Increasing your self-awareness may necessarily require an increase in your awareness of the unconscious defenses that may contribute to your blind spots and denial. To a large extent, our defenses are considered a normal and acceptable way of dealing with some of the conflicts that we confront on a daily basis. Most of us will use many different defense mechanisms in the course of our lives, although there may be one primary defense that dominates.[5] If not carried to extreme levels, our defenses may improve our lives by reducing the anxiety, depression, and lowered self-esteem we might otherwise experience.

Some defenses are more maladaptive than others,[34] and some personalities have an overreliance on defense mechanisms. Individuals with these personalities may not be as connected to the realities of daily life. It may help your journey of self-discovery to become familiar with the more common defense mechanisms. It is important to keep in mind that a reduction or abandonment of one's defenses may result in an increase in anxiety and/or depression. If some level of anxiety or depression becomes a part of your journey, conducting your journey with the help of an experienced and knowledgeable professional is recommended and may greatly enhance the experience.

Here are descriptions of some of the more common defense mechanisms:[1,5]

Denial: Denial involves the refusal to consciously acknowledge the existence of some anxiety-causing conflict, thought, emotion, impulse, desire, behavior, or external event. For example, alcoholics or drug addicts may deny they have a problem, or an abused wife may refuse to admit to herself that she is abused for fear of being a single parent and losing her abusive partner's financial support or help with child rearing if she stands up to the abuse. While all of us use denial to some extent, when carried to extremes denial can completely destroy a family's or individual's ability to function rationally. In some cases, serious denial may endure for a lifetime. If it is someone else, it may not be possible to talk to them because they just do not want to hear you at the deepest level. For some people, the need for an honest conversation with themselves may never become a part of their conscious awareness.

Rationalization: Rationalization involves creating a fictional view or explanation that is less threatening than the original view or the actual explanation. For example, an individual who has just been fired from a good job will now conclude the job was just a dead-end position with an obviously incompetent boss.

Projection: Projection involves attributing one's own uncomfortable thoughts and feelings to another person as a way to avoid anxiety from internal conflict. This may appear as a tendency to blame others. The individual who has uncomfortable thoughts about having an affair may project these thoughts onto the spouse and wonder if his or her spouse is thinking about having an affair.

Displacement: Displacement involves transferring emotional or behavioral responses from an anxiety-causing person or object onto another person or object that is experienced as less threatening. For example, an individual who is angry at his boss may go home after work and unload his anger onto his spouse or children—or kick the dog.

Humor: Humor as a defense involves reducing stress or anxiety by focusing on the humorous side of the stressor or anxiety-causing event. The difference between humor as an unhealthy defense mechanism and humor for healthy and effective stress relief may be a fine line.

Acting Out: Acting out is the direct expression of unconscious internal conflicts and desires, or as a response to external stressors, through outward behavioral expression, rather than thinking about the actual issue and consciously experiencing the emotions involved. To avoid the anxiety from consciously experiencing conflicts, desires, or stressors, individuals may have temper tantrums, commit crimes, have promiscuous sex, abuse their spouse or children, etc. Acting out as a defense helps to avoid emotional conflict, but not all bad or negative behavior is the result of acting out.

Passive-Aggression: Passive-aggression involves subtle and indirect—that is, passive—aggression toward other people. The indirect aggression may involve a refusal to perform or complete expected behaviors as part of a job or relationship, while always having some excuse for the failure. The indirect aggression typically involves underlying feelings of resentment or anger. Blaming others or circumstances for practically anything is common. This defense is described as a separate personality in Part III.

Fantasy: Some individuals dealing with loneliness, fear of intimacy, an eccentric personality, etc., may seek comfort in a fantasy world, which may include imaginary friends. Focused on the fantasy world inside their minds, these individuals may appear aloof to others.

Affiliation: Affiliation involves dealing with internal conflict and emotions or environmental stress by seeking help and support from other people. Sharing some of our problems with others is, of course, quite normal and can be very beneficial. In some cases, though, an individual may expose too much, too often, to the wrong people or talk to too many people.

Anticipation: Anticipation involves reacting emotionally or behaviorally to possible future events or planning reactions in advance of an event. This defense is common among shy people who become anxious at just the thought of attending a future social event and find some reason why they just cannot attend.

Devaluation: Devaluation involves ascribing exaggerated negative traits to oneself or to other people.

Idealization: Idealization involves ascribing exaggerated positive traits to oneself or to other people.

Intellectualization: Intellectualization involves an overuse of thinking, including an overemphasis on analysis and details, but with little or no emotional content. This overthinking is a way of avoiding uncomfortable or anxiety-provoking thoughts, feelings, or impulses. The analytical but emotionally unavailable spouse may involve an overuse of this defense.

Omnipotence: Omnipotence involves dealing with internal conflict and emotions or environmental stressors by acting as if you possess some special ability or power or simply acting superior to other people. Look for this one among members of various religious or political organizations and cults.

Suppression: Suppression involves intentionally choosing not to think about uncomfortable or anxiety-producing thoughts, feelings, impulses, desires, or experiences.

Repression: Repression involves the unconscious expulsion of anxiety-causing thoughts, feelings, impulses, or desires. The memory of actual experiences may also be expelled from conscious awareness. Yet feelings related to the anxiety-causing events may remain without any conscious awareness of their origin.

Reaction Formation: Reaction formation involves avoiding uncomfortable or anxiety-causing thoughts, feelings, desires, and behaviors by substituting thoughts, feelings, desires, and behaviors that are essentially the opposite. For example, the individual who feels an overwhelming attraction to pornography may preach unceasingly against pornography and organize political-action groups to advocate stricter antipornography laws. Reaction formation may be accompanied by repression.

Sublimation: Sublimation involves channeling uncomfortable feelings or impulses into socially acceptable outlets, such as channeling anger into a fitness program.

Dissociation: Dissociation involves a breakdown in the normal functions of consciousness, memory, behavioral responses, or perceptions of self or the environment. The individual may lose usual thought processes and memories of events. Dissociation may involve replacing unpleasant emotions with other emotions and may be associated with more highly emotional personalities, such as the histrionic personality. Dissociation may be experienced by victims of child abuse as they attempt to block painful memories and feelings.

Introjection: Introjection involves unconsciously internalizing the attitudes, values, or ideas of someone else into one's own personality. Individuals may internalize the teachings of their parents, resulting in a conscience that is based on their parents' values. A mid-level manager may internalize his boss's abusive nature to avoid the guilt he might otherwise feel after enforcing abusive rules and regulations.

If only we might examine our footprints once
in a soft mix of earth and water
we may come to know the power of our footsteps
of a quick decision
and thus practice the graceful skill of stepping lightly.

From "Meditations"
By William Ladnier

ACKNOWLEDGMENTS

EVERY NOW AND then a batch of raw talent presents itself to me in a way that commands my attention. How fortunate to be walking down a street fair in Portland, Oregon and come across such a phenomenal artist as Hilary M. Larson, whose extraordinary talent graces the pages of this book. It was also serendipitous to meet poet William Ladnier in Manitou Springs, Colorado. I suggested the idea for a beginning and an ending poem for this book, and within about 10 minutes, Will handed me a prototype introductory poem. I want to thank my publisher, Karen Pickering of Colorado Springs, for guiding me through the publishing process. I also want to thank the employees at various Whole Foods Markets in the Dallas area for allowing me to sit in their café areas and work for hours at a time, year after year. Ditto for the great employees at the Gloria's and Blue Goose restaurants on Greenville Avenue in Dallas, and the Wild Goose Meeting House and Rico's Café in Colorado Springs.

Artist: Hilary M. Larson
lilhilpdx@gmail.com
www.lilhilillustrations.weebly.com

Poet: William Ladnier
ladnierw@gmail.com

BIBLIOGRAPHY

1: DSM-5 (2013). Diagnostical and Statistical Manual of Mental Disorders (5th ed.). American Psychiatric Association.

2: The Allstate Foundation: allstatefoundation.org.

3: Kopp, S. (1972). *If You mMeet the Buddha on the Road—Kill Him: The Pilgrimage of Psychotherapy Patients.* New York: Bantam Books.

4: Frankl, V. (1946). *Man's Search for Meaning.* New York: Washington Square Press.

5: Sadock, B.J., Sadock, V.A. (2007) *Synopsis of Psychiatry.* New York: Lippincot Williams Wilkins.

6: O'Donohue, W., Fowler, K.A., & Lilienfeld, S.O. (2007). Introduction: Personality Disorders in Perspective. In O'Donohue, W., Fowler, K.A., & Lilienfeld, S.O. (Eds.), *Personality Disorders: Towards the DSM-V* (pp. 1–20). Thousand Oaks: Sage Publications, Inc.

7: Cloninger, C.R. (1987). A systematic method for clinical description and classification of personality variants: A proposal. *Archieves of General Psychiatry,* 44, 573–588.

8: Widiger, T.A. (2007). Alternatives to DSM-IV. In O'Donohue, W., Fowler, K.A., & Lilienfeld, S.O. (Eds.), *Personality Disorders: Towards the DSM-V* (pp. 21–40). Thousand Oaks: Sage Publications, Inc.

9: Bernstein, D.P., & Useda, J.D. (2007). Paranoid personality disorder. In O'Donohue, W., Fowler, K.A., & Lilienfeld, S.O. (Eds.), *Personality Disorders: Towards the DSM-V* (pp. 41–62). Thousand Oaks: Sage Publications, Inc.

10: Mittal, V.A., Kalus, O., Bernstein, D.P., Siever, L.J. (2007). Schizoid personality disorder. In O'Donohue, W., Fowler, K.A., & Lilienfeld, S.O. (Eds.), *Personality Disorders: Towards the DSM-V* (pp. 63–80). Thousand Oaks: Sage Publications, Inc.

11: Bollini, A.M., Walker, E.F. (2007). Schizotypal personality disorder. In O'Donohue, W., Fowler, K.A., & Lilienfeld, S.O. (Eds.), *Personality disorders: Towards the DSM-V* (pp. 81–108). Thousand Oaks: Sage Publications, Inc.

12: Bancroft, L. (2002). *Why Does He Do That?* New York: Penguin Group.

13: Patrick, C.J. (2007). Antisocial personality disorder and psychopathy. In O'Donohue, W., Fowler, K.A., & Lilienfeld, S.O. (Eds.), *Personality Disorders: Towards the DSM-V* (pp. 109–166). Thousand Oaks: Sage Publications, Inc.

14: Bradley, R., Conklin, C.Z., Westen, D. (2007). Borderline personality disorder. In O'Donohue, W., Fowler, K.A., & Lilienfeld, S.O. (Eds.), *Personality Disorders: Towards the DSM-V* (pp. 167–202). Thousand Oaks: Sage Publications, Inc.

15: Blagov, P.S., Fowler, K.A., Lilienfeld, S.O. (2007). Histrionic personality disorder. In O'Donohue, W., Fowler, K.A., & Lilien- feld, S.O. (Eds.), *Personality Disorders: Towards the DSM-V* (pp. 203–232). Thousand Oaks: Sage Publications, Inc.

16: Levy, K.N., Reynoso, J.S., Wasserman, R.H., Clarkin, J.F. (2007). Narcissistic personality disorder. In O'Donohue, W., Fowler, K.A., & Lilienfeld, S.O. (Eds.), *Personality Disorders: Towards the DSM-V* (pp. 233–278). Thousand Oaks: Sage Publications, Inc.

17: Herbert, J.D. (2007). Avoidant personality disorder. In O'Donohue, W., Fowler, K.A., & Lilienfeld, S.O. (Eds.), *Personality Disorders: Towards the DSM-V* (pp. 279–306). Thousand Oaks: Sage Publications, Inc.

18: Bornstein, R.F. (2007). Dependent personality disorder. In O'Donohue, W., Fowler, K.A., & Lilienfeld, S.O. (Eds.), *Personality Disorders: Towards the DSM-V* (pp. 307–324). Thousand Oaks: Sage Publications, Inc.

19: Bartz, J., Kaplan, A., Hollander, E. (2007). Obsessive-compulsive personality disorder. In O'Donohue, W., Fowler, K.A., & Lilien- feld, S.O. (Eds.), *Personality Disorders: Towards the DSM-V* (pp. 325–352). Thousand Oaks: Sage Publications, Inc.

20: Morey, L.C., Hopwood, C.J., Klein, D.N. (2007). Passive aggressive, depressive, and sadistic personality disorders. In O'Donohue, W., Fowler, K.A., & Lilienfeld, S.O. (Eds.), *Personality Disorders: Towards the DSM-V* (pp. 353–374). Thousand Oaks: Sage Publications, Inc.

21: Westen, D., & Shedler, J. (1999). Revising and assessing Axis II: Developing a clinically meaningful and empirically valid assessment method. *American Journal of Psychiatry*, 156, 258–272. Cited by Levy, K.N., Reynoso, J.S., Wasserman, R.H., Clarkin, J.F. (2007). Narcissistic personality disorder. In O'Donohue, W., Fowler, K.A., & Lilienfeld, S.O. (Eds.), *Personality Disorders: Towards the DSM-V* (pp. 233–278). Thousand Oaks: Sage Publications, Inc.

22: Kernberg, O. (1975a). *Borderline Conditions and Pathological Narcissism*. New York: Jason Aronson. Cited by: Levy, K.N., Reynoso, J.S., Wasserman, R.H., Clarkin, J.F. (2007).

Narcissistic personality disorder. In O'Donohue, W., Fowler, K.A., & Lilienfeld, S.O. (Eds.), *Personality Disorders: Towards the DSM-V* (pp. 233–278). Thousand Oaks: Sage Publications, Inc.

23: Turner, S.M., & Beidel, D.C. (1989). Social phobia: Clinical syndrome, diagnosis, and comorbidity. *Clinical Psychology Review*, 9, (p. 3–18). Cited by Herbert, J.D. (2007). Avoidant personality disorder. In O'Donohue, W., Fowler, K.A., & Lilienfeld, S.O. (Eds.), *Personality Disorders: Towards the DSM-V* (pp. 279–306). Thousand Oaks: Sage Publications, Inc.

24: Bornstein, R.F. (1992). The dependent personality: Developmental, social, and clinical perspectives. *Psychological Bulletin, 112, 3–23.* Cited by Bornstein, R.F. (2007). Dependent personality disorder. In O'Donohue, W., Fowler, K.A., & Lilienfeld, S.O. (Eds.), *Personality Disorders: Towards the DSM-V* (pp. 307–324). Thousand Oaks: Sage Publications, Inc.

25: Bornstein, R.F. (1993). *The Dependent Personality.* New York: Guilford Press. Cited by Bornstein, R.F. (2007). Dependent personality disorder. In O'Donohue, W., Fowler, K.A., & Lilienfeld, S.O. (Eds.), *Personality Disorders: Towards the DSM-V* (pp. 307–324). Thousand Oaks: Sage Publications, Inc.

26: Pincus, A.L., & Wilson, K. R. (2001). Interpersonal variability in dependent personality. *Journal of Personality*, 69, 223–251. Cited by Bornstein, R.F. (2007). Dependent personality disorder. In O'Donohue, W., Fowler, K.A., & Lilienfeld, S.O. (Eds.), *Personality Disorders: Towards the DSM-V* (pp. 307–324). Thousand Oaks: Sage Publications, Inc.

27: Bornstein, R.F. (1995). Sex differences in objective and projective dependency tests: A meta-analytic review. *Assessment*, 2, 319–331. Cited by Bornstein, R.F. (2007). Dependent Personality Disorder. In O'Donohue, W., Fowler, K.A., & Lilienfeld, S.O. (Eds.), *Personality Disorders: Towards the DSM-V* (pp. 307–324). Thousand Oaks: Sage Publications, Inc.

28: Shapiro, D. (1965). *Neurotic Styles.* Basic Books.

29: Beck, A.T., Freeman, A., Davis, D.D., & Associates (2004). *Cognitive Therapy of Personality Disorders* (2nd ed.). New York: Guilford Press. Cited by Bartz, J., Laplan, A., Hollander, E. (2007). Obsessive-compulsive personality disorder. In O'Donohue, W., Fowler, K.A., & Lilienfeld, S.O. (Eds.), *Personality Disorders: Towards the DSM-V* (pp. 325–352). Thousand Oaks: Sage Publications, Inc.

30: Herbert, J.D. (2007). Avoidant personality disorder. In O'Donohue, W., Fowler, K.A., & Lilienfeld, S.O. (Eds.), *Personality Disorders: Towards the DSM-V* (pp. 279–306). Thousand Oaks: Sage Publications, Inc.

31: Quinn, B.P. (1998). *The Depression Sourcebook.* Lincolnwood, Illinois: Lowell House.

32: *Passive-aggressive behavior.* Wikipedia.

33: DSM-IV-TR (2000). *Diagnostical and Statistical Manual of Mental Disorders* (p. 789). American Psychiatric Association.

34: Skodol, A.E., & Bender, D.S. (Eds.). (2009). *Essentials of Personality Disorders* (pp. 37–62). Arlington, VA, American Psychiatric Publishing, Inc.

35: Oldham, J.M., Skodol, A.E., & Bender, D.S. (2009 Introduction. In Oldham, J.M., Skodol, A.E., & Bender, D.S.

(Eds.), *Essentials of Personality Disorders* (p. xv). Arlington, VA: American Psychiatric Publishing, Inc.

36: Oldham, J.M. (2009). Personality disorders: Recent history and the DSM system. In Oldham, J.M., Skodol, A.E., & Bender, D.S. (Eds.), *Essentials of Personality Disorders* (pp. 3–12). Arlington, VA: American Psychiatric Publishing, Inc.

37: Heim, A.H., Westen, D. (2009). Theories of personality and personality disorders. In Oldham, J.M., Skodol, A.E., & Bender, D.S. (Eds.), *Essentials of Personality Disorders* (p. 13–36). Arlington, VA: American Psychiatric Publishing, Inc.

38: Grilo, C.M., McGlashan, T.H. (2009). Course and outcome. In Oldham, J.M., Skodol, A.E., & Bender, D.S. (Eds.), *Essentials of Personality Disorders* (pp. 63–82). Arlington, VA: American Psychiatric Publishing, Inc.

39: Torgersen, S. (2009). Prevalence, sociodemographics, and functional impairment. In Oldham, J.M., Skodol, A.E., & Bender, D.S. (Eds.), *Essentials of Personality Disorders* (pp. 83–102). Arlington, VA: American Psychiatric Publishing, Inc.

40: Cohen, P., & Crawford, T. (2009). Developmental issues. In Oldham, J.M., Skodol, A.E., & Bender, D.S. (Eds.), *Essentials of Personality Disorders* (pp. 123–142). Arlington, VA: American Psychiatric Publishing, Inc.

41: Johnson, J.G., Bromley, E., & McGeoch, P.G. (2009). Childhood experiences and development of maladaptive and adaptive personality traits. In Oldham, J.M., Skodol, A.E., & Bender, D.S. (Eds.), *Essentials of Personality Disorders* (pp. 143–157). Arlington, VA: American Psychiatric Publishing, Inc.

42: Westen, D. & Gabbard, G. (2002). Developments in cognitive neuroscience: *Journal of the American Psychoanalytic Association*. Vol 50, pp 99–134. Cited by Gabbard, G.O. (2005). Psychodynamic approaches to personality disorders. *Focus*, vol 3, no. 3, (p. 363). focus.psychiatryonline.org.

43: Unterberg, M.P. (2003). Personality disorders in the workplace: Shaking down the con man. http://managedhealthcareexecutive.modernmedicine.com.

44: Oldham, J.M., Skodol, A.E., & Bender, D.S. (2009). Introduction. In Oldham, J.M., Skodol, A.E., & Bender, D.S. (Eds.), *Essentials of Personality Disorders* (pp. 375–398). Arlington, VA, American Psychiatric Publishing, Inc.

45: Dreikurs, R. (1993). *The New Approach to Discipline: Logical Consequences.* Plume. Penguin.com.

46: Evans, P. (1992). *The Verbally Abusive Relationship*. Avon, MA: Adams Media.

47: Roberts, B.W., & DelVecchio, W.F. (2000). The rank-ordered consistency of personality traits from childhood to old age: a quantitative review of longitudinal studies. Cited by: Grilo, C.M., McGlashan, T.H. (2009). Course and outcome. In: Oldham, J.M., Skodol, A.E., & Bender, D.S. (Eds.), (2009). *Essentials of Personality Disorders.* Arlington, VA, American Psychiatric Publishing, Inc., pp. 63–82.

48: Costa, P.T., & Widiger, T.A. (2002). *Personality Disorders and the Five-factor Model of Personality* (2nd Edition). Washington, DC, American Psychological Association. Cited by: Cohen, P., & Crawford, T. (2009). Developmental issues. In: Oldham, J.M., Skodol, A.E., & Bender, D.S. (Eds.), (2009). *Essentials of Personality Disorders.* Arlington, VA, American Psychiatric Publishing, Inc., pp. 123–142.

49: Unterberg, M.P. (2009). Personality disorders in the workplace: Shaking down the con man. http;//www.modern medicine. com/ modernmedicine/psychology.

50: Rettew, D.C. (2009). Avoidant personality disorder. http://emedicine.medscape.com/article/913360-overview.

51: Bhatia, S.K., & Bhatia, S.C. (2009). Childhood and adolescent depression. Internet.

52: Heise, L.L. (1994). Gender-based abuse: the global epidemic. In: Dan, A.J., (Ed.), Reframing Women's Health: Multidisciplinary Research and Practice. Thousand Oaks, California: Sage Publications, 1994: 233–250. Cited by: Eyler, A.E. & Cohen, M.C. (1999). Case studies in partner violence. *American Family Physicians,* 60 (9).

53: Koplewicz, H.S. (2003). More than moody: Recognizing and treating adolescent depression. *The Brown University Child and Adolescent Behavior Letter.*

54: Jamison, K.R. (1995). *An Unquiet Mind.* Alfred A Knopf.

55: Zanarini, M.C., Frankenburg, F.R., Hennen, J., Reich, D.B. & Silk, K.R. (2005). The McLean study of adult development (MSAD): Overview and implications of the first six years of prospective follow-up. *Journal of Personality Disorders,* 19 (5): pp 505–523.

56: Hyman, B.M. & Pedrich, R.N. (2003). *Obsessive-Compulsive Disorder.* Brookfield, Connecticut: Twenty-First Century Books.

57: Phillipson, S. *The right stuff: Obsessive-compulsive personality disorder: A defect of philosophy, not anxiety.* http://www.ocdonline.com/ articlesphillipson.php.

58: Phillipson, S. *The understanding and treatment of the obsessional doubt related to sexual orientation and relationship substantiation.* http://www.ocdonline.com/articlesphillipson.php.

59: Phillipson, S. *God forbid.* http://www.ocdonline.com/articlesphillipson. php.

60: Phillipson, S. *Rethinking the unthinkable.* http://www.ocdonline.com/articlesphillipson.php.

61: Phillipson, S. *Guilt beyond a reasonable doubt.* http://www.ocdonline. com/articlesphillipson.php.

62: Yabroff, J. (2008). *Take the bananas and run.* Newsweek, August 18 & 25, p. 56.

63: Phillipson, S. (2010). *Speak of the devil.* http://www.ocdonline.com/articlephillipson3.php.

64: Yoffe, E. (2009). *But enough about you... What is narcissistic personality disorder, and why does everyone seem to have it?* http://www.slate.com/id/2213740.

65: Hyman, B.M. & Pedrick, C. (2005). *The OCD Workbook.* Second edition. Oakland, California: New Harbinger Publications, Inc.

66: Hecht, A.M., Fichter, M. & Postpischil, P. (1983). Obsessive-compulsive neurosis and anorexia nervosa. *International Journal of Eating Disorders,* 2: 69–77. Cited in: Hyman, B.M. & Pedrick, C. (2005). *The OCD Workbook.* Second edition. Oakland, California: New Harbinger Publications, Inc.

67: Yaryura-Tobias, J.A. & Neziroglu, F.A. (1997b). *Obsessive-compulsive disorder spectrum: Pathogenisis, diagnosis, and treatment.* Washington DC: American Psychiatric Press. Cited in: Hyman, B.M. & Pedrick, C. (2005). *The OCD Workbook.* Second edition. Oakland, California: New Harbinger Publications, Inc.

68: Freeston, M.H. & Ladouceur, R. (1997). What do patients do with their obsessional thoughts? *Behavior Research and Therapy,* 34(5): 433–446. Cited in: Hyman, B.M. & Pedrick, C. (2005). *The OCD Workbook.* Second edition. Oakland, California: New Harbinger Publications, Inc.

69: Steketee, G.S. (1993). *Treatment of Obsessive-Compulsive Disorder. New York*: The Guilford Press. Cited in: Hyman, B.M. & Pedrick, C. (2005). *The OCD Workbook.* Second edition. Oakland, California: New Harbinger Publications, Inc.

70: Rachman, S. & de Silva, P. (1978). Abnormal and normal obsessions. *Behavior Research and Therapy* 16: 233–248. Cited in: Hyman, B.M. & Pedrick, C. (2005). *The OCD Workbook.* Second edition. Oakland, California: New Harbinger Publications, Inc.

71: March, J., & Mulle, K. (1998). *OCD in Children and Adolescents: A Cognitive-Behavioral Treatment Manual.* New York: The Guilford Press. Cited by: Hyman, B.M. & Pedrick, C. (2005). *The OCD Workbook.* Second edition. Oakland, California: New Harbinger Publications, Inc.

72: Cozolino, L. *The Neuroscience of Human Relationships* (pp. 256–257). New York: W.W. Norton & Company.

73: Vogel, C. (2006). A field guide to narcissism. *Psychology Today,* January/February.

74: First, M.B., & Tasman, A. (2010). *A Clinical Guide to the Diagnosis and Treatment of Mental Disorders.* John Wiley & Sons, Inc.

75: Stout, M. (2005). *The Sociopath Next Door.* Random House Inc.: New York.

76: Zimmerman, M. (1994). Diagnosing personality disorders: a review of issues and research methods. *Arch Gen Psychiatry,* 51: 225–245. Cited by: Skodol, A.E. (2009). Manifestations, clinical diagnosis, and comorbidity. In: Oldham, J.M., Skodol, A.E., & Bender, D.S. (Eds.). (2009). *Essentials of Personality Disorders.* Arlington, VA, American Psychiatric Publishing, Inc., pp 37–62.

77: Harvard School of Public Health (2001). *Dating violence against adolescent girls linked with teen pregnancy, suicide attempts, and other health risk behaviors.* Boston, MA. http://www.hsph.harvard.edu/news/press-releases/archives/2001-releases/press07312001.html.

78: Taylor, C.A., Manganello, J.A., Lee, S.J., & Rice, J.C. (2010). Mothers' spanking of 3-year old children and subsequent risk of children's aggressive behavior. *Pediatrics,* Vol. 125 No. 5 May 2010, pp. e1057–e1065 (doi:10.1542/peds.2009–2678).

79: Berlin et al. (2009). Correlates and consequences of spanking and verbal punishment for low income white, African-american, and Mexican-American toddlers. Child Development, 80 (5).

80: Carducci, B.J. (2000). *The new solution.* Psychology Today, January 1.

81: Carducci, B.J. (2008). *Are we born shy? Genetics, environment, and bashfulness.* Psychology Today, June 16, 2008.

82: Zimbardo, P.G. (1977). *Shyness: What Is It? What to Do About It.* Addison-Wesley, New York.

83: Asendorpf, J.B. (2010). Long-term development of shyness: Looking forward and looking backward. In: Rubin, K.H., & Coplan, R.J. (Eds.), *The Development of Shyness and Social Withdrawal* (pp. 157–175). New York: Guilford.

84: Crozier, W.R. (2010). Shyness and the development of embarrassment and the self-conscious emotions. In: Rubin, K.H., & Coplan, R.J. (Eds.), *The Development of Shyness and Social Withdrawal* (pp. 42–63). New York: Guilford.

85: Schmidt, L.A., Buss, A.H. (2010). Understanding shyness: Four questions and four decades of research. In: Rubin, K.H., & Coplan, R.J. (Eds.), *The Development of Shyness and Social Withdrawal* (pp. 23–41). New York: Guilford.

86: Hastings, P.D., Nuselovici, J.N., Rubin, K.H., Cheah, C.S. (2010). Shyness, parenting, and parent-child relationships. In: Rubin, K.H., & Coplan, R.J. (Eds.), *The Development of Shyness and Social Withdrawal* (pp. 107–130). New York: Guilford.

87: Rapee, R.M. (2010). Temperament and the etiology of social phobia. In: Rubin, K.H., & Coplan, R.J. (Eds.), *The Development of Shyness and Social Withdrawal* (pp. 277–299). New York: Guilford.

88: McNeil, D.W. (2010). Evolution of terminology and constructs in social anxiety and its disorders. In: Hofmann, S.G. & Dibartolo, P.M. (Eds.), *Social Anxiety: Clinical, Developmental, and Social Perspectives* (pp. 3–21). New York: Elsevier.

89: Henderson, L., & Zimbardo, P. (2010). Shyness, social anxiety and social phobia. In: Hofmann, S.G. & Dibartolo, P.M. (Eds.),

Social Anxiety: Clinical, Developmental, and Social Perspectives (pp. 65–93). New York: Elsevier.

90: Miller, R.S. (2010). Are embarrassment and social anxiety merely distant cousins, or are they closer kin? In: Hofmann, S.G. & Dibartolo, P.M. (Eds.), *Social Anxiety: Clinical, Developmental, and Social Perspectives* (pp. 93–118). New York: Elsevier.

91: Stravynski, A., Kyparissis, A., & Amado, D. (2010). Social phobia as a deficit in social skills. In: Hofmann, S.G. & Dibartolo, P.M. (Eds.), *Social Anxiety: Clinical, Developmental, and Social Perspectives* (pp. 147–181). New York: Elsevier.

92: Wenzel, A. (2010). Relation to clinical syndromes in adulthood. In: Hofmann, S.G. & Dibartolo, P.M. (Eds.), *Social Anxiety: Clinical, Developmental, and Social Perspectives* (pp. 183–205). New York: Elsevier.

93: Reich, J. (2010). Avoidant personality disorder and its relationship to social phobia. In: Hofmann, S.G. & Dibartolo, P.M. (Eds.), *Social Anxiety: Clinical, Developmental, and Social Perspectives* (pp. 207–222). New York: Elsevier.

94: Detweiler, M.F., & Comer, J.S. (2010). Social anxiety in children and adolescents: Biological, developmental, and social considerations. In: Hofmann, S.G. & Dibartolo, P.M. (Eds.), *Social Anxiety: Clinical, Developmental, and Social Perspectives* (pp. 223–270). New York: Elsevier.

95: Amir, N. & Bomyea, J. (2010). Cognitive biases in social anxiety disorder. In: Hofmann, S.G. & Dibartolo, P.M. (Eds.), *Social Anxiety: Clinical, Developmental, and Social Perspectives* (pp. 373–393). New York: Elsevier.

96: Heimberg, R.G., Brozovich, F.A., & Rapee, R.M. (2010). A Cognitive behavioral model of social anxiety disorder: Update and extension. In: Hofmann, S.G. & Dibartolo, P.M. (Eds.), *Social Anxiety: Clinical, Developmental, and Social Perspectives* (pp. 395–422). New York: Elsevier.

97: Kashdan, T.B., & Weeks, J.W. (2010). Social anxiety, positive experiences, and positive events. In: Hofmann, S.G. & Dibartolo, P.M. (Eds.), *Social Anxiety: Clinical, Developmental, and Social Perspectives* (pp. 447–469). New York: Elsevier.

98: Powers, M.B., Capozzoli, M.C., Handelsman, P., & Smits, J.A.J. (2010). Comparison between psychosocial and pharmacological treatments. In: Hofmann, S.G. & Dibartolo, P.M. (Eds.), *Social Anxiety: Clinical, Developmental, and Social Perspectives* (pp. 555–575). New York: Elsevier.

99: Otto, M.W., Hearon, B.A., & Safren, S.A. (2010). Mechanisms of action in the treatment of social anxiety disorder. In: Hofmann, S.G. & Dibartolo, P.M. (Eds.), *Social Anxiety: Clinical, Developmental, and Social Perspectives* (pp. 577–598). New York: Elsevier.

100: Lang, P.J. (1979). A bio-informational theory of emotional imagery. *Psychophysiology*, 16, 495–512. In: Hofmann, S.G. & Dibartolo, P.M. (Eds.), *Social Anxiety: Clinical, Developmental, and Social Perspectives* (pp. 396–422). New York: Elsevier.

101: Gabbard, G.O. (2005). *Psychodynamic Psychiatry in Clinical Practice.* Fourth edition.

102: Skodol, A.E. (2005). Manifestations, clinical diagnosis, and comorbidity. In: Oldham, J.M., Skodol, A.E., & Bender, D.S. (Eds.), *Textbook of Personality Disorders.* Arlington, VA, American Psychiatric Publishing, Inc., pp 57–87.

103: Schiffmana, J., Nakamuraa, B., Earleywineb, M., & Labriec, J. (2003). Symptoms of schizotypy precede cannabis use. *World Psychiatry, 2 (3)*.

104: Roberts, B.W., Wood, D., & Caspi, A. (2008). The development of personality traits in adulthood. In O.P. John, R.W. Robins, & L.A. Pervin (Eds.), *Handbook of Personality* (3rd ed., pp. 375–398). New York: The Guilford Press.

105: Caspi, A., Elder, G.H., & Bem, D.J. (1988). Moving away from the world: Life-course patterns of shy children. *Developmental Psychology*, 24, (pp. 824–831). In O.P. John, R.W. Robins, & L.A. Pervin (Eds.), *Handbook of Personality* (3rd ed., pp. 375–398). New York: The Guilford Press.

106: Botwin, M., Buss, D.M., & Shackelford, T. (1997). Personality and mate preferences: Five factors in mate selection and marital satisfaction. *Journal of Personality* (pp. 107–136). In O.P. John, R.W. Robins, & L.A. Pervin (Eds.), *Handbook of Personality* (3rd ed., pp. 375–398). New York: The Guilford Press.

107: Caspi, A., & Roberts, B.W. (1999). Personality continuity and change across the life course. In L.A. Pervin & O.P. John (Eds.), *Handbook of Personality: Thewory and Research* (2nd ed., pp. 300– 326). New York: Guilford Press. Cited by B.W. Roberts, D. Wood, & A. Caspi (2008). The development of personality traits in adulthood. In O.P. John, R.W. Robins, & L.A. Pervin (Eds.), *Handbook of Personality* (3rd ed., pp. 375–398). New York: The Guilford Press.

108: Roberts, B.W., Walton, K., & Viechtbauer, W. (2006). Patterns of mean-level change in personality traits across the life course: A meta-analysis of longitudinal studies. *Psychological Bulletin*, 132 (pp. 1–25). Cited by Cited by B.W. Roberts, D. Wood,

& A. Caspi (2008). The development of personality traits in adulthood (p. 388). In O.P. John, R.W. Robins, & L.A. Pervin (Eds.), *Handbook of Personality* (3rd ed., pp. 375–398). New York: The Guilford Press.

109: Rochman, B. (Feb 6, 2012). Why spanking doesn't work. *Time Magazine: Healthland.* healthland.time.com/2012/02/06/why-spanking-doesnt-work/?xid=newsletter-weekly.

110: Park, A. (April 12, 2010). Spanking kids leads to more aggressive behavior. *Time Magazine.* http://forum.psychlinks.ca/ parenting/22641-spanking-kids-leads-to-more-aggressive-behav- ior.html.

111: Haley, J. (1987). *Problem-solving Therapy*. San Francisco: Jossey-Bass.

112: Lerner, H. (1997). *The Dance of Anger*. New York: Harper Collins.

113: Bowen, M. (2004). *Family Therapy in Clinical Practice*. Lanham, Maryland. The Roman & Littlefield Publishing Group.

114: Nichols, M.P. (2010). *Family therapy: Concepts and methods*. Boston: Pearson Education, Inc.

115: Nichols, M.P. (1984). *Family Therapy: Concepts and Methods*. New York: Gardner Press, Inc.

116: Haley, J. (1986). *Uncommon Therapy*. New York: W.W. Norton & Company, Inc.

117: Bowen, M. (2004). *Family Therapy in Clinical Practice* (p. 537). Lanham, Maryland: The Roman & Littlefield Publishing Group.

118: Prochaska, J.O., Norcross, J.C. (2010). *Systems of Psychotherapy: A Transtheoretical Analysis.* Belmont, California: Brooks/Cole.

119: Minuchin, S. (1974). *Families and Family Therapy.* Harvard University Press.

120: Bowen, M. (2004). *Family Therapy in Clinical Practice* (p. 540). Lanham, Maryland

121: Combrinck-Graham, L. (2006). *Children in Family Contexts: Perspectives on Treatment.* New York: The Guilford Press.

122: Cozolino, L. *The Neuroscience of Human Relationships.* New York: W.W. Norton & Company.

123: Russek, L.G., & Schwartz, G.E. (1997). Feelings of parental caring predict health status in midlife: A 35-year follow-up of the Harvard mastery of stress study. *Journal of Behavioral Medicine,* 20, 1–13. Cited by: Cozolino, L. (2006). *The Neuroscience of Human Relationships* (pp. 218). New York: W.W. Norton & Company.

124: Cozolino, L. *The Neuroscience of Human Relationships* (p. 262). New York: W.W. Norton & Company.

125: Fox, G. (2006). Development in family contexts. In: Combrinck-Graham, L. (Ed.) *Children in Family Contexts: Perspectives on Treatment* (pp. 26–50). New York: The Guilford Press

126: Josephson, A.M. (2006). Family therapy in an age of biological psychiatry. In: Combrinck-Graham, L. (Ed.) *Children in Family Contexts: Perspectives on Treatment* (pp. 71–89). New York: The Guilford Press.

127: Keith, D.V. (2006). The family's own system: The symbolic context of health. In: Combrinck-Graham, L. (Ed.) *Children in Family Contexts: Perspectives on Treatment* (pp. 333–355). New York: The Guilford Press.

128: Fox, G. (2006). Development in family contexts (pp. 28–29). In: Combrinck-Graham, L. (Ed.) *Children in Family Contexts: Perspectives on Treatment* (pp. 26–50). New York: The Guilford Press.

129: Keith, D.V. (2006). The family's own system: The symbolic context of health (p. 333). In: Combrinck-Graham, L. (Ed.) *Children in Family Contexts: Perspectives on Treatment* (pp. 333–355). New York: The Guilford Press.

130: Bowen, M. (2004). *Family Therapy in Clinical Practice* (p. 534). Lanham, Maryland. The Roman & Littlefield Publishing Group.

131: Bowen, M. (2004). *Family Therapy in Clinical Practice* (p.536). Lanham, Maryland. The Roman & Littlefield Publishing Group.

132: Bowen, M. (2004). *Family Therapy in Clinical Practice* (p.542). Lanham, Maryland, The Roman & Littlefield Publishing Group.

133: Stout, M. (2005). *The Sociopath Next Door* (p. 2-3), Random House Inc.: New York.

134: Watamura, S.E. & Brown, S.M. (2017). *Parental History of Adversity and Child Well-being: Insights from Colorado*. Colorado Department of Human Services Office of Early Childhood (OEC) & University of Denver. Colorado.gov.

135: Hare, R.D. (1999). *Without Conscience.* The Guilford Press: New York.

136: Rivers, C.T. (2014). *Personality Disorders & Mental Illnesses.* Self-Published.

137: Hare, R.D. (1999). *Without Conscience.* (p. 211). The Guilford Press: New York.

138: Paul, Deanna (November 26, 2018). *U.N. finds the deadliest place for women is in the home.* Article based on the United Nations Office on Drugs and Crime. *Global study on homicide: Gender related killing of women and girls (2018).*

139: American Psychiatric Association (2020). *What are anxiety disorders?* https://www.Psychiatry.org/patients-families/anxiety-disorders/what-are-anxiety-disorders

140: National Institutes of Mental Health (2020). *Anxiety disorders.* https://www.nimh.nih.gov/health/topics/anxiety-disorders/index.shtml

141: Mayo Clinic. *Anxiety disorders: symptoms and causes.* https://www.mayoclinic.org/diseases-conditions/anxiety/symptoms-causes/syc-20350961

142: National Institutes of Mental Health (2020). *Panic disorder: When fear overwhelms.* NIH Publication No. 19-MH-8077

143: Goldman, R. (2017). *7 steps for getting through a panic attack.* https://www.healthline.com/health/anxiety/panic-attack-self care-strategies

144: Mayo Clinic (2020). *Anxiety disorders: Symptoms and causes.* https://www.mayoclinic.org/diseases-conditions/anxiety/symptoms-causes.syc-20350961

145: Holland, K. (2020). *Everything you need to know about anxiety.* https://www.healthline.com/health/anxiety#disorders

146: American Psychiatric Association (2020). *What is posttraumatic stress disorder.* https://www.psychiatry.org/patients-families/ptsd/what-is-ptsd

147: Mayo Clinic (2020). *Panic attacks and panic disorder: Symptoms and causes.* https://www.mayoclinic.org/diseases-conditions/panic-attacks/symptoms-causes/syc-20376021

ABOUT THE AUTHOR

DR. JOHN B. EVANS is a therapist specializing in individual, marriage, family, and group therapy, including parent/child/adolescent conflict, abusive relationships, and personality issues. Dr. Evans received his PhD in clinical social  work from the University of Texas—Arlington (1994). Dr. Evans also received a master's degree in mental-health counseling from Texas A&M University–Commerce (1988), a second master's degree in social work from the University of Texas–Arlington (1997), and a bachelor of arts in philosophy from the University of North Texas (1977). Dr. Evans currently resides in Colorado Springs. You may contact Dr. Evans at thedrjohn@thedrjohn.com.